Other Books by Jane Ann McLachlan

Historical Fiction:
The Sorrow Stone
The Lode Stone
The Girl Who Would Be Queen

Memoir:
IMPACT: A Memoir of PTSD

Creative Writing:
Downriver Writing: The Five-Step Process for Outlining Your Novel

Books by J. A. McLachlan

Science Fiction and Fantasy:
Walls of Wind
The Occasional Diamond Thief
The Salarian Desert Game
Midsummer Night Magicians

The Girl Who Tempted Fortune

Jane Ann McLachlan

This book is dedicated to all who have suffered the slights of prejudice, whether on account of their race, color, gender, social or financial status, or any other superficial excuse people make to look down on others.

May you, in your own way, rise above their expectations of you as gloriously as Philippa and Raymond rose above the limits their society tried to set for them.

The Angevin Line in the Kingdom of Naples
from Charles I to Joanna and Maria

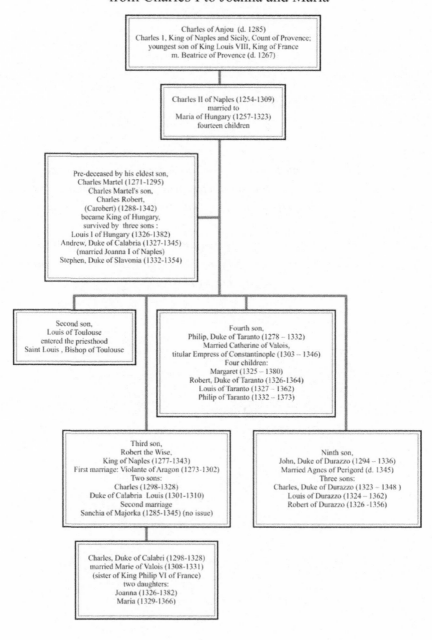

Charles of Anjou (d. 1285)
Charles 1, King of Naples and Sicily, Count of Provence;
youngest son of King Louis VIII, King of France
m. Beatrice of Provence (d. 1267)

Charles II of Naples (1254-1309)
married to
Maria of Hungary (1257-1323)
fourteen children

Pre-deceased by his eldest son,
Charles Martel (1271-1295)
Charles Martel's son,
Charles Robert,
(Carobert) (1288-1342)
became King of Hungary,
survived by three sons :
Louis I of Hungary (1326-1382)
Andrew, Duke of Calabria (1327-1345)
(married Joanna I of Naples)
Stephen, Duke of Slavonia (1332-1354)

Second son,
Louis of Toulouse
entered the priesthood
Saint Louis , Bishop of Toulouse

Fourth son,
Philip, Duke of Taranto (1278 – 1332)
Married Catherine of Valois,
titular Empress of Constantinople (1303 – 1346)
Four children:
Margaret (1325 – 1380)
Robert, Duke of Taranto (1326-1364)
Louis of Taranto (1327 – 1362)
Philip of Taranto (1332 – 1373)

Third son,
Robert the Wise,
King of Naples (1277-1343)
First marriage: Violante of Aragon (1273-1302)
Two sons:
Charles (1298-1328)
Duke of Calabria Louis (1301-1310)
Second marriage
Sanchia of Majorka (1285-1345) (no issue)

Ninth son,
John, Duke of Durazzo (1294 – 1336)
Married Agnes of Perigord (d. 1345)
Three sons:
Charles, Duke of Durazzo (1323 – 1348)
Louis of Durazzo (1324 – 1362)
Robert of Durazzo (1326 -1356)

Charles, Duke of Calabri (1298-1328)
married Marie of Valois (1308-1331)
(sister of King Philip VI of France)
two daughters:
Joanna (1326-1382)
Maria (1329-1366)

CONTENTS

CAST OF CHARACTERS

Philippa of Catania – a young Sicilian girl who is hired as wet-nurse to the infant Prince Charles during his father, Prince Robert's campaign to reclaim Sicily for King Charles II of Naples.

Characters from Philippa's Past (1298-1344):

Guilio: Philippa's first husband, presumed dead by everyone in Naples.
Antonio: Philippa's son by Guilio, also presumed dead by the Neapolitans.
Maroccia: Philippa's mother
Cicillia: Philippa's maid
King Charles II of Naples: King of Naples with a claim on Sicily, father of Prince Robert and nephew of Louis IX, King of France.
Prince Robert: Crown Prince of Naples, later known as Robert the Wise, King of Naples.
Princess Violante: First wife of Prince Robert, mother of his sons Louis and Charles.
Prince Charles: second son of Robert and Violante, born in Sicily during Prince Robert's failed campaign to reclaim Sicily for his father, King Charles II
Queen Sancia: King Robert's second wife, who becomes Philippa's friend and supporter.
Raymond of Campagno: An Ethiopian slave freed by King Charles of Naples, rewarded and promoted many times for his competent and loyal service to King Charles and then King Robert.

Characters from Philippa's Present (March-December, 1346):

Joanna: Queen of Naples, daughter of Prince Charles, granddaughter of King Robert the Wise.
Maria: Joanna's only living sibling, second in line for the throne of Naples after Charles Martel.
Prince Charles Martel: Joanna's and Andrew's infant son and only child, heir to the Kingdom of Naples, born three months after his father's murder.
Raymond (*seneschal of Queen Joanna's court*) and **Robert** (*grand seneschal of the Kingdom of Naples under Queen Joanna's reign*) Philippa's sons by her second husband.

Sancia: Philippa's granddaughter, married to the Count of Marcone, daughter of Philippa's son, Robert, and close friend since childhood of Queen Joanna and her sister, Princess Maria.

Robert of Taranto: The Duke of Taranto, Joanna's cousin, the same age as her. He desires to marry Joanna to secure the crown of Naples for himself.

Louis of Taranto: Robert of Taranto's brother, one year younger. He also wants to marry Joanna and raises an army of mercenaries to fight his brother Robert's army for her hand.

Charles of Durazzo: The Duke of Durazzo, Joanna's cousin, married to her younger sister Maria.

Prince Andrew of Hungary: Joanna's cousin and first husband, wed when they were children. He was murdered on September 18, 1345.

King Louis of Hungary: Prince Andrew's older brother, bitterly determined to avenge the murder of his brother, and convinced he is the rightful heir to the crown of Naples.

Charles of Artois: King Robert's acknowledged bastard son, strong supporter of Queen Joanna.

Bertrand of Artois: Charles of Artois' son.

The Count of Terlizzi (*marshal of the realm*) and **Nicholas of Melizanno**: Two of Joanna's councilors and supporters.

Hugo del Balzo: A courtier in Joanna's court, in league with the Dukes of Taranto and Durazzo.

Bertrand del Balzo: Hugo's cousin, chief justice of the kingdom. Authorized by Pope Clement VI to prosecute those guilty of Prince Andrew's murder in order to placate King Louis of Hungary.

Maroccia: Philippa's great-granddaughter, daughter of Sancia and the Count of Marcone

Note: The characters Guilio, Maroccia, and Antonio in Philippa's past, (her husband, mother, and son in Sicily) are fictional. Philippa was hired as wet-nurse to Prince Charles, so she must have been a young mother. It's unlikely an unwed mother would have been considered an appropriate wet-nurse for a prince, but nothing is known of her family in Sicily. The ladies' maids, including Cicillia, are also fictional; records were not kept of maids, unless they rose to the heights of court life, as did Philippa. All other characters are real historical people, depicted as accurately as I am able based on their recorded letters and actions, and my research into the period they lived in.

Chapter 1

March 5, 1346
Queen Joanna's Court, Naples

I peer through the carriage window anxiously as it rattles down the steep road toward Naples' busy center. Even up here away from the city center the streets are crowded, forcing the horses to curb their gait.

"Can you not hurry?" I call to the driver.

His back stiffens. He turns with a tight-lipped smile, forming a respectful reply.

"No matter," I say, restraining my impatience. "I see you are doing your best." I pull my head back inside the carriage.

The crowd has unnerved me. I am used to crowds at market, though I have not done my own marketing for many years. Naples is always full of people, unlike the small village where I was born. But this is a different kind of crowd altogether. As if to prove the point, my carriage curtains are pulled aside and a man's face peers in. I lean away, startled. One of my guards riding beside the carriage shouts and the curtain falls back, but it does not silence the angry voices outside. I would cover my ears, but even alone inside my carriage I refuse to show fear.

"Death to the king-slayers!"

"Why have the culprits not been brought to justice?"

"Who is so base as to shelter a murderer?"

Those comments in the last vein rattle me most, for they are aimed at Queen Joanna herself and everyone knows it, though none of this rabble would dare name her directly.

The carriage has been creeping along the streets. It stops entirely now. I sit still, waiting for it to start again as it has twice already, afraid to look outside my window. When the curtain is pulled back again I gasp, covering it with a cough.

"Pardon, my Lady, but the driver says he cannot go further. The crowd is too thick for people to move aside even if they wanted to." Giovanni is sweating though it is not yet summer. He has been my faithful guardsman since he was a lad. His hair is graying now, but he is still strong and quick, trained by my husband and loyal to death.

I think a moment, listening to the ugly rumble of voices outside the carriage. This is no time for Queen Joanna's councilors to be walking the streets.

This is also no time for her chief advisor to be absent. "Dismount and walk with me. Tell the other guards, also." I rise and climb stiffly out while they tie their horses to the carriage. They surround me for the walk through Naples to Castle Nuovo, three strong, armed men. I hope it will be enough.

The walk takes twice as long as it should. We are jostled and pushed in the narrow streets despite my guards' attempts to shield me. They would like to be up on their horses ploughing through this mass of commoners, I see it in their faces. They are accustomed to fighting from above, if it comes to that. But I have hated horses ever since my first wild ride on one and Giovanni has been with me long enough not to suggest we ride.

We pass the magnificent Duomo, contracted by King Charles I. A few streets later we reach the Basilica San Lorenzo Maggiore, commissioned by his son, King Charles II. I stop there to rest. My guards look about constantly. Their nervousness affects me. As soon as my breathing calms and my legs cease to tremble we continue, passing the Basilica San Domenico Maggiore under the

2

Dominicans' benevolent watch, and on to the Franciscans at the Basilica Santa Chiara, where King Robert the Wise, my beloved prince, lies at rest. The basilicas and monasteries built by the Angevins lie along the streets of Naples like stepping stones leading me to Castle Nuovo.

In the Piazza del Gesu, in front of Santa Chiara, I stop to rest again. We are only a dozen streets away from the royal castle. The square is thick with milling people, citizens from as far away as Salerno and Capua, from the look of their clothing and worn footwear. All demanding justice for Prince Andrew—whom they hated and feared while he lived. What has riled them so? The blackguard prince has been dead six months now. Tommaso Mambriccio, Prince Andrew's chamberlain and a victim of his vicious nature, has been convicted and executed for the crime, although no one believes he acted alone. But a semblance of justice has been done, and a healthy heir is now lying in the royal nursery. The royal line will continue smoothly, which is all these tradesmen and merchants should care about.

I look around the square. This unrest is the work of others, preying on the people's baser natures. I know those behind it, subtle and sly and ambitious men: Robert, Duke of Taranto, Queen Joanna's cousin, who wants the crown for himself and means to frighten Queen Joanna into marrying him; and Charles, Duke of Durazzo, another scheming cousin, who wants Joanna destroyed so he and his wife, Joanna's younger sister Maria, can inherit. Villains both! Robert of Taranto is the more vicious, an arrogant, cruel bully, no better than Joanna's dead husband. She will never marry another such. But Charles of Durazzo is more treacherous, a man who changes his loyalty as easily as he does his garments. Did I not support his marriage to Maria? He has forgotten that debt, for now he publicly links my family with those accused of the conspiracy to murder Prince Andrew. As if we would be so stupid as to participate in regicide, no matter how appealing the thought in Andrew's case.

But anyone who stands beside Queen Joanna against either of those two ambitious dukes is likely to be accused of the crime.

"My Lady," Giovanni whispers. He is as tense as a drawn bow, examining the congested square we must cross. Have I misjudged the danger? Well, I have no choice but to continue now. I nod to Giovanni and walk briskly into the crowd.

Angry voices assault my ears and the heat of bodies packed together presses on me. I bend my head, praying not to be recognized. Behind me I hear the thunder of horse's hooves. My guards pull me into a doorway, their faces tight, scowling. A dozen mercenaries ride by, careless of the people dodging out of their path. Lord Louis' hired soldiers. I wish them a speedy victory for Joanna's sake and an even quicker departure for the sake of Naples. Behind them the people surge back, their voices more bitter than ever.

Perhaps it was something in my expression as I watched Louis' mercenaries ride by, or only that I looked up, exposing my face. People in the square are pointing at me. "She is the one who turned our young queen against her rightful lord!" a woman calls.

"She murdered our poor prince!" a man's voice shouts. Calls of "Conspirator!" and "There she is!" rise around me. My guards circle, their backs pressing against me, swords drawn. Three men against hundreds.

Sweat breaks out under my court gown, and my breath comes quick and shallow. I pull myself up, straight and tall. "Do not be afraid," I tell my men. "Help is coming." Maybe it is and maybe not, but a crowd is a wild animal; it can sense fear. The scent of fear is the scent of prey, and I am no prey. I do not intend to die today.

"Seize the whore!" someone shouts. A hand grabs my arm, yanking me sideways. My guard's sword swings, opening the arm to the bone and spraying my sleeve with blood.

Those near us cringe back, but there are others behind them, pushing forward. The false courage I gave my men will not hold long. I do not bow my head or close my eyes but in my mind I call out to my great-grandmother, a woman of power and prophecy, to intercede for me. I look above the crowd at Santa Chiara, with its spire pointing to Heaven, and there, on the steps of the basilica, I see Hugo del Balzo, the Count of Avellino, Queen Joanna's seneschal in Provence, surrounded by a dozen men-at-arms. He looks straight at me with his slow, cold smile, and turns away.

The crowd dances back and forth around us, those behind pushing forward and those immediately in front of my guards' swords holding back. It is only a matter of time before the standoff breaks. My men will die defending me. "Giovanni," I say softly. He hears me though he continues to watch the enemy. "Giovanni. My husband would not sac—"

A volley of hoof beats approaches from the left. I pause to look up and nearly weep for joy when I recognize royal livery. "For Queen Joanna!" I cry, raising my blood-spattered arm. My men glance up, still watching the crowd. "A la Reigne!" Giovanni shouts, brandishing his sword.

The horses swerve toward us across the square, the soldiers' swords unsheathed but unnecessary as people fall away before them. I recognize their captain now, my son Robert, seneschal of the Kingdom. His face is a mixture of fear and fury as he thunders toward us. He has heard my call, recognized my voice among so many. No doubt he came out searching for me, alarmed at my delay.

One of my men turns to stare at me, white-faced. I laugh softly under my breath. Help has come! The rumors of my ability to prophesy will continue.

When they reach us my son leans down and swings me up behind him. Giovanni lifts as my son pulls, making my ascent appear effortless, worthy of the queen's chief advisor. Robert says nothing. He wants to upbraid me but dares not. I am still his mother, and Queen Joanna's advisor, for all that he holds the highest position in the kingdom. My men leap up behind three of the soldiers as the crowd surges forward again.

Someone yells "Do not let her escape!" A hand grabs my leg and pulls. Perched sideways behind the saddle I feel myself slipping. Robert's sword flashes, followed by a scream. The hand, no longer attached to its arm, falls to the ground as my son pulls me back and wheels his horse, shouting, "Way for the queen's guard!" I grab his waist and hang on, my dignity shattered as we gallop for the castle.

Soon the towers of Castle Nuovo rise ahead, with more armed guards at its gates. I would get off here and walk, surely we are safe now, but my son does not slow down. The gates open as soon as he is recognized and he charges through, with me clinging desperately to him. He must always make his point, my son. Nevertheless I take the warning, despite the unnecessary emphasis.

Faithful Giovanni is there to catch me as I tumble down the horse's side, making it look as though he is simply lifting me down. He does not release his grip until I am steady on my feet. I nod when I am ready, and he steps back.

Robert swings down beside me, throwing the reins to a waiting boy. "Madam Mother," he enunciates precisely. He bows his head briefly, turns on his heel and stalks into the castle. Giovanni frowns. I raise an amused eyebrow at him before following my son.

Robert is speaking with his brother Raymond when I enter the queen's presence chamber. I note the fierce tension in his shoulders and Raymond's stricken expression as he leans towards him, their voices low. A private conversation about their stubborn mother, no doubt, who insists on traversing the volatile city so she can sleep in her own house.

I glance around the room. Most of the queen's councilors are already here, mingling with her ladies-in-waiting while they wait for Queen Joanna to appear and lead them into her privy chamber. Raymond breaks off what he is saying and comes over as soon as he sees me.

"Thank God you are safe!" His voice is hushed, pitched only for my ears.

I smile and pat his arm.

"No, Mother, do not dismiss my concern. You must stay at court until this is resolved. I cannot have you travelling through these streets."

"I am well, Raymond," I say. And then, because I feel his hand on my arm trembling, I relent. "I will not distress you and your brother again," I promise him. "I will send for my things." I had already made the decision when Giovanni stood ready to die for me, but I prefer the appearance of conceding to another's fear.

Raymond nods, blinking in relief. He is seneschal of Joanna's court, a man proven in battle like his brother. His tender heart is a side of him only those he loves may see. He takes a deep breath and straightens, becoming again the court seneschal.

The door to the queen's bedchamber opens. My granddaughter Sancia stands in the frame, looking about the room. She sees me and calls out formally, "my Lady Philippa, Her Majesty the Queen would speak with you."

I smile at her as I cross the room, noting the swell of her gown. She will have to go into confinement this autumn. I wish she was already safely tucked away in her husband's summer residence, away from Naples and all this upheaval. She smiles back at me and steps aside so I may pass through the door.

Joanna is standing in the window alcove with her back to the room, gazing out. The window faces the inner courtyard but at the angle she is standing she can see the front gate and further, beyond the moat and grounds to the narrow streets of Naples. From here she will not be able to see the anger on her peoples' faces, but she can hear through the half-open window the low, bitter rumble of voices in the distance, so different from the normal cheerful bustle of Naples' streets. I cross the room and curtsey low before her, drawing her gaze from the window.

"There is no need of that between us." She gestures for me to rise.

My knees creak in agreement as I rise but I will make no concession to my age when I am at court.

7

Joanna turns back to the window. "They are so angry. Why are they so angry?"

We are alone in the room so I put my hand on her shoulder. She leans, very slightly, into my touch. I have known her all her life, this fair-skinned, yellow-haired beauty, not yet twenty and ruler of the most celebrated kingdom after France itself. Her love of Naples is second only to her love of God, and her people have always returned that love. This rift in her kingdom is tearing her apart.

"It is not their own anger you are hearing, Your Majesty."

Her mouth twists in a bitter smile. "A message from my cousin, the Duke of Taranto. What more can I do to pacify Lord Robert?"

"You have given him lands and titles already."

"I will never marry him." She looks out over her city, her voice low and fierce. "Surely you do not advise it?" She glances at me, her eyes narrowed.

"I do not." He would have us murdered, every one of Joanna's friends and advisors. He would murder her the day after their wedding if he could, to be the sole monarch of Naples.

Her face clears at my agreement. I cannot resist the urge to stroke her cheek. So much like her grandfather in his youth, my beloved Prince Robert.

"Louis is not at all like his brother." Joanna smiles. Handsome, blond, and amusing, Louis of Taranto, the Duke of Taranto's younger brother, has always been her favorite. I look steadfastly out the window. Somewhere, outside of the city, the two brothers' armies are battling for power even as we speak. Louis is very much like his brother.

"He has promised he will protect my advisors. They will be his advisors when we marry." Her voice is quiet, as though she fears the walls will hear us.

Does she, also, believe her husband's murderers are among her favorites? Prince Andrew had threatened to execute most of her court and councilors as soon as he was crowned, a good enough reason to want him dead. Does she wonder if I or my sons were involved? I do not need protection, I want to say, shunning any association with the gruesome murder. But I hold my tongue. I have just walked through the outraged city. The innocent do need protection here.

"Then we must pray for Louis' victory," I say calmly.

She nods, accepting my advice. Louis will receive the funding he needs.

"And Charles?" A bitter topic, for she loves her sister Maria, as do I.

"He is with Lord Robert," I tell her flatly. Then, to soften the truth she must hear, I add, "The Duke of Durazzo is not a man to listen to his wife."

She turns back to the window. "What have they made my people believe?"

I consider everything I saw and heard today. She must know where she is vulnerable. "That you are to blame for the long delay in prosecuting those responsible for the foul murder of your husband. That you are protecting those involved. Lord Louis has lost favor because of his hated mercenaries."

"They are not saying I was involved?" she whispers, her face pale.

"They stop short of it."

She grips my hand. "What am I to do?"

"What you have always done, Your Majesty. Reach out to those who support you. Negotiate with those who do not. Accept your God-given duty to rule the Kingdom of Naples as your Grandfather intended. Protect your people from themselves." This last makes her smile, as I intended. I would like to leave her with that smile, but there is one more warning I must deliver. The face I saw in the crowd, a face she trusts and should not. I open my mouth but before I can speak, the door to Joanna's bedchamber opens again.

Joanna glances over my shoulder. "Ah, you have come to tell me my councilors are waiting. Escort me, then."

I turn to see Hugo del Balzo hold out his arm to her.

Chapter 2

Autumn, 1298
Trapani, Sicily

Philippa!" my sister's voice called.

I frowned down at the warm river. I had slipped away from the other girls doing the foreign soldiers' laundry to be alone for a while. If I stayed quiet, Anya might not see me. Mama would have to do herself whatever task she had sent Anya to fetch me for. I stepped backward nearer the shrubs on the shore and beat the soldier's uniform as quietly as possible with the wide smooth rock I had retrieved from my hiding place under the bushes. The rough material lay heavy between my hands, clouding the river water with a week's dust and sweat. I wrinkled my nose.

Robert of Anjou arrived months ago with his smelly army to take Sicily for his father, King Charles II of Naples. So far they had captured the port town Catania and moved inland to our little town, Trapani, where they set up their military encampment.

I have heard he has yellow hair and blue eyes and skin so fair you could nearly see through it. I tossed my head—that!—for his foreign looks. We did not want a French King in Sicily. When the traitor, King James II of Aragon, sold Sicily to Robert of Anjou's father three years ago, we would have none of his foreign French ways. Instead we offered our fealty to James of Aragon's younger brother, Frederick III. He will never allow this young crown prince of Naples to claim us! I gave the uniform a satisfying smack with my stone.

"Philippa," my sister called again from the riverbank.

I held up the uniform to see if it was clean enough. Whatever outcome we prayed for, we were practical in Trapani. The citizens of Catania, many of whom had lost fathers, sons, and husbands in the battle, might resent Prince Robert's few victories, but those of us who lived beside his temporary encampment could recognize a profitable situation. An army must eat. Someone must catch the fish and raise the chickens, cook their meals and wash their clothes. Prince Robert, wishing not only to subdue us but to rule us, kept to a minimum the violence an army generally visits on a conquered town. They paid a fair price for our fish and farm goods, respected our women for the most part, and paid for their drinks. And there was no denying the charm and dashing figure of the twenty-year-old prince and the young wife who could not bear to be separated from him and so had accompanied him on campaign. The tale was too much for many of our village girls, who sought their own romance among his men—until their handsome soldier left them with an empty promise and a swelling belly.

It could be worse, my mother said. Princess Violante's presence ensured a certain amount of decency among Robert's men, more than we had expected. She was, after all, Violante of Aragon, the sister of our King Frederick. We were her people. If she could fall under the spell of this French prince, how could we not?

I stopped my scrubbing and looked down into the water, trying to catch my reflection. I was lighter-skinned than most Sicilians, with thick, dark hair and darker eyes. Since my son's birth my figure had filled out into that of a woman, although my skin was now once again firm and tight. Men looked twice at me behind my husband's back.

"Philippa!" This time it was my mother's voice calling my name. I straightened quickly. Why would she come herself to fetch me? There was something strange in her voice, it sounded sad and frightened and eager, all at the same time.

The skin on my back prickled. I shivered despite the hot sun beating down. I became intensely aware of the hard brilliance of the light on the river, the warm water lapping at my knees where I stood with my skirts hitched up to my thighs, the soft mud of the riverbed squishing between my toes. The scent of the woods and the moist air rising from the water in the heat of the sun were poignantly sweet to me. The chatter of the other girls, the ones I had left to steal a few moments alone with my thoughts, echoed softly over the water like music, mingling with the birdsong in the treetops. Precious, all of it. I wriggled my toes and swirled my fingers through the river water as if to memorize the feel of home, of standing here in my river, careless and contented, a simple fisherman's daughter.

"Come, Philippa," my mother scolded from the bank, having known exactly where to look for me. "Anya will finish the laundry."

I waded up out of the river, leaving the soldiers' clothes floating in the water. I passed my sister without a word, handing her my smooth rock to beat them with, as though I was handing my old life over to her. My mother watched me.

"Your son is fine," she said, turning to lead me along the path toward our village.

I flushed and bit my lip. But why should I be worried about Antonio? He was a strong infant, and my mother-in-law worried enough for us both.

My mother walked quickly, without speaking. I let my skirts down as I followed her, the strange dream-state that had overcome me in the river, gone now. There was no reason to think this summons any different than a dozen others this summer, when I was needed to assist her with a birthing. My mother was the best midwife in Sicily. She had been teaching me since I was a child to find and prepare the herbs that eased a birth and cooled a fever, and teas that strengthen and revive a woman. When my woman's courses began I started going with her to the birthings.

This was no different, I told myself, wishing I had not given Anya my stone, becoming a little annoyed. My mother always knew when a woman was going to have her child, before she was sent for. She could have told me this morning to expect a summons when I passed her hut. I went over in my mind the wives and foolish girls I knew who were with child, but none of them was near her time. An early birth, then? I thought of my friend Elina. She wasn't at the river today. I hurried to catch up with my mother.

"Once I've delivered the babe and cut the cord, I must tend to the mother. You know what to do," she said, before I could speak.

"Swipe out his mouth clear of mucus with my finger, and see that he cries," I answered immediately.

"And if he doesn't?"

"Press gently on his chest, or place him on his stomach and rub his back." I had done this many times, yet my voice shook as I recited it. Always, the moment she handed me the tiny infant, silent and weary from his struggle into life, my heart filled with fear that this one might not live. For that brief moment my pounding heart was the only noise I could hear and my hands shook so that I feared I would drop the slippery babe. Then I would hear the tiny wail, turning my terror to sudden joy.

"You mustn't tremble!" My mother stopped and faced me, her voice fierce. "Your hands mustn't shake! You must be as confident as I am, firm of voice if you speak at all. No one may see your fear!"

She had told me this before, but never so fiercely. It was our job to calm the women, to shore up their courage as much as to bring forth their babes. I nodded, but my mother grabbed my shoulders and shook me roughly.

"No one must see a moment's doubt in you, nor a speck of fear in your eyes. Your life depends on it!"

I gaped at her, stumbling backward as she let me go. My life depended on it?

"You're so young," she murmured, regarding me as I caught myself and straightened.

"I'm a woman grown and a mother myself!" I answered hotly, and with some bitterness as well. I had not wanted to marry Guilio.

He was nearly as old as my father, and what did I care if he owned two fishing boats? My mother had supported me; for once she had stood up to my father, saying I was too young. "Thirteen summers is long enough for me to feed and clothe her!" he roared, striking my mother across the side of the head so hard she fell against the wall. He glared at me. "You'll never be hungry, girl. And he'll choose another if I ask him to wait." I did not hide the mutiny in my eyes, but I did not bother arguing. Clearly Guilio had offered him money.

I loved my baby, though, my dear little son, no older than the new moon. I hated to leave him with my mother-in-law, but Guilio insisted I go back to doing the soldiers' laundry as soon as my bleeding stopped. I saw Guilio's house—our house—as we approached the village. Would I have time to feed Antonio before—

"Pay attention!" my mother snapped. "This's your chance, daughter. This is it, if you dare to take it!"

I knew at once what she meant, and grew still. How often had she quoted to me the words her mother's mother said when I was born: *This girl will travel far from home and rise high above her station. She will be mother to a queen—*

Always she stopped abruptly, with a frown, as though there was something more; something she would not have me know.

I never told my mother her grandmother's prophecy was foolish, that she must have suffered the weakness of mind that those who live too long are subject to. Of course the prophecy was ridiculous. My husband would not leave this village, nor ever allow me to, and even if I were not married, the daughter of a fisherman will never be the mother of a queen. So I had not worried myself over the unspoken end of the prophecy.

Nor did I now. I only stood there, thinking of the possibility of escaping my life...

I pulled myself to my full height—I am tall, as tall as any woman in Trapani, and not yet full grown—and looked my mother in the eye. "I'm not too young," I said. "And I'm not afraid." I added that because I was afraid and needed to hear myself deny it. Guilio would beat me if he learned I was even thinking of taking his son and leaving him. And if I was still alive after he tired, my father would finish the job. But was it possible? Could I escape?

My mother made a small gesture, something between a nod and a shrug, and began walking again. I had to hurry to keep up. Whoever needed us was not to be kept waiting.

As we neared my parent's hut I saw a horse. At least this soldier was acknowledging his paternity. Perhaps he would even marry the girl—

Two men came round the side of the hut, one of them leading a second horse. I stopped short when I realized they were wearing royal livery. They caught sight of us, or rather of my mother. The older one snapped his fingers and reached for his horse's reins as the younger swung up into his saddle. My mother hurried forward, murmuring something about herbs and healing, and ducked into the little hut. I stood there gawking until the mounted man, with an impatient gesture, stretched out his arm for me.

I looked around foolishly, hoping to see another woman from our village. Only my mother? Only my mother and me, barely out of girlhood? Only the two of us to midwife a royal birthing? For that was surely who we were being summoned to attend. Everyone knew the wife of the conqueror, Robert of Anjou, was with child.

Had they not sent for a doctor? Had they not thought to bring a royal midwife on campaign with them? I have only been a woman for two summers, assisted my mother at six births, seven if you count the stillbirth… the blood drained from my face. If the queen's babe—

The young man frowned. I swallowed, raised my chin, and stepped forward, lifting my hand for him to grasp. He pulled me up onto his horse. I kept going, straight over the other side, and grabbed at him. He laughed as he reached back to steady me. I straightened, stiff and angry, letting go of him at once and holding the saddle instead. The horse stamped and blew out a snort of air as if it, too, was laughing.

My mother, holding her basket of herbs in one hand, allowed the other soldier to swing her up behind him. She settled gracefully, her knees tightening against the horse's sides as though she had always ridden. I tried to squeeze my legs against the beast beneath me, but who would have thought a horse's back was so wide? I held tight to the saddle. The horse's hair was soft against my calves where my skirt had ridden up. I thought it would be coarse, like the mane and tail, but it was as soft as a rabbit's skin, and warm.

With a sharp kick the men wheeled their mounts into a gallop and it was all I could do to hang on. Beneath me I felt the great beast's muscles bunched, tight and hard, its hooves pounding against the ground tearing up clods of earth as we raced into town and along the narrow streets. I gripped the saddle till my fingers cramped, swearing to myself that if I did not fall off and get trampled I would never climb onto a horse again.

When the beige peaks of the tents became visible in the distance I risked my life to lean sideways and peer around the soldier's back. Even dwarfed by distance, the size of the encampment stunned me. Our village would fit into a corner of it. Smoke from campfires hung above it mottling the sun like the coat of a sickly beast. As we approached the wind shifted, carrying the smell of smoke and boiling fish, horse dung and human waste and sweat. I'm no stranger to such scents but I would have pinched my nose if I had not been too frightened to loosen my hold on the saddle.

I must have made a sound for the man in front of me laughed. "The cess pits are on this side, girl. The tent you are going to will smell sweeter."

I was not so certain of that, having cleaned the fluids of afterbirth before. I shrugged although he could not see me.

By now we had reached the first tents. I peered around, expecting to see hundreds of men, but only a handful were walking about, practicing their swordplay or sitting in front of campfires. I realized the bulk of the army and probably Robert of Anjou himself, were away fighting Frederick III. Only those who were wounded or left behind to hold the area would be here.

Our horses pranced and tossed their heads at being reined in as we trotted through the encampment. The soldiers looked us over and several called out rude remarks. I became aware of my bare feet and long legs against the side of the horse, and tried to pull my skirt down lower. One of the soldiers reached to stroke my leg as we passed him, saying something which made his fellows laugh. I kicked out at him. The horse shied sideways, nearly dislodging me.

"The Princess has sent for these women!" the guard on my mount shouted.

The men stepped back. Their eyes still undressed me, as men will do, but they kept their hands and their comments to themselves. So the Anjou prince protects his wife's women, I thought. A little emboldened, I glared back at them.

We stopped before a large light-colored tent. Pennants bearing the colors of Aragon fluttered from its peaks. Nearby stood an even larger tent hung with pennants bearing the colors of the French Anjou line, and others the purple of royalty.

My escort turned in his saddle, gripped my arm, and swung me down in front of the first tent. I stumbled, not having expected such a quick descent, and my legs being sore from the ride, but he held my arm a moment as if he had expected it so I did not fall. My mother was already walking toward the door, which was guarded by two armed men. She glanced behind at me with a look of annoyance. I took a step. My legs held. After a few more unsteady steps they regained the feel of solid land. I hurried to catch up.

The air was hot and still inside the tent. I got a sense of spaciousness and a quick sight of the ornate bed at the far end before the flap fell shut behind me, leaving us in darkness. I stumbled forward, nearly tripping on the edge of a thick tapestry which provided the tent with a floor. The luxurious softness of it was unfamiliar to my bare feet. I tried to side-step off it, horrified that my feet would dirty it, but it filled the area of the tent. Beside me my mother made a slight sound, a warning. I remembered that we were about to midwife a royal princess.

I blinked, trying to adjust my eyes to the dimness. The window flaps had been tied shut to keep vapors out; only what little light seeped through the sides of the tent alleviated the darkness. How would we see to birth a child in here? Surely we would make a mistake in our blindness.

Beware of tempting Fortune. A saying in our village whenever someone tried to improve their station, came to me. There was no doubt we were tempting Fortune today. I made a quick sign of the cross to avert the consequences Fortune might visit on us for our audacity.

"Your Majesty," my mother said, sinking into a curtsey. Behind our skirts her hand gripped mine hard enough to hurt. I dropped down, hoping my long skirt would hide my clumsiness, for I had never curtseyed and did not know what to do with my legs. I bent them as low as I could and hoped for the best. They were trembling again and I was not sure I would be able to get back up. I schooled my voice so it sounded more confident than I felt, or at least less terrified.

"Your Majesty," I echoed.

"You may approach," a thin voice whispered from the bed. At first I did not understand, the voice was so strained and the Italian words spoken in the heavy accent of Aragon.

My mother rose slowly from her curtsey and walked without haste to the bed on which Princess Violante lay. I gritted my teeth and forced my legs to straighten. For a moment I feared they would not, that I would have to crawl across the room, but they held me and the delay gave my eyes time to adjust to the darkness.

The princess's breathing was shallow and quick, more like gasps, loud in the quiet tent. I did not like the sound of it, and was sure my mother would not, but her face was impassive and I schooled mine to show nothing either.

A lady's maid, sitting on a stool by the bed, rose quickly and stepped back for us, her face a mixture of terror and relief as she turned responsibility for her mistress over to us. My heart almost stopped when I saw the princess's face, white as death, covered with a sheen of sweat and etched with lines of pain that made her look as old as my mother. She bore it bravely, but the weakness of her voice when she bid us approach was not a good sign.

"Your name?" she whispered when my mother drew near.

"Maroccia, Your Majesty." She hesitated. My mother was not given to bragging, she had no need to; but even I could see the princess's fear in her eyes and smell the sharp odor of it in her sweat. The room was thick with everyone's fear; I could taste it lying heavy on the air.

"I am the best midwife in Trapani, perhaps in all Catania," my mother said calmly. "You are safe in my care, Princess."

The princess closed her eyes. I wanted to close mine too. What had she promised? This woman was dying, my mother had to know that. I glanced furtively sideways. The lady's maid had heard, her eyes were wide with sudden hope. She would repeat that promise. Even if my mother got away before the prince returned it would not matter; she had given her name: Maroccia the midwife.

"How long has she been in labor?" my mother asked, rolling her sleeves back.

"Since yesterday, noon." The maid's voice shook.

A servant girl came in, carrying the fresh bowl of water my mother had ordered. She set it on a table near the bed and curtseyed. She made it look easy.

My mother nodded, as though a full day of labor was perfectly ordinary. "May I examine you, Your Majesty?" she asked, reaching for the cover and drawing it back when the princess whispered her assent. Her lips barely moved as she spoke. The drawn sheet revealed a slender body soaked with sweat and the swollen mound of her belly. I could see it ripple under her shift with the movements of her babe and the intense contractions that shook her.

19

My heart pounded in my ears. The princess was at the end of her endurance; she was going to die. In my mother's care. And possibly the babe as well if we could not get him out quickly. In my care. And then I did not want him birthed, all I could see was the moment he would be handed to me, expiring as I touched him. What would they do to us? If both the princess and her infant died in our care, what would this foreign warrior prince do to us? Like a children's game of pass-the-stick, I wanted to put my hands behind my back, refuse to take the babe. I took a step backward, as though I could retreat from this place, from this hour, when my life hung in the balance, as tremulous as the life of this unborn infant.

My mother glanced at me, a look that said she knew the danger we were in, and knew that I knew it. She lowered her lashes and dipped her chin, a tiny movement demonstrating the mixture of power and obeisance that all who deal out life and death owe to the gods. The submission of a midwife. I dipped my chin, but I did not lower my lashes. I would meet whatever fate decreed with my eyes open. I must accept the consequences of this day, but I would not submit. I stepped forward.

My mother saw my response but our exchange was so quick no one else caught it. Her strong hands had not paused in their exploration of the princess's abdomen, while the lady's maid gently wiped the beads of sweat from her mistress's forehead. The servant girl returned with a second bowl of fresh water for the infant. She plopped it gloomily on the table as if to say, why bother? My mother sent her to fetch some freshly-pressed olive oil. The maid raised her eyebrows at that, but my mother paid her no attention.

"I must reach inside, Your Majesty," my mother said, rubbing her hands with the olive oil when it arrived, to make them slick. "It will be painful but I must know how your baby lies."

Watching her, I felt my armpits moisten, and the undersides of my breasts. I could see beneath her reassuring murmur the tension in her face. *Don't let it be crosswise,* I thought, over and over, a silent prayer. A woman had died this summer giving birth to an infant that had not turned into the opening of her womb, but lay crosswise against it. True, my mother had been attending another birth, but the outcome might well have been the same even with my mother's skill.

Gently my mother massaged the opening with the oil before sliding her hand inside. The princess groaned. My mother made a soothing sound, as she would to any birthing woman, her face still and concentrated as she felt for the babe. I watched her closely, praying for a smile, an easing of her facial muscles, any sign that all was well. But her eyes were still distracted, though she appeared calm and assured when she withdrew her hand.

"Your womb is open, Your Majesty. It won't be long now," she said. She let the princess have a moment with that news, her mouth smiling in response to the sigh of relief it invoked, but the smile did not reach my mother's eyes. There was worse news to come. "Can you walk, Your Majesty? The infant hasn't found the opening, but I'm hopeful he'll do so with a little encouragement."

Walk? The princess was so depleted she labored to breathe. How would she find the strength to rise from this bed, let alone walk? But somehow she did, and I admired her for it. We held her between us, half dragging her around the hot tent, my mother watching her taut belly beneath the linen shift the whole while. When she had contractions we let her rest against us, then urged her once again to walk. Her feet stumbled over the tapestry, sometimes dragging as we held her up, but she made no complaint. I began to pray silently for her. Not only because she was royalty and I feared reprisal; I wanted her to live because she deserved to, so valiantly she bore her pain and struggled to birth this child. When she could no longer move her feet and her head drooped listless on my mother's shoulder, we let her lie back down. My mother reached inside her again, and again the smile she presented to the princess did not reach her eyes.

"A sharp knife and a bit of twine," she ordered the servant girl. "And a strip of cloth two fingers wide, as long as my forearm." She reached into her basket and handed the girl a small packet. "Boil these herbs into a tea. The princess will need it to regain her strength after the birth." Turning back to the bed she said, "Your Majesty, I'll have to reach in once more and guide your baby out. It'll be painful, I'm afraid." She glanced at me and I nodded, to let her know I was ready.

I was not at all ready. I nodded because I knew if I spoke my voice would be shaking. All the lady's maid would need to prove our incompetence when the princess died along with her infant would be to remember my shaking, stuttering voice. But it was not ignorance that made me shake, it was the terrible knowledge that the babe was lying crosswise in the womb.

My mother bent her head down and reached into the womb, frowning with concentration. The brave young princess groaned, her face twisted with pain, but she endured it and lay still. I imagined my mother's fingers exploring the tiny body inside, searching for the feet to grasp onto, for she would not be able to turn its head down now. I held my breath.

Slowly my mother's hand emerged, covered in blood and brownish matter, holding tight to a little foot. One foot. I groaned under my breath. She could not pull the babe out by one foot. The other leg would get caught and if she pulled too hard it would tear his mother apart. At the very least the other leg would be broken, or this one disjointed, and what good was a lame prince to his father?

My mother did not pull on the foot. She reached for the strip of cloth which she had greased with olive oil, and tied one end tightly to the little ankle. Then—my mouth fell open in disbelief—she pushed that foot gently back inside. After a moment's groping her hand emerged again, this time holding the other foot! Grasping it firmly in one hand she gently tugged on the cloth until the second little foot emerged beside it.

"Bear down now, Your Majesty!" she said, her voice sharp and authoritative. The poor princess pushed, grunting, her face scrunched up with the effort like any peasant woman. "Push!" my mother cried, "Push harder!" The princess, near fainting, did her best.

The legs appeared, and the scrawny little torso, impossibly small. My mother reached her fingers in to secure the arms, and the next push revealed more of the torso and two tiny fists. I was relieved until I looked at my mother's face, tense and sweating. There was no room for my mother's hand now; she reached in only two fingers, feeling for something…

The cord! I had forgotten the cord. I imagined it circling the tiny neck—

"Push!" my mother said urgently, but the princess gave no response. Her face had gone slack. I leaned over her quickly and nodded to let my mother know she was still breathing, though faintly. My mother's face was grim as she pulled the babe's head out. The cord was twisted around its neck, but my mother had wedged two fingers between the neck and the cord. Only, how long had it been there, strangling the infant? My mother pinched the cord and cut it quickly, tying it with the twine when the baby's neck was free.

She handed the infant to me. I had no choice but to take him. He was covered in blood and smelling of gore and lay still, so very still in my hands. I pinched open his mouth and wiped my little finger round inside, clearing out the mucus and birth liquid, and leaned my ear against his mouth and nose, praying to hear even the smallest gasp of breath. His face was slack and his lips were cold and I could barely breathe myself, listening for him to. He was so tiny in my hands, with the lightness of a new, unsullied soul barely attached to its morsel of flesh. Lighter than a single breath. "Breathe!" I whispered urgently, with my ear against his little blue lips.

My mother had once breathed her own breath into a newborn, wanting the infant to live. It had, but it was ever after attached to her, and she to it, so that the mother became jealous and did not call on her for the next birthing.

"A child carries its mother inside it," my mother warned me after that. "Sometimes you see her in the child's eyes, in the shape of the mouth or the tilt of a chin. There is no room for another, as well."

The princess's little son lay unmoving in my hands. I swiped inside his mouth again but it was clear. He had come too far and the journey had been too long; he had no strength left for breathing. "Please breathe," I whispered again, rubbing his little back harder. We would be hanged, or worse. Desperate, I looked to my mother but she and the lady's maid were occupied with the princess, who lay as still and pale as her babe. The servant girl backed away from the bed, clutching the untouched mug of tea. They were both going to die!

I bent my head and blew my breath into the infant's mouth. I waited, and blew again, and felt it emerge through his tiny nose. He could not keep it inside him. I pinched his nose and blew again, willing him to take it into his lungs and learn to breathe. And again, before I could stop myself. *Breathe!* I ordered, silently.

He gave a little gasp, so faint I nearly missed it. I waited, not breathing myself, until I felt his little breath against my cheek. I watched him open his eyes, squinting and blinking in the dim light of the room. We stared at each other, he and I, so close I could not tell his sweet breath from mine, until the servant girl touched my arm. Her eyes were huge, incredulous, as she held out a cloth for me to wipe him with, and his swaddling clothes.

He gave a little mewl as I cleaned him, and pursed his lips, his little brow puckered as if he wondered where his milk was. My breasts wept in sympathy. Without thinking I pulled aside my bodice and slipped my nipple into his mouth.

Across the tent, the princess gave a low moan. My mother laughed softly with relief.

The servant girl crossed herself.

24

Chapter 3

March 5, 1346

Queen Joanna's Court, Naples

Hugo del Balzo is dressed in silks as though he were a prince, stopping just short of wearing purple. About his neck is a crusader's cross, bejeweled and finely wrought. The way he stands, the way his eyes take in the room to see who is noticing while he leans in conversation with the queen, always fingering the cross on his chest, makes me cold. A vain and dangerous man; his show of piety does not fool me. Those who are truly pious cannot see it in themselves, judging themselves unworthy, like Queen Joanna and her Grandfather, King Robert. Or else they try to hide it, fearing others will perceive it as a weakness. Which it is, for goodness blinds a person to the wickedness in others. Such as Hugo del Balzo, who pulls piety over his face like a mummer's mask. I was hopeful when he rode off on crusade, but the Saracens have disappointed me. Now he is back, after a visit with the Pope, which I also find suspicious. Regrettably, del Balzo cannot be kept out of council—he is Joanna's seneschal in Provence—so perhaps it is best my warning was preempted. I will speak to her when I have more certain proof of his treachery.

Joanna leaves her chamber with her small hand resting on del Balzo's arm while I follow behind. She stops inside her presence chamber and steps apart from him. Del Balzo bows, not quite as low as he should for his sovereign queen but near enough that he thinks

Joanna will not notice. I see a tiny tightening between her shoulder blades and smile to myself. Like most of the men in her court, he underestimates her. I have encouraged her not to enlighten them, to let her youth and beauty make them careless.

I note del Balzo's expression when Joanna leaves him to speak to Robert. He cannot bear that my son's position as seneschal of the Kingdom of Naples is higher than his as seneschal of Provence.

Charles of Artois approaches me. "I hear you were delayed by the disorder in our city?" he asks quietly.

I am not surprised that he has already learned of my morning's adventure. My sons trust him. Charles of Artois is the closest thing to an ally our family will ever have among the proud Neapolitan lords. The bastard son of King Robert the Wise, he knows what it is to be an outsider, to depend upon the benevolence of others and have to earn whatever position he achieves. Like us, he lost two strong supporters in the death of King Robert three years ago, and his wife, Queen Sancia, last year. His name and his son's name, like ours, have been linked to Andrew's death, only in their case I suspect it is accurate.

"It was disconcerting," I acknowledge. "I had not realized the situation had gone so far."

He nods thoughtfully. "It may be wise to leave the city."

"Wiser to remain."

"Yes. There is danger either way for those of us too close to the throne and yet not close enough."

I bend my head. He is closer than we are to safety, with half a royal bloodline. As he well knows. "God will protect the innocent," I answer mildly.

"I would like to see Him kept busier than that."

I allow myself a *huff* of amusement.

"Councilors," Joanna says. She leads us into her privy chamber. My sons follow close behind her with Hugo del Balzo behind them, his mouth pursed as though he has just eaten something foul. I enter last, watching the other councilors, who they speak to, who they sit beside. Allegiances change at times like this. The guards close the door behind me.

Joanna sits at the head of her council table, a signal that the rest of us may be seated.

Prepare yourself!

The room lurches beneath me before I have time to see who has spoken. I grab the back of my chair. An earthquake, I think, my heart pounding, my throat frozen silent. But when I look about the room, dizzy and shaken, no one else appears to be affected. Their attention is focused on my son Raymond, who is rising from his chair to speak. I swallow and sink down onto my seat. The two words still ring in my ears, spoken in the harsh accent of Catania, on the island of Sicily. Impossible. No one here but I has ever been to Catania, and I abandoned my childhood accent long ago.

That is how I know it is my great-grandmother, speaking to me from the grave. My mother warned me of her prophecies. I never met her and would not recognize her voice, but it is just as I have imagined. And I, the most composed, most stoic of courtiers, who never gives away anything I do not wish to have noted, I shiver as I take my seat, overcome with a sense of doom.

Raymond glances at me without pausing in his speech. He is a sensitive one, my Raymond, always aware of others. I have no doubt he has noted my pale face and indrawn breath, but he makes no sign of it, allowing me to regain my composure with dignity. I straighten my back and raise my chin. Let come what will, I will meet it as I always have. My other son, Robert, shifts in his chair, his attention fixed—pointedly?—upon his brother.

We three are once more among Queen Joanna's councilors, reinstated after the birth of her son to our former wealth and positions: Raymond as seneschal to the court, Robert as grand seneschal of the kingdom of Naples, and I as Queen Joanna's oldest, most trusted advisor. Secure once again.

"We must act now, before the situation gets out of hand, to ensure the safety of the citizens of Naples," Raymond is saying.

He is introducing his new law, a positive action, but I am still caught in the echo of that spectral warning and open to nameless fears. I recall my great-grandmother's prophecy at my birth, as my mother told it to me. A shudder sweeps through me before I can prevent it. No, I realize as my heartbeat resumes, I did not move. It is all happening inside me, this creeping sense of dread that chills me to the soul. Why now? Why is she speaking to me now?

My son's forceful voice brings me back to the council room. His every move and expression exude confidence and strength. I bask in it, pull some of it into myself. We trained our boys well, their father and I.

But he is gone and I am aging; I imagine things, my thoughts wander. I am prey to foolish fears. I have known worse crises than this in my sixty long years. Was I not certain that we were lost, our family ruined, when Pope Clement VI ordered our exile from court last year and Queen Joanna complied? Yet I hid my fear and denied Clement's accusation that I and my family had "provoked mischief" between Queen Joanna and her husband Andrew. We refuted it calmly, and not overmuch, as though it was too foolish to bear much discussion. Which it was; that pup Andrew needed no help in debasing himself, may God forgive me for speaking ill of the dead.

And here we are once again in the most vaunted positions in the kingdom, secure in Queen Joanna's affections. I dismiss the premonition. It is foolish and the chill that stays with me is only a symptom of my aged bones.

"I have therefore issued a decree prohibiting any man to bear arms in public within the city," Raymond finishes, laying his royal decree upon the council table with a flourish.

Joanna, of course, has already seen it; she is watching her councilors to see their reactions, as I taught her. "Let nothing surprise you," I told her, when as a young child she began attending her grandfather's council meetings. Since then, with a face as stoic as any great statesman, she has weathered many surprises. None, however, from me and my family, who serve her more faithfully than Pope Clement VI serves God.

I make my own survey of the councilors' faces.

Catherine of Valois, mother to Joanna's warring suitors, has taken up the decree and is reading it carefully. Trying to determine how to turn it to her advantage, as always. Our goals are the same for now: to keep Joanna secure in her crown and marry her to Louis, Catherine's favorite son. Oh, we are not allies. She is the Empress of Constantinople and the sister of the King of France, while I am the daughter of a fisherman. Even worse, my husband was a slave before King Robert elevated him; our children and grandchildren look nothing like these fine French aristocrats. No matter how high we have risen in Naples' cosmopolitan court, no matter that our son is now Count of Eboli and our granddaughter the Countess of Marcone, for Catherine of Valois we will always be what we were born. Well, she is not alone in that. So we are not allies, but today we are not enemies, for I, too, would see Joanna wed to Louis. Because it is true that he has sworn to protect Queen Joanna's intimates when she marries him, and innocent though we are, I and my family may need his protection.

On Raymond's left the Count of Terlizzi, marshal of the realm, nods vigorously in support of Raymond's decree. Like Joanna, he has already seen it. I would be ashamed if any son of mine did not know to prepare his allies and surprise his enemies.

Beside Terlizzi, Nicholas of Melizzano, having glanced at Joanna first, allows himself a careful nod of agreement. His expression gives little away, but there is a bead of sweat on his forehead. He knows he is balanced on a sword. He has ever been Joanna's man, and Andrew threatened him many times because of it. An impulsive man, easily frightened and prone to sly reprisals, he was certainly part of the conspiracy to murder Andrew. He thought Joanna wanted it also, and he was partly right, but more than partly wrong. For now Joanna is being accused of the crime by her Hungarian in-laws, and here in Naples she is accused at the very least of harboring the murderers. A teeter to the left or the right, and Melizzano will be dispensable.

Across the table, Catherine favors Terlizzi and Melizzano with a single scornful look. I feel it as much as see it from where she sits two seats up from me. Utterly predictable, all three. I am briefly amused.

Hugo del Balzo sits across from Catherine. I have been watching him most carefully, with no inclination at all toward humor. His face is bland as he looks at my son; only a tiny narrowing of his eyes and a slight flare of his nostrils, gone in a second, reveal his true feelings.

"There are mercenaries in the streets," he drawls, leaning back in his chair. He glances at Joanna. The mercenaries are Louis' army, paid for by Joanna, to fight his brother the Duke of Taranto's legitimate soldiers. Joanna meets del Balzo's look coolly. "Men will not part with their weapons when the streets are not safe," he finishes, as though he meant no more. He looks at Raymond directly. Again that slight flaring of his nostrils. "How will you enforce such a decree?"

Charles of Artois glances at me quickly. His look is meant as a warning. He can afford to give it, for he has royal blood; King Robert acknowledged him and none can deny it.

I have already seen the danger, but what can I do? What can Raymond do? He is seneschal of the court, it is his duty not only to make laws, but to enforce them.

"I will ride out myself, with the queen's men, and see that it is obeyed," my son says.

For a second time I feel the room sway beneath me. I press my arms hard against the table, willing myself still. It is the hardest thing I have ever done, keeping my mouth closed, swallowing the cry of protest. Oh my son! My son, Raymond!

Hugo del Balzo slowly smiles.

Chapter 4

Autumn, 1298
Trapani, Sicily,

Little Charles wanted to feed whenever he was awake. My Antonio was a placid babe, content to wait for his milk, but this little prince was furious for my breast as soon as he awoke. His little red face and pummeling fists made me laugh, and the sudden easing after his first few desperate gulps filled me with a tenderness I tried to hide. This was not my child. Princess Violante watched us jealously, her breasts bound, waiting to grab him from me as soon as he stopped suckling. I reminded myself that I had my own Antonio waiting for me as she took Charles from my arms, his eyelids drooping over those huge blue eyes, his little body relaxed and satisfied.

I tried not to watch her cuddle him, tried not to think of the ache in my own arms, reminded myself that I was a mother, too. But that only made it worse, for I could not hold my own child, I was not there with him to see the daily changes as he grew. Was he smiling now? Was he beginning to babble baby talk? My mother-in-law had found a neighbor to nurse him alongside her own newborn. Was my son gazing up at her, reaching to touch that other woman's cheek while she fed him, the way Charles patted mine?

My mother came daily to check on Princess Violante and baby Charles. When I had been there five days, I took her aside while the princess played with Charles. "It's time I returned to my son," I told my mother. She had warned me never to speak of Antonio in front of anyone, so I had to whisper, huddled in a corner with her. "You must find another woman to wet-nurse the prince." I glanced over enviously to where Princess Violante sat holding her son.

"He's a beautiful child," my mother observed. "You'll miss him."

"I miss my own son!"

"Antonio is happy and healthy."

"He needs his mother." I took a deep breath to still the tremble in my voice.

"Guilio's bought him a new swaddling cloth, soft and warm, to wrap him in. He commissioned Giovanni the carpenter to build a cradle. Your son lives like a little prince."

The extravagance left me speechless. I knew how pleased Guilio was to finally have a son, but a cradle?

"The head cook for the camp has ordered his servants to buy their fish from your father and your "uncle" Guilio. That's why your son lives this way."

"Uncle?"

"I told the princess your husband was lost at sea," she said in a low voice only I could hear.

My mouth fell open. "Why would you tell her that?"

"So you wouldn't be sent home to him."

I wondered how Guilio would like being thought my uncle. Then I pictured him selling his entire catch to the royal cook and boasting about it to the other fishermen. He liked it very much, I was sure.

"What are you whispering about?" Princess Violante demanded from across the room.

"Only a little family news, Your Majesty," my mother said smoothly. "Philippa's brother has got engaged, her father's bought his own boat. We owe you much for your generosity to our family."

"How nice that you, at least, are doing well." The princess's expression was sour with pain and weariness. She nodded to the nurse to take Charles. My mother hurried to her side, murmuring how well she was doing, how brave she had been, how proud she must be of her fine, handsome son, until the princess's frown cleared.

"My lord husband will be happy." She smiled, pleased with herself. When my mother handed her a mug of healing herbs she drank it down without a fuss. "He will be pleased with you and your daughter, also, for saving our lives. Yes I know how close—" she broke off with a shiver. "But every day I am stronger." She handed my mother the empty mug. "The prince will hear what you did. You will both be rewarded."

She was like that, unpleasant and generous alternately. Royals are always that way, my mother had warned me. I must be careful, consider their pleasure in everything I said and did. As if my mother had known a lot of royalty. But she was right about this one. She glanced at me now. I looked away. I did not want a reward, I wanted Antonio, my own little boy, to cuddle whenever I pleased.

My mother's right eyebrow arched, the only change in her steady gaze. I sighed.

As if I had ever lived such a life. I could cuddle my son when the house had been cleaned and Guilio's fishing nets untangled and his clothes washed for the next day, if I was not too tired. I could play with our child when I had finished the soldiers' laundry I must take in and had fetched our daily water and cooked my husband's meal. I could hold Antonio as long as I wanted in the night to keep him from crying while Guilio slept. Now I understood why Guilio had not sent word ordering me home to work myself to exhaustion for him. I was here, making him a rich man. He would not welcome me home while there was money to be made.

Violante would soon leave her confinement and Charles would go to the day nurse. He would stop needing to feed so often; then I would be able to slip away to see my son. I smiled at Princess Violante, and offered to comb her hair while her lady read to her. I knew how she liked it combed now, and had learned how to braid it up from watching her lady's maid. My mother nodded, satisfied, and left.

A few days later we received news that Prince Robert had lost a skirmish. He was coming back to the castle to regroup and allow his men a brief rest. A flurry of activity followed throughout the encampment as unused tents were readied for weary men and cots prepared for the wounded. Extra supplies were purchased, fish and game salted. The cook came to the door of our tent himself to enquire of the princess which delicacies the prince favored. The preparations revived her, even if she could only have her maid relay her instructions while she was still bleeding. No man wished to be emasculated by the strength of her feminine element at this time.

I helped Violante's maid wash and comb out her hair. Even with the extra attention it was thin and dull. We wiped the princess's sweat away with rosewater and put her into a clean night robe, and I braided up her hair, hiding it under a clean white cap. The princess supervised all this attention, looking into her glass anxiously, changing her cap and collar several times, never content with what she saw. Nor would I be if I was her, but I lied for her sake, most convincingly. I had learned from her maid how to make myself agreeable. I watched now as her jewels were brought to the tent and held up against her neck and ears to determine which would look prettiest with her gown. I memorized the name of each stone.

Neither the maid nor I mentioned what we were both thinking while we primped Violante to please her husband: that Prince Robert had another woman come to his tent at night when he was in camp. Childbirth is a lengthy business, and a man is a man. I pitied Violante, who had faced down death so bravely and had so few natural assets to combat this. But she had one.

"Hold your baby when he comes," I suggested. "The prince will find you the most beautiful woman alive with his son in your arms."

She looked at me and I feared she would take it wrong, but then she smiled and clapped her hands for him. The nurse lifted Charles from his cradle and put him in her arms, sound asleep and bound to his swaddling board. It was an uncomfortable armful but she looked down at Charles, her face flushed with love, and she was indeed a pretty sight when Robert of Anjou came into the room.

I curtsied as the door opened, like all the other women except the princess. They kept their heads bowed so I did also, wondering how long we must stay like this. Prince Robert swept by us as though we were furniture, straight to his wife's bedside. "Un autre fils!" he cried, and though I did not understand the foreign words his joy was obvious.

I looked up, unable to help myself, and saw him present her with a new chain for her neck. It gleamed golden in his hand, with blue stones—sapphires, I reminded myself, having seen them in the brooch she was wearing. He took the infant from her so she could have her maid clasp the jeweled band around her neck. I looked up fully then, still crouched in my curtsey.

He stood by the princess's bed, his profile to me as he looked down at his son. He was taller than any man I knew, his body taut with muscle, powerful. No wonder he was unconcerned about coming into his wife's birthing chamber. The idea that this young prince, whose very presence radiated virility, could be emasculated was absurd. His head was bent down to his son's face, murmuring words in that musical language of his as a woman might do to her child, but nothing about this hardened soldier was womanish.

He was younger than his wife, whom I suddenly pitied, for no woman could be beautiful beside this man. Even in the dull light of the room his yellow hair shone like the sun. I had never seen such hair. His eyes were pale, as blue as the sea, a startling shade. His skin was fairer than any in Sicily, despite the golden touch of the sun, so that he looked like a shining statue. I could not look away; I feared if I did he would disappear and I would never see such a man again. *Robert of Anjou*, I whispered under my breath, naming him, making him real. No one had told me the French were so beautiful, only that they were foreign. As foreign as gods, I thought. Why ever had we not wanted a French king? What did it matter that no one in Sicily spoke French? This young warrior-prince would surely speak

Italian and if he did not, who cared what he was saying as long as that rich, mellow voice kept speaking?

I forgot the cramp in my legs, the sore spot in my back. I could have bent there staring up at him forever. If only I had been able to wash my hair and change my cap and collar as Princess Violante had. As if I had a second cap or any collar at all! I had never longed for fancy things but I did now, for him. I wanted to make him see me, notice me, even once.

He kissed Charles on the forehead and handed him back to his nurse—oh, how I wished I was the day nurse and not merely the wet nurse. Did their hands touch when she took Charles? What would it be like to touch this prince? He bent over Violante and kissed her full on the lips, murmured something that made her blush and smile, and then he left us. He had not once glanced at me. The princess had not told him how I—my mother and I—had saved her life and his son's. I was sorry, but I could not blame her. It was impossible to collect one's thoughts in his presence. Surely we were all of us only now coming out of a spell cast by the golden prince who had just left us.

I did not see Prince Robert again before he led his men back into battle a few days later. I prayed that he would not be killed, and it was a small step from that to praying he would win over Frederick III. If he were our crown prince he might stay in Sicily. Even after I returned home to Antonio and Guilio, I might hope to see him riding past sometimes.

I looked at Princess Violante differently after that visit. To think she was married to such a man. She was not much to look at, but he had kissed her in front of us all and made her blush. I tried not to think of that kiss, of how his hand must have felt, warm on her cheek, of what he might have whispered, but I began to watch her, how she moved her hands, how straight she sat with her head held high. It no longer looked proud or vain to me, but womanly and desirable. Strong. A strong man likes a strong woman, a woman who knows her worth, my mother had often told me. I had thought that foolishness, not seeing it in my father or Guilio or any of the boys I knew, who wanted submissive women. Now I remembered Violante's quiet courage in the face of her likely death and Prince Robert's expression when she sat holding his son so straight and proud before he kissed her. My mother was right. I straightened my back, even when I was feeding Charles, and tried to remember to hold my head up.

The next time my mother came I asked her, since they had money enough now, to bring me some shoes. I was ashamed of having bare feet here, where even the servant girl wore woven slippers. Hers were not good, softened leather, and not dyed in blue or green or russet like the princess's and her maid's, but even they looked better than my dirty bare feet. As my mother prepared to leave I suddenly realized I had forgotten to ask about Antonio. It was too late now. Charles was complaining in his cradle and he could go from whimpering to screaming in the time it took to cross the room if I did not put him to the breast quickly enough. Princess Violante hated to hear him cry. Well, my mother would be back and I could hear about my son then, I told myself as I lifted little Charles from his cradle and loosed him from his swaddling board.

When the princess stopped bleeding the tent door was thrown open and the window flaps tied back. Charles and his nurses were moved into a smaller tent nearby, which became the nursery. We opened the window flaps to let in some light; Charles was now several weeks old and need not be protected from a mild daytime breeze. The princess visited every day, but my mother had no more excuse to come. I was free to play with Charles after his feedings when the nurse and I were alone with him. Since it made her job easier the nurse was happy to leave him with me until he had to be bound back onto his swaddling board. I wondered if Antonio's legs were growing crooked, for we did not use swaddling boards as the nobility did but wrapped our babies only in their swaddling cloths. My mother had assured me his legs were straight, but I knew Charles' would be straighter.

We waited for news of the war. Now and then a wounded soldier would ride back to recover and tell us of a recent skirmish. At first the news was good, but then more wounded men began to arrive and their news was of losses and retreats. Soon every face I saw as I walked about the camp looked glum, including mine.

Violante's footstep outside the tent was my cue to pop Charles into his cradle if I was holding him. The nurse began to do the same; the princess was a jealous mother and now that the war was going badly it took very little to set her off. We curtseyed to the floor when she came through the door, and stayed there till she motioned us up.

Back straight, head bent, I chanted to myself as she stood looking us over critically. A messenger had come this morning from the most recent battle. We had not heard the news but we had seen the faces of those who had. My stomach was in knots with fear for the prince. Violante's face was not as anguished as I was sure it would be if he had been wounded, or worse. But who could tell with royalty what their face might show?

"I will speak with you later this afternoon," Violante said to the nurse. She turned to me. "And you, can you not wear another kirtle? I am tired of seeing you in those rags!"

"I have no other clothes, Your Majesty."

She looked down at me, eyes narrowed. "Then have your father order you one. He is doing well enough now, thanks to our generosity. And have it made in the French style. I am tired of looking at dowdy, dark Sicilian clothes and frowning faces!"

I forced myself to smile at her, still bent low in my curtsey. Fortunately, the princess had never learned to look at a person's eyes when they smiled. Royalty does not need to know the value of the smiles given them.

"What is there to smile at?" she shrieked. "Get up! And see that you have a better kirtle tomorrow!" She left the room with a swirl of silk, graceful despite her petulance.

I rose from my curtsey and looked down at my kirtle. It was not the bright blue of the princess's silks, but there was a bluish hue to it, and despite being only rough homespun it was nearly new; I only wore it in the evenings. I had been married in it. If Princess Violante wanted to see rags, she should see what I wore to do my chores at home: the dull grey skirt I had worn to save her baby's life!

I took a breath. It was no use being annoyed or embarrassed. Let the nurse smirk at me from across the room. At least Prince Robert was unharmed. Violante would not have been able to say "*our* generosity" so casually if he were dead.

"What will you do when they leave and King Frederick III learns you served them so faithfully?" I asked the nurse. The same could be said to me, of course, but I wanted the smirk gone from her face.

"Nothing, for when they leave, I will go with them. The baby will need his nurse on the journey," she answered.

I gaped at her. Such a thing had never occurred to me. I had hoped to escape my life for a little while, had thought now and then that if they stayed… But to go to Naples with them? Across the sea to a foreign land? It was inconceivable. I looked at the nurse's smirking face. And yet… who would feed Charles on the journey?

No. I pushed the idea from my head. My home was here.

The next day another messenger came. I was in the princess's tent, braiding up her hair and helping her to dress, for her maid was ill. Violante sent me away, but it was clear what the message was, for as soon as the man left her tent, Princess Violante ordered all their belongings packed up. I learned it would be several days before Prince Robert and what was left of his men arrived, but she was determined to be ready. She sent two dozen armed men—nearly all those she had here in any shape to fight—to Catania to hold the town. If Catania rebelled in a show of loyalty to Frederick III, they could cut off Robert's retreat to his ships. For the first time I saw fear in her eyes, but it did not deter her, rather it spurred her on.

Later that day one of the cook's helpers arrived at the nursery tent with a yellow kirtle in her arms. "The princess says when she gets back to civilization," she wrinkled her nose in a fair imitation of

Violante in a certain mood, "this will no longer be in style, so you may as well have it. You will have to let the hem down yourself."

I let her lay the kirtle over my arms in a daze. It was a brilliant yellow, like the sun, and made of fine linen! The color was perfect for me, with my black hair and dark eyes. My skin was fairer than it had ever been from staying inside the tent with Charles so much of the day. I would look like a lady in this gown! I blinked back tears. Guilio would never let me keep it, but at least I could wear it here for the next few days.

"Princess Violante wishes to speak with you. Someone will come to take you to her tent later today. You are to wear this." The girl smiled, a mixture of envy and good will, and left me with my yellow linen miracle.

I draped it over a chest and stared at it as I fed Charles. The next time the tent door opened it was my mother. "I heard," she said, walking briskly toward me. "So they will leave us now."

I pressed my finger against my breast, breaking Charles' hold, and eased him off my nipple. He had already stopped suckling but protested anyway as I handed him to his nurse. I motioned toward my yellow kirtle, unable to hold in my smile.

Her eyes lit up. "You're going with them!"

"Of course not." I frowned at her. She knew I had a husband even if no one else knew. "It's only a gift for my services. She didn't want to bother packing it. Will you help me lower the hem?" I did not add that I had only a few days to wear it; she would know that.

"I will be going with them to Naples," the nurse said, standing up proudly after depositing her charge in his cradle. Violante had asked her to accompany them home the day the messenger came. The woman had been crowing about it to anyone who entered the nursery tent. Not many did, so she was desperate enough to boast to my mother. Everyone else was busy getting ready to leave as soon as the prince and his men arrived. King Frederick III had soundly beaten Prince Robert and was preparing to drive him out of Sicily.

My mother and I hemmed in silence. When it was done she insisted on washing my hair before I put it on and had me send for some water. Borrowing three hairpins from the nurse, who sulked unwillingly but was afraid to refuse my mother, the woman who had saved the princess's life, she braided up my hair. I closed my eyes as she lifted the beautiful gown over my head and pulled it down around me. I had never felt anything so light and cool. It was like walking inside a breeze. I blushed, feeling as though I was wearing nothing but my shift.

My mother looked at me astonished. "How did I not know you were so beautiful?" she said, making me blush even more.

"Better not get used to it," the plain nurse said. "You will have no occasion to wear it here when the prince and princess are gone. Unless you want to announce to King Frederick III that your loyalties were not with him."

"She can't have given it to you now, for no reason..." my mother murmured, paying no attention to the nurse's envious words.

"I told you, Mother, she didn't want to pack it." I twirled like a child, watching the skirt swirl out around me.

The door to the nursery opened. I stopped twirling, embarrassed.

"I have come to take you to Her Highness' presence chamber." The princess's guard stood at the opening, looking me over approvingly. Would I never stop blushing?

My mother beckoned me. "A moment, please," she said to the guard as I followed her into a window alcove.

"She'll ask you to go with her," she said quietly. "You must say yes."

"I... I can't," I stammered. "You know I can't, Mother!"

"You were bound to go with them the moment I called you from the river."

"Why me? Why not my sister? Why—"

"Because you are bold and quick-witted enough to succeed. Now go!"

"Wait! What if she doesn't want me to bring Antonio?"

41

She looked at me as though I were simple. "Of course you can't bring Antonio. I told the princess your babe died soon after it was born."

I stared at her, horrified, and crossed myself.

"Do you think your husband'd let you leave if you tried to take his son?"

Never. I didn't have to think to know the answer. Which showed I had not thought about it at all. Guilio was an indifferent husband but he was proud as a cock strutting about the hen-yard crowing the praises of his son. He had had only daughters with his first wife, sickly infants who mostly had not lived long. He was constantly fussing over Antonio who was since birth as strong and healthy as I have always been.

"If you try to take the child he'll show up and make a scene. Princess Violante will look a fool, not knowing her own servant was married and had a son."

"And whose fault is that?"

"D'you imagine you're irreplaceable, daughter? That there are no other girls in Catania willing to wet-nurse the son of the crown prince of Naples?"

I shook my head miserably, looking at my feet. "I can't leave Antonio," I mumbled, near to crying. "How I've missed him these past weeks!" Antonio was my son, not Charles, however beautiful and sweet Charles might be. Charles could never take Antonio's place in my heart.

"Young Francesca's daughter died of a fever last week," my mother said. I felt her watching me although I would not look up. "Shall I tell her Violante of Aragon is looking for a wet-nurse for her son? Would you rather Francesca goes to Naples while you stay here with Guilio?"

"No!" I whispered fiercely. I looked at her, wretched with indecision.

"You must go," she said. "I'll watch out for Antonio. He'll be happy and well cared for with his father."

Still I could not go. My feet were stuck to the floor, my heart as heavy as an iron bolt holding me in place. I wanted to stand there forever and never have to make this terrible choice. What kind of woman would desert her own child?

"You must go, Philippa," my mother said again. "It's your destiny. My grandmother foretold it at your birth."

"Beware of tempting Fortune."

My mother snorted. "Good advice for foolish, fearful people."

"How does it end, the prophecy?"

"How can anyone know?" She looked surprised—eyes wide, brows drawn together in a puzzled frown. If I had not seen her fool others so often—women in labor who needed reassurance, my father who would not have let her keep a penny to buy us clothes if he had known what she was really paid—it might have worked.

"You always stop before it ends. Don't lie to me, mother. I'll know. If I'm to go away and leave Antonio, I want to know it all. Or else I won't go."

She watched me, considering. Weighing my resolve against hers. My mother could prophesy a little. Not like my great-grandmother, and not for anyone she cared about. But even with strangers she never told them how they would die, or any other awful thing she saw. "It does no good," she said, "and often does harm. A man told he'll die in his sleep is afraid to sleep. Finally, exhausted, he succumbs to sleep on his fishing boat and falls overboard. A woman is told her husband will desert her. From then on she looks at him with suspicion and imagines he's sleeping with every woman who looks at him. Eventually, her distrust and accusations drive him to leave her. The prophecy comes true in the telling. Because of the telling." No matter how much money she was offered, no matter if my father beat her half to death, she would not tell if she saw tragedy or death in a person's future.

"I won't leave without knowing," I repeated. "And then none of the prophecy will come true and you'll know what I think of prophecies." I snapped my fingers scornfully, because what I thought of my great-grandmother's prediction, of its power or lack of power over me, was the important part for my mother.

"Then you'll have to stay," she said.

"So be it," I answered, but it hurt me. It pierced me to the core, the thought of staying when I was so close to… escape. To a life at a royal court, to wearing garments like this yellow kirtle and having food sent to me when I was hungry and discussing what was happening in the world, if only with the other servants. To being able to see Robert of Anjou again. I had to reach the point of losing all of it to know how much I wanted it. Needed it. I would suffocate here, married to Guilio, taking in laundry, mending his fishing nets and cooking his dinners…

"Tell me, Mother," I pleaded. "I already know it's bad, or you would've told me. I know no prophecy is binding. We're bound to the wheel of Fortune only by our own accord. But if you keep it secret it will haunt me. I'll imagine ten new things each night, every one worse than whatever my great-grandmother saw. There's greater power in secrets than in prophecies!"

"Enough!" the guard called across the room. "Who are you, to keep Her Royal Highness waiting?"

"She's coming," my mother called, pretending to adjust my gown. "It's your own choosing, then," she murmured, and leaning close, she told me.

I went with the guard, and when Violante asked me to come with her to Naples as Charles' wet-nurse, I curtsied low and said I would go. I kept my eyes downcast walking back to the nursery and tried to think of Antonio, to remember his little face and be sad. But it was blurry in my mind. When had I stopped thinking about him? I wanted to weep. I told myself I would never see him again, trying to make myself weep.

But my heart was as light as a bird and all I could see when I closed my eyes were the white sails of the Neapolitan ships in the harbor at Catania that would carry me far away.

Chapter 5

March 6, 1346
Queen Joanna's Court, Naples

I walk with seeming carelessness toward a window overlooking the courtyard, where I can look down at my son and the soldiers assembling to go with him. Behind me Joanna's ladies-in-waiting chatter as they play cards or bend over their needlework. I lean through the open shutters, pretending to want a little air, and let their feminine voices fade behind me.

In the courtyard Raymond is giving instructions to a dozen soldiers of the queen's guard before they ride out to enforce his decree. "Do not attack, no matter what you hear." His voice carries up to me.

"You mean we are to let them insult us, or Her Majesty the Queen?" one of the men demands. His unlined face is frowning, his voice high with the indignation of youth.

"We are not charged by the queen to attack her subjects," Raymond answers sharply. "Only draw your sword if I give the sign, or if you yourselves are attacked."

"And if they won't surrender their weapons peacefully?" This one is older, his voice level. He watches Raymond's face as he waits for his answer.

"Then we will take their swords by force." Raymond pauses, looking around at his men. "Prepare yourselves for some resistance, but we will meet it together. Preferably without harming anyone."

Or letting yourselves be harmed, I think, wishing I could call it down to him. It is not my place to correct the court seneschal; bad enough if his men catch his mother watching over him, a man of forty-two years. I should withdraw, but I cannot make myself, not even when they mount and turn their beasts toward the gate. The courtyard is suddenly loud with the neighing of horses, the jangle of bridles as they shake their heads trying to take the bit, the stamp of shod hooves against the hard ground. The swords in the men's scabbards slap against their leather leg-guards as they wheel their horses. The gate opens noisily. Raymond twists in his saddle to glance up at me. There is humor and affection and exasperation all in that quick glance before he turns back and touches his spurs to his horse's flanks. They canter through the gate, my son in the lead. I watch until they disappear into the twisting, narrow streets of Naples. Six of Louis' mercenaries fall in behind them, close enough to lend assistance if needed but far enough to avoid any association with the queen's guard. Raymond has agreed to this precaution at my insistence, but he would not agree to more than six. The mercenaries have hidden their swords under their cloaks at his insistence, and no doubt have an arsenal of knives hidden under their garments. I take comfort in those hidden weapons guarding my son and his little band.

When they are out of sight, I still stand there listening. There is a current of discontent running through this city I know so well. I hear the low grumble of its citizens arguing, shouting an insult or two to show their anger but in the end obedient to the law. It is what I expect to hear; what I hope to hear, and nothing more.

It is not only the forces of Robert, the Duke of Taranto and Charles, the Duke of Durazzo who are riding through Naples fully armed, but Louis' mercenaries also. Robert of Taranto would have his men storm the palace and take Joanna by force if it were not for Louis and his mercenaries also riding through the city streets. There are skirmishes daily between the two forces; may God protect any honest citizen caught between them. How will Raymond convince either side to lay down their weapons inside the city boundaries? He knows it is a lost cause, I have told him so and he agreed, but how can he maintain his position if he refuses to enforce the queen's laws? How will he keep the respect of the men he commands? Louis has promised to order his mercenaries to hide their weapons and not to draw their swords in the city. If Raymond can make Taranto's and Durazzo's men do the same, at least there will be fewer deadly clashes in our streets.

"Grandmother, come and sit. Uncle will be back when he is assured the new law is being obeyed. You cannot stand there the whole afternoon." My granddaughter Sancia touches my arm, drawing my attention away. "He is the seneschal of the royal court. He will be safe in Naples; none would dare touch him." She frowns, puzzled by my distress.

It is a trap. I do not say this out loud. She will not believe it, will think me imagining things in my age. The foolish fears of an old woman. I glance again at the window. Ah, but I thought I heard my great-grandmother's voice yesterday—perhaps young Sancia is not far wrong. I let her draw me back into the room. Still, I do not close the window shutters and I choose the chair nearest it.

Hugo del Balzo is in audience with Joanna in her privy chamber. Right where he cannot be blamed if anything happens.

That is my secret thought, but I will blame him. If anything happens to my son, I will know he had a hand in it no matter where he hides.

Robert is in there with them. Why would del Balzo want my son with them? Del Balzo hates my family, he would not ask for one of them present, not even the grand seneschal of the kingdom, when he meets with the queen. I stare at the closed door of the queen's privy chamber. Joanna seeks my counsel always, but I still have not voiced my concerns about del Balzo to her.

Hugo del Balzo is her appointed man as much as my sons are, and he is just back from a crusade in the Holy Land, which makes him halfway to being a saint in her eyes. She knows he has spoken against Louis, whom she loves, has even accused her of protecting those who are guilty of her husband's murder. In her mind this makes him a man of strong principles, for she knows he is at least partially right. Joanna does not want to learn who murdered Andrew, since he was most at enmity with those closest to her. Del Balzo is speaking the truth: if she can, she will protect them, and Louis has promised to help her. But she cannot appear to be doing so. Her people would not stand for it. The pope would not stand for it. They would believe the rumors that she herself was involved in Andrew's murder if it was apparent that she was shielding the real murderers from justice.

She knows we are innocent, I and my family. She has brought us back to court to show her trust. But if we are accused it will not matter. I who have served her all her life and her royal parents and grandparents before her, more loyally than any in her kingdom, I whom she loves, must ride out this storm on prayer and hope and whatever strength and courage I can find within myself.

"Grandmother?" Sancia has been talking to me. I have not heard her; I am too busy listening for sounds outside the window. I nod and smile anyway. She is making a little gown for the coming babe. This will be her second. She has a daughter already and hopes for a boy.

"Yes, your husband the Count will want a son," I agree. I consider getting up and going to the window again. Will I hear anything here, inside the room? But I do not want to call attention to the window, someone might ask for the shutters to be closed. What could I say? That I must listen in case the seneschal of the court calls for his mother?

I am being foolish. My husband, if he were still alive, would chide me for it. *Fear is our enemy,* he told me more than once. *Fear is the traitor that will open the gate to all our other enemies.* We were fearless, he and I, utterly fearless, rising like cream together in the Neapolitan court, raising our children, sons to be warriors as well as courtiers, daughters who would marry well. A stalwart little army in place of relatives and ancestors and a bloodline to call on. Our own strength and boldness fuelling theirs.

Now it is only mine, and I am faltering.

How can I keep them all safe, my children and my grandchildren and now great-grandchildren? Stand fast, I want to tell them. I have a terrible dread that if one of them should fall, even one, the rest will topple like a deck of cards all leaning one on the other.

"Hold fast," I say to Sancia.

"Grandmother?" She looks at me puzzled, frowning.

"Hold fast to your little ones," I amend. "They grow up so quickly."

Her brow clears. "They do! Maroccia is already walking. You must come and see her walk, Grandmother."

I smile as always at mention of my great-granddaughter. I told Sancia stories of my mother, Maroccia the midwife, while she was expecting; I often think of my mother now that I am old. It was a pleasant surprise when Sancia named her daughter Maroccia. I have been told she looks like me, but it is her namesake she takes after, her complexion the same sun-kissed Sicilian shade as my mother's. The first time I held her, she opened her eyes and looked solemnly up at me. I was surprised to see they were a deep blue. "As blue as the sea," I murmured, looking down at my great-granddaughter and remembering my long-ago passage to Naples. "She will carry us all into the future."

Sancia looked at me alarmed. She thought I was prophesying for her newborn daughter, and it is possible I was, although initially I thought only of the natural progression of a family.

I smile at Sancia now, returning my thoughts to the present, and promise her I will come soon. If this conflict between the royal cousins ever ends, I will go to see little Maroccia walk.

Sancia invites me to play a hand of cards. I agree, touched by her attempts to distract me. We join a table. She is gracious when I play badly and cheerfully pays when we lose. I excuse myself from another game and return to my chair by the window. Across the room the court musician begins to play for us. I am annoyed at first, for his song covers the distant noises coming through the window, but the music calms me and soon I am dozing in my seat.

I wake suddenly to the sound of cries in the courtyard. Sancia jumps up and goes to the window. I push myself stiffly to my feet and hurry after her.

It is the young knight, the one who wanted to draw his sword if the queen was insulted. He has ridden through the partly opened gate, shouting.

Blood on his livery, blood on his sword still clutched in his hand, blood on his horse. *Where are the others? Where is Raymond? Where is my son?* I look to the gate, willing myself to see the others galloping in behind him.

No one is there.

No one else is coming home.

The boy is still shouting. A single word, repeated: "Treachery!"

He tries to dismount and falls sideways, into the arms of a palace guardsman who has run to him.

"Treachery," the young man moans as he is carried across the courtyard and inside.

"Summon the queen!" My voice cracks, the words coming out a thin croak. Sancia looks at me wide-eyed. I turn toward the palace guard standing stiffly at the door of Joanna's privy chamber and take a deep breath. "Summon Queen Joanna," I order in a voice that carries across the room. "Something has happened that she must know about."

He hesitates, looking at the closed door.

I draw myself up to my full stature. "Summon Her Majesty! At once!"

He snaps to attention and reaches for the handle to the door, but it is pushed open from inside. Joanna strides out, Robert right behind her. He looks around the room quickly until he finds me, the alarm in his eyes increasing when he sees my face. Behind them del Balzo follows, his eyebrows arched as though he is surprised, but a tiny lift at the corners of his lips denies it.

Joanna cuts across the room toward to door of her presence chamber. She glances at me briefly as she passes. "Come!"

I would have followed anyway but now I hurry to walk with her and Robert, explaining in a low voice what I have seen as we go through to the outer chamber and down the wide stairs. Halfway down we are met by one of the guards I saw assisting the wounded boy inside.

"Your Majesty." He bows low. His livery has red stains upon it. I look aside.

"What is it? What has happened?" Joanna demands without stopping her descent.

"One of your men," the guard turns, trying to keep up with his sovereign, trying to catch his breath—fear? "One of the men who went out this morning with the court seneschal has returned!"

"One of them? And the others?" Joanna is nearly at the bottom of the stairs. She glances sharply at the silent guard, and hurries on. I see the young man lying on a marble bench inside the door. The guard who carried him there quickly stands at attention when he sees his queen. His livery is covered in the boy's blood. "Bring the court physician," Joanna snaps at a hovering servant. "You!" to the first guard, "Take two men and go out to the gate. I want the guard on it doubled."

By now she has reached the wounded man. "Tell us what happened," she says in a gentler voice.

"We were betrayed," he gasps. His face is pale, his voice already weaker than it had been in the courtyard. The blood on his clothes is bright and wet. "We heard raised voices in the market square. When we got there, several men were arguing. Two of them drew weapons on each other. Lord Raymond rode toward them, urging us to follow." He is stopped by a fit of coughing. A line of blood trickles from the side of his mouth. I wipe it away, the habit of a woman trained in healing, and urge him to continue.

"I was behind the last man. I drew my sword but Lord Raymond did not, nor the others, they were waiting for his signal. He called to the arguing men, ordered them to put down their weapons. But they ignored him, seeming to fight until he got near, then suddenly all together they turned their weapons on us! More men ran out from the market stalls where they had been hiding, cutting us off. Our men tried to draw their weapons but they were surrounded by men already armed. They dragged them down off their horses—" he is sobbing, his left side and leg soaked with fresh blood. He coughs again, a terrible, wet sound.

"Raise him!" I say. The guard beside him helps him into a sitting position, holding him up. The cough eases. "Can you continue?" I ask, trying to sound concerned, compassionate, when in fact I am desperate to hear the rest.

"Lord Raymond warned us to watch for groups of men wearing the colors of Taranto or Durazzo. But these were all dressed plainly, as simple citizens. Even the mercenaries missed it, and they were too far behind us when it happened…" His voice is weak, his eyes drift upwards.

"Lord Raymond?" Robert prompts.

"He called retreat!" The boy's eyes are wild, his voice no more than an urgent whisper. "He ordered us to retreat but I was the only one who could. I had already drawn my sword, they couldn't get near to pull me down—" he gasps. Blood drips steadily from his thigh onto the floor. I want to urge him to stop, the exertion is killing him. I want to scream, *What happened to my son?*

"Did you see what happened to Lord Raymond?" Robert asks again, calm and controlled.

"They have taken him. They… they killed the others, but took him alive. He was still yelling "Retreat!" trying to save us as they dragged him away." He gasps for breath, staring at us wildly. "Too late! They were dead, the others are all dead!"

"Where have they taken him? Did you see who it was? Who was leading them?"

Joanna lays her hand lightly on Robert's arm. The boy is struggling for breath and the physician has arrived.

"The Duke…" the boy gasps. "The Duke of Taranto…" He falls into a faint.

My son Robert stares at me. I stare back at him, too numb to cry out. The Duke of Taranto, Robert of Taranto, that arrogant, cruel, ruthless man has taken Raymond.

I know exactly what he wants with my son.

Chapter 6

Autumn, 1298
Trapani, Sicily

I woke to the thunder of horses' hooves. I ran to the door of the nursery tent and peered out into the darkness. The entire encampment was waking to the commotion of horses neighing and men calling and servants running in every direction. I called out to one as he ran past toward the royal tents, but he would not stop to give me the news. Light flared in the night as the cooks lit the kitchen fires. In that uneven light I saw Prince Robert surrounded by half a dozen men, commanders of his army. Even in the night he was unmistakable, with his yellow hair and fair skin and dominating height. My heart skipped faster as he strode past. I gave a silent prayer of thanks to Saint Martin of Tours for the golden prince's safe return from battle.

Princess Violante appeared at the opening of her tent. She gave a glad cry on seeing him. He turned and went to her. I listened shamelessly from the shadow of the nursery tent which stood beside the princess's tent.

"We must get to our ships as soon as possible."

"What, now? This very night?"

"As soon as we have eaten and rested our horses. King Frederick's army is not far behind us. We will have to leave whatever is not packed."

"Everything is packed. We can leave as soon as I am dressed and the tents taken down."

"A true princess," he murmured, kissing her forehead.

I touched my own forehead as though I felt his lips there while I watched him walk back to his commanders. He must be weary, having fought a battle, then riding hard to get here, but his stride was long, the muscles in his legs taut under his hose, the arm he had put around his wife...

"Wake the prince's son and get him ready for travel!"

I whipped my hand away from my forehead and turned to see Princess Violante frowning at me. I dropped a hasty curtsey as she disappeared inside her tent.

I shook the nurse awake, surprised that she could sleep through all the din, then woke little Charles and put him to my breast. He was sleepy and drank little. I gently slapped his feet to keep him awake. When a soldier stuck his head inside our tent, demanding we leave so he could take it down, I gave up and handed Charles to his nurse. "We will be ready directly," I told him. While the nurse bound Charles to his swaddling board I considered quickly what to wear. We would be travelling hard, then taking to open water. I did not want to soil my fine new kirtle. My hand hovered over my drab homespun robe.

Outside I heard Charles' voice calling a command to his men. *You are no longer a fisherman's daughter!* I told myself as I tossed it onto the dirt and pulled on the yellow linen kirtle. I would take nothing of my old life with me.

A soldier lifted me onto the bedding wagon where I sat holding baby Charles. Beneath us the royal blankets and feather mattresses made our ride as soft as floating on a cloud, despite the rattling pace of the wagon. The night was still dark as we made for the sea and safety.

Catania was several hours' ride away, and then the port beyond it. I had never travelled so far from home. Charles slept in my arms as we passed the huts of my village and left them behind. The

Sicilian nurse sat up front with the driver, a soldier who spoke only French, all three of us silent, alone with our thoughts. As the night wore on I thought of my mother and sisters, my son Antonio. I felt myself surrounded by strangers. What was I doing, fleeing into the unknown, alone and unprotected? More than once I imagined myself setting Charles down and jumping off the wagon to run home. If I had been wearing the drab blue dress Guilio had given me I might have done so, but I was in the beautiful yellow kirtle with its promise of an enchanted life, and now and then, in the night wind, I thought I heard my great-grandmother calling me toward the future she had predicted.

I tried not to think what would happen to me if we were caught. My new kirtle clearly proclaimed me a traitor to King Frederick. I would be lucky to receive a quick death if his men caught me. Charles' nurse was dressed in the plain, dark Sicilian robe of a village wife. Now that it was too late I understood why she had dressed that way, ready to pass herself off as a loyal Sicilian. The bundle of her new clothes lay in the wagon near me, beside a small packet of herbs my mother had insisted on giving me for the journey. If we were stopped, I would be caught with both. I shivered though the night was warm, but I stayed where I was, rocking Charles and humming softly to distract myself.

When we finally arrived at the harbor I reached for the packet of herbs, hesitated a moment, then grabbed the nurse's bundle and slung them both over my shoulder. Tightening my hold on Charles, I slid down off the wagon. Dawn was breaking. Servants and soldiers rushed about shouting instructions. Horses, protesting loudly, were being coaxed over a gangplank onto a ship tied to the small wharf. Three other ships bobbed on the water a short distance away. I saw two rowboats, heavily laden, making their way toward those ships, and two others in the shallows being loaded with goods from the wagons. I looked around for Violante but could not see her in the dark crowd of bodies.

"The princess asks for her son," a soldier said, appearing beside me. He looked me up and down appraisingly.

"I'm Prince Charles' nurse. Take us to the princess," I said.

"And who is she?" He nodded toward the front of the wagon where the day nurse in her worn dark clothes was being helped down from her seat.

"A Sicilian woman. A camp follower." I began walking away from the wagon. "Do you mean to keep Princess Violante waiting?"

I heard him chuckle as he caught up with me and took the lead, forcing a path through the crowd. It quickly closed in again behind us, swallowing us in the press of weary bodies and the dim light of early dawn.

Despite the commanders shouting at the men for greater speed, the sun was full up by the time we set sail. The wind whipped my hair about my head and flung salt spray onto my cheeks, and the ship bobbed on the water like a twig heading out into the endless sea. I stood on the deck holding another woman's baby, watching my country, my home, and everything familiar slipping away. I was a stranger among these people with my sun-browned skin and black eyes and my foreign accent. I knew little of their ways and less of their city. When my usefulness was over I would be nothing to them; less than nothing, an embarrassment in their polished, sophisticated court. I trembled on the deck, unbalanced as much by the thought of what I was doing as by the movement of the sea beneath me. I stared hungrily at the receding shore of Sicily, imagining myself leaping into the briny water and swimming home like a fish. Only I could not swim. I was a girl who waded in a shallow river to wash laundry, not a shining silver fish at home in the open sea. I was tethered to this boat and the choice I had made.

She will travel far from home, my great-grandmother foretold at my birth. But it was not my great-grandmother's prophecy that had brought me here. It was my mother's implacable will. And mine, I added in fairness. I straightened my back and raised my chin. And mine.

At least I had not been caught escaping with the invaders. I would not be executed as a traitor in my yellow dress. It occurred to me then that I was leaving forever. As long as King Frederick III ruled Sicily, I could never return. I stared out at my island, trying to commit to memory this last sight of my home.

A blur on the land caught my attention. Shielding my eyes I thought I saw a dust cloud far inland. King Frederick! This close he had been behind us! This close I had come to an agonizing death! The chance I had taken frightened me more than the choice I had made. A choice that had, in part, been made for me. I would have cursed my mother if the knowledge that I would never see her again did not tighten my throat until I nearly choked on unshed tears.

A cry rose up around me as others noticed the dust cloud and began pointing to it. After the discouragement of failure and a humiliating retreat, this small victory, escaping intact from King Frederick's late-arriving army, lifted the soldiers' spirits. They stood cheering from the decks of all four ships. I imagined King Frederick and his soldiers gnashing their teeth and shooting their arrows harmlessly into the sea as we sailed out of reach jeering at them, and I added my voice to the general merriment. The day nurse, who had been waving frantically from the beach in her Sicilian clothing, looked behind her and ran from the harbor to hide among the townsfolk. I laughed loudly. How she had mocked me when she thought she was chosen to accompany the princess and I was not!

The noise woke little Charles. He made a face and soiled his clout.

"That for King Frederick III," I said. Those near enough to see the baby's red, distracted face laughed at my joke and passed it on. I had never had so many young men smiling their approval at me, and not only because of my wit. I smiled back saucily, thinking myself one with them now.

I expected the joke to be soon forgot, but more and more men looked my way. Assuming they were interested in their prince's son, who most of them had not yet seen, I held him so his pretty little face was clearly visible. But many of the admiring looks—and the comments that accompanied them—were clearly meant for me. I attributed it to the yellow kirtle, which conferred a portion of its beauty onto me, but I flushed with pleasure nonetheless.

Charles took that moment to announce his hunger. Emboldened by the success of my first quip, I made a second: "The son of the crown prince of Naples has an appetite for Sicily and he will have her soon enough."

It was a bawdy joke, not the kind Violante or her lady's maid would have made, but the soldiers roared their approval, repeating it to others as I made my way below decks to find a quiet place to change and nurse Charles.

The laughter followed me downstairs to the little cabin Charles and I had been given. I was smiling as I stepped inside, pleased with myself. These Neapolitans liked me! I sighed deeply, feeling the long night's tension leave me. I had taken a step that could not be taken back; I had no home but with them from the moment I stepped on board this ship. But it would be all right. I could make them like me. I changed Charles' clout and put him to my breast.

My eyes drooped wearily. It had been a long, hard ride through the night. Charles was still sucking intermittently, half asleep against my breast. I did not want to waken him; he had slept so little the night before and been too unsettled to nurse this morning. I jiggled him a little to get him to take some more. I was so tired. I slid down off the little stool onto the floor where I could lean back against the wall, and closed my eyes...

"I will not have my son raised by a trollop! Where is his nurse?"

I looked up, startled, from the floor where I had been dozing against the wall. The front of my kirtle was unlaced and my shift pulled down, exposing my breasts. Charles lay across one of them, having fallen asleep suckling. Princess Violante stood over me in the little cabin, glowering. Behind her, her lady's maid smirked down at me.

"Where is Charles' day nurse?" the princess repeated.

"She... she saw the Sicilian army coming and ran into the town to hide," I answered, somewhat honestly.

Violante's face changed, surprise, then anger.

"I'm not a woman of loose morals, Your Majesty," I protested, sitting straighter and pulling my shift up and the front of my kirtle together over my breasts, an awkward maneuver while holding a sleeping baby. "I've known no man but my husband." I let my voice tremble and my eyes water, since she believed he was dead. Behind the princess her maid pursed her mouth, making a small sound of disbelief.

"I have heard the lewd comment you made to entertain my husband's soldiers!"

I gaped at her. *It was only a joke,* I wanted to say, *to make them laugh.* But looking up at her stern face I realized how vulgar it sounded. "I swear to you, my Lady, I only meant that your son will see the Kingdom of Sicily as his own one day. It is my firm belief." I let the tears fall now, real tears, for if she turned her back on me what would become of me? Better I had stayed the poor wife of a cruel man then to arrive unprotected and alone in a foreign city.

The princess looked down at me silently. "I have heard your mother was a seer," she said. I flushed but said nothing to deny it. She nodded, slightly mollified; less by my assurances of chastity, I suspected, than by the knowledge that there was no one else on the ship to feed and care for her son. "See that you speak more circumspectly in the future," she said. "And lay the prince in his cradle! He is not a pauper to sleep on the floor."

In fact he was sleeping on me, but I scrambled up to obey her. His clout was heavy and warm so I reached for a clean one and a cloth. By the time I had untied it she was gone, and the sly maid with her. I had no doubt who had passed on the news of my jest to her.

I cleaned the baby's bottom and bound him to his swaddling board. His eyes were drooping as I lay him in his cradle. I had been told we would be two days at sea—I had until then to convince the princess she could not do without me. I sat beside the cradle and rocked it while I thought.

I was ashamed of my foolish joke now. It was the comment of a coarse fisherman's daughter. If that was how people saw me I knew where I would end up when we reached Naples. I could not change my parentage but I had two days at sea to recreate myself. The dress was a start. I had learned to sit and walk with my back straight, to hold my head high, from watching Violante and her maid. I had begun to listen to the way the princess spoke, as well. She did not shorten her words or let them spill out of her mouth quickly but said each one distinctly, knowing her audience would remain attentive until she was finished. As though every sentence was a formal announcement. I would have said that was the mark of a royal used to being listened to, but I noticed her lady's maid spoke the same way.

I had never had much occasion to speak. People seldom addressed me except to issue an order. But after my first sight of the prince, I tried whenever I had the opportunity to speak more slowly, to avoid shortening my words into the dialect I was used to. *Patois*, I heard Violante's maid call it, sneering. She mocked me once when I tried to speak as she did, but Violante told her it was a good thing when people improved themselves and everyone could do with some improving. Then the news came that Robert had been defeated, and in the rush to pack and my expectation that I would return to Guilio, I stopped concerning myself with all of that. Now I promised myself that when this boat docked outside of Naples I would leave it with a straight back, my head held high, and speaking Italian the way the princess spoke it.

Sitting on the little stool rocking Charles' cradle with my foot, I straightened my back and lifted my chin. I raised my hand to feel my hair. I'd twisted it up quickly but it had come undone in the ride and been blown into tangles by the wind off the sea. I removed the three pins my mother had borrowed from the nurse, and found several more in her bundle which I had taken. She had not wanted it with her in the wagon in case we were caught, but had not hesitated to lay it down beside me, so I felt I had earned it. I combed my fingers through my hair, easing out the tangles as best I could, and braided and pinned it up as I did the princess's. There! I would make myself into a lady. I smiled down at sleeping Charles. Not just a lady; I would make myself into the kind of person who could be the mother of a prince.

But first I had to convince Princess Violante to keep me in her service. It would not be enough to care for Charles, or to help the princess dress and do up her hair; any nurse or lady's maid could do those things. No, I had to convince her I was special. That she needed me and only me.

I sighed. My mother was the one she would have treasured: a healer, a seer, a trained midwife. I was only her daughter, her mostly unwilling apprentice. True, I had saved Charles' life with what she had taught me but much had happened since then, and he had been so healthy no one remembered his uncertain birth. If they did I would certainly not be put aside, but I would not be thanked for pointing out their robust little prince had been a sickly newborn. If only I could do something as noteworthy as save a royal life again.

I remembered the packet my mother had given me. Where had I put it? The nurse's bundle which I had rummaged through for hair pins lay scattered on the bed. I tossed aside the clothes and other items that had spilled out of it, pulled down the blanket and lifted the straw mattress. Where had I dropped my mother's packet? She had insisted I take it with me, else I would have left it behind with my Sicilian robe. I searched the little cabin from end to end and finally found it lying against the wall behind Charles' cradle.

I opened it out on the small table beside the bed. Anise for headache and digestion, also for nausea; we made that into a tea for women suffering the sickness of carrying a child. Motherwort which we sometimes used to begin the birthing process, and dried yarrow and valerian which eased pain and helped induce sleep after a difficult labor. Did my mother mean me to earn my way as a midwife? There was ginger root and comfrey root for stomach ailments, willow bark ground into a powder for fever, and sage leaves to make a healing compress for wounds.

Why had she chosen these of all the herbal remedies she and I had made together? The sage perhaps because she feared we might meet resistance in our escape, but as for the others—no one on this ship was with child and surely there were more experienced midwives than me in Naples. One had to be careful with yarrow and ginger root. Taken together they could sometimes induce the heat and sweat common to a fever...

I looked down at Charles just beginning to wake in his cradle. The symptoms did not last long and there was no after effect. In fact, the patient often felt much better, having flushed out the bad humors within him. But Charles was just a baby.

I could not believe I was even considering this. But Princess Violante intended to send me away for a single foolish remark, even after I had saved her child's life and left my home to serve her.

Charles whimpered from his cradle, his mouth pursing as it did when he was hungry. I loved him; I would never hurt him. He turned his head from side to side, searching for me. It was me he wanted, not his mother. He would miss me if I was sent away, he would cry for me and I would not be there to comfort him. He began to cry now, a petulant little wail. I wanted to pick him up, my arms trembled with the need to comfort him and I felt my breasts grow damp in answer to his crying. I had to do it now before I lost my nerve. I ran to the door.

"Boil some water and bring it to me," I told the guard standing just outside. "And bring me two mugs and a large wash bowl at once."

I closed the door and paced the room while I waited. Charles' howls got louder. I loosened his swaddling cloths and lifted him up. Immediately he began rooting, searching for my breast. When I put him down again he cried harder. Would his mother hear him and come to see why I was neglecting my charge? I could not feed him yet, I needed him to be hungry.

The mugs and the bowl arrived. I used my dinner knife to grate a small piece of ginger root and a little yarrow in the bowl, releasing the juice and pungent odors, which I tipped into one of the mugs. In the other mug I put some of the willow bark powder. When the hot water arrived I poured a little into each mug to make a tea, and the rest into the wash bowl. I packed up the herbs and hid them while I waited for the tea to cool enough for Charles to drink. Meanwhile Charles howled and flailed his little arms, demanding his milk. My arms shook as I removed his gown and his clout, and every noise outside the cabin terrified me. Someone would come, I was sure of it, and demand to know what I was doing. What would I say?

I dipped a clean washing cloth into the ginger and yarrow root tea and let Charles suck on it. He scrunched up his face over the taste, which made me laugh, but he was hungry and sucked vigorously. I kept dipping the cloth into the mug and letting him suck until most of the tea was gone. The water in the bowl had cooled a little now; still quite warm but not so much as to burn his tender skin. I sat him in it and splashed the warm water onto his chest and his shoulders while he sucked the last of the tea from the cloth. He was still hungry and complaining of it so I leaned over and let him have my breast as he sat in the water.

His little body was hot against me, his cheeks flushed. I took him off my breast before he was finished eating. It hurt to let him cry when I could easily satisfy him, but I needed a crying baby, flushed and hot, not a contented one. I took him out of the water before it cooled and dried and dressed him and wrapped him tightly in a blanket to hold in the warmth.

Now I wanted Violante to come and prayed that every step I heard outside the cabin would be hers. At last she did.

"Why is he crying?" she asked, hurrying across the room to pick him up. "Why are you not rocking him? He should not be left to cry! And why is he wrapped in this heavy blanket?"

"I was rocking him, Your Majesty," I said, forcing myself to sound calm, confident. "He has a fever."

"A fever?" She drew back, stricken, torn between comforting her son and avoiding his disease.

"It is an infant's malady, you will not get it," I told her. "Babies often die of it."

I paused while she gasped in horror.

"But I noticed his ailment in time, and have made him a healing tea with herbs I brought with me. I am confident he will recover, Your Majesty. And I will buy more of the herbs when we arrive in Naples, in case the fever returns."

"He is so hot," she cried, taking him from me and kissing his flushed cheeks. "Are you certain he will recover?"

"Very certain, Your Majesty. I have seen this before. It is a good thing I brought the herbs with me." I brought forward the mug I had set aside with the willow bark tea, cool now, and dipped Charles' sop into it, and let him suck on it as she held him. She murmured her gratitude in a broken voice that shamed me, kissing her son's eyes, his hot forehead, the silky yellow cap of his hair. He was quiet in her arms, sucking the sop drenched in willow tea.

He would not take much. After a while I said, gently, "May I, Your Majesty?" and put my hand to his forehead. I feigned relief and told her the tea was working, he was cooler now. Once again I was shamed by her relief and gratitude. She sat him on her knee and played with him until he became fussy.

I did not like the sound of his whine. He had not actually been ill, he should not be so weary, almost lethargic. His little body was cool now, clammy with sweat. My mother made her patients drink ale when they sweat like this, but I dared not give a baby ale.

"He is quite cool now," the princess said happily.

"Perhaps he has regained his appetite. That would be a good sign." What would I do if he would not suckle? I was terrified I had harmed him. How could I ever have taken such a risk? He was adorable and he trusted me completely, and I had done something

65

awful to him. I wanted to cry, but I took him calmly when Violante handed him to me. She was looking only at him or she would surely have seen in my eyes the fear and regret I felt, however much I tried to hide it.

Charles would not take my breast himself. I had to place my nipple in his mouth and stroke his little back. But then he suckled, and soon he was eating in earnest.

"See, Your Majesty, he is fine now," I said, as relieved as she was. We laughed together fondly at the sound of his noisy gulping as he pulled on my breast.

"You have saved my son's life twice," Violante said when I handed him back to her, fed and satisfied. He made a gummy grin up at her as if in agreement, but I bowed my head, unable to meet her eyes.

She took it as modesty and vowed that I would be rewarded, that I need never fear for my future, that she was sorry if her earlier words had caused me distress.

My cheeks burned. "Your Majesty," I cried. "You were right to chastise me! But I have learned from it. I will never from this day do anything to make you regret your faith in me. I swear it! I swear it by my mother who I will never see again!" I meant it, I meant it desperately. I saw how such a life might change me, the insecurity and falseness of a royal court, but I would not let it! I could not look at baby Charles who I had so nearly murdered, or this impulsive princess who had placed her trust unwisely, but wept onto the floor at her feet.

Violante saw my tears, or perhaps it was the mention of losing my mother. She touched my bent head, and when I looked up a tenderness had come into her face that made me weep all the harder. I promised myself that I would never betray her again, not for any reason.

"You did not mean to be vulgar," she reassured me. "You are very young. Perhaps you did not understand how a rough soldier would take your words."

My sob turned into a hiccup. She thought all this regret was over an ill-considered joke. "I... I would not want to think I disappointed you," I managed.

"I am certain you will not," she said quietly.

That afternoon the wind rose. By evening a storm had blown in. The guard at my door came in with a second man, one of the sailors, to make sure everything in my cabin was secure. The bed and table were built out from the walls but Charles' cradle had to be tied down securely. They left me a fishnet to wrap over it to prevent him from falling out if things got that bad. I nodded, frightened. "You will likely be sick," the sailor added briskly. "Try to spare the mattress." He handed me the bucket he had brought with him.

Our ship tossed on waves so tall I could not see their peaks through the little window in my cabin. When Charles cried I sat on the floor beside his cradle and stroked him, singing a little song he liked. I was afraid to pick him up for fear a sudden swell might make me drop him. Fortunately, I was not sick beyond a mild queasiness and as the storm passed, that did also.

The waves were still steep, rocking the boat so that it was difficult to walk, but the worst was over when I opened my door and looked out. The hallway was empty. Looking down it I noticed the door to another cabin swinging open. From inside I heard a voice moaning. Charles was sleeping soundly in his cradle so I made my way down the hall holding onto the walls, and looked in. Princess Violante lay on her cot groaning in misery, her face pale with a greenish cast. On a second cot her maid lay in the same condition. I hurried to the princess. Her eyes opened as I felt her forehead for fever.

"Charles—?" she managed before a retch shook her. She heaved fruitlessly; there was nothing left in her stomach save a small dribble of bile.

"Charles is fine, Your Majesty," I assured her. "He is sleeping now."

She nodded and closed her eyes again.

"Are you ill?" I asked.

"It is just the sea. I am always ill on the sea." Her voice was weak and her head lolled sideways but I was reassured. I had heard the fishermen in my village laugh while recounting tales of 'land-loving men' aboard their boats having this same reaction.

Two men appeared at the cabin door carrying emptied buckets and a washbasin of water.

"You are not ill," one of them observed. He handed me the washbasin.

After I had washed the princess' face and her maid's, I ordered boiling water sent to my cabin to make a tea, and two mugs. Anise for nausea. My mother had thought carefully when choosing the herbs she gave me.

I was kept busy tending Charles as well as his mother and her maid the rest of the night and the next morning. When at last everyone slept, I stumbled up to the deck to get some fresh air, steadying myself with one hand on the walls and holding in the other a chunk of bread and some cheese the cook had given me.

It was a great relief to get away from the close quarters and the smell of vomit. The wind was still brisk and the salt air was bracing. I leaned against the railing and ate my simple dinner.

"So you are Philippa the Catanian."

I turned with a start and found myself staring into Prince Robert's intensely blue eyes. He stood behind me, quite alone. For a moment I gawked like an idiot, then sank into a deep curtsey just as our ship hit a steep swell. I lost my footing completely and would have fallen across the deck had he not grabbed my arm and pulled me up. I had so longed for him to notice me, even once, but all I could think was that my hair was a mess and I smelled of his wife's vomit and his son's spit-up.

"Are you not afraid to be out here in this rough weather?" His smile lit up his eyes and showed his even, white teeth. I stared, caught myself and looked away. My arm burned where he held it, but in so delicious a way I wanted him never to let go. I hardly dared breathe.

"Apparently not," he answered himself, letting go of my arm. He looked over my shoulder at the sea.

What must he think of me, standing here speechless? And smelly! "On the contrary, Your Majesty. I have always enjoyed a wild wind," I said breathlessly, wondering if I could move a bit, to get downwind of him. "And the salt air is… refreshing." I shrugged helplessly, acknowledging the obvious.

"You have been ill."

"Not I. I have been tending your—another, who is."

"My wife does not have a stomach for the sea." His lips quirked, almost a smile.

"All the more admirable of her to venture onto it, then."

"Well said, Philippa of Catania." He turned that dazzling smile on me again. "I hear that you have foretold my son will… enjoy the fruit of Sicily." He glanced with amusement at my ripe breasts, swollen with milk.

A hot blush spread over my face; I could not help raising my arm to cover my chest. "A poor choice of words, Your Majesty." I would gladly have ripped my tongue out to undo that ill-considered jest. Then I heard the other word he had used: *foretold*. Did he think it was a prediction? I wasn't a seer like my mother. It had been a joke to make the soldiers laugh! But I couldn't take it back now. *Could not. I could not take it back*, I corrected myself. At least I could sound like a Neapolitan lady if the foolish substance of my words could not be retracted. I looked up at him. He was watching me, waiting for an explanation. I looked away quickly, my heart pounding. Whatever should I say?

"Fortunate is the man who sits at the bottom of Fortune's wheel, for when her wheel turns, he will rise." I blushed, hearing how pompous it sounded, but it was all I could think of. My mother had said it once to console me when Guilio had beaten me, only she had said "girl'.

"Philosophy from a Sicilian wet-nurse? Or another prediction?" He looked amused but there was a challenge in his voice.

The boat dipped into a wave. I grabbed the railing, my balance shaken, precarious. I was about to confess I could not see the future, but just then the clouds parted. A beam of sunlight caught us, the crown prince of Naples with his golden hair and sea-blue eyes and I in my yellow kirtle, and set us ablaze with light. I took a breath to steady myself against the swells and lunges of the sea, and thought of my mother when she was seeing for someone.

Was I going to do this? Dared I pretend to tell a crown prince's future? Before I could change my mind I covered my face with my left hand, blocking the light. I pictured the prince's face, more lined than his youth could explain, and his eyes, steady and direct. But there was sorrow there, and uncertainty, hidden in their depths. Was there not a rumor he had been cruelly imprisoned in his youth by our former King James II of Aragon? I drew in my breath. Pitching my voice as low as I could, I said with a certainty that surprised me, "Your Majesty, you will rise. You who have sat at the bottom of Fortune's wheel, for the rest of your life you will climb as high as the wheel can turn, and all who are loyal to you will rise with you." I moved my hand from my face and dared to look him in the eyes. "This is not flattery, my Lord. Have I not left everything behind to align myself with your household? Would I do so if I had not seen your future?"

He looked me over thoughtfully. I could not tell whether I had convinced him or not. I suspected he did not mean me to.

"You are an interesting girl, Philippa of Catania," he said.

Chapter 7

March 6, 1346
Queen Joanna's Court, Naples

How can this be happening?" Joanna stares round the table at my son Robert, Louis of Taranto, and me, ensconced in her privy chamber. Her face is pale, her eyes wide and startled. "I am the rightful queen of Naples! King Robert named me his heir. Every noble in the land knelt and swore fealty to me when I was still a child. They swore their allegiance again at my coronation. I rule by the right of God, anointed by His Eminence, Pope Clemente VI! They defy God to rise against their anointed Monarch!" She pauses, breathless.

Louis sits watching her. He, too, swore obedience to her. He, too, would not hesitate to break that oath to wear the crown of Naples, if he had not found a way to secure them both.

"My people love me!"

Not at the moment. I grit my teeth to restrain my impatience. We are here to discuss what can be done, not to console a frightened young woman. Joanna is deeply shaken to let her self-control slip so much.

"Your people are the pawns of ruthless men," Louis, an equally ruthless man but one who is on our side, says calmly.

Enough. "Your Majesty, you are the rightful ruler. And it is time to rule."

Joanna blinks at my stern tone, but her breathing slows and her pallor begins to improve. After a moment she straightens, glances round the table at us, and says, "What do you advise?"

The men relax. Robert wants to take a contingent of knights and rescue his brother. He makes the suggestion carefully, referring to Raymond as 'the seneschal of your court'.

"We cannot appear to be harboring a man accused of regicide," Louis says.

We? They are not joined yet. The queen has chosen him for her champion, but I have privately warned her against aligning herself publicly with him, whatever she promises in private. Louis' mercenaries are not popular in Naples.

I focus on this to avoid the larger insult. My son had nothing to do with the murder of Andrew and they both know it. None of my family would be so stupid as to join such a cause for precisely this reason: we would be the first accused.

"The queen cannot send her own guard out against her people," I say. Robert looks at me as though I have just murdered his brother. He may be right. But Louis has no intention of fighting for Raymond. The prize, for him, is the crown. He will defend Joanna's favorites to encourage her to marry him, but only when it does not obstruct his goal. I must not force his hand now. And I will not let Robert go out as blithely unprotected as Raymond did.

Louis looks at me with surprised approval. As though I am not ten times the experienced courtier he will ever be. "Joanna must maintain the support of her people," I say, looking at Robert.

Or we are all dead. After the training I gave him he knows the end of my sentences. I want him to think of his wife and children, of Raymond's wife and children, of their niece Sancia, and little Maroccia.

In fact, I am thinking of him. My Robert with his father's complexion and features would be instantly recognized and set upon, and then they would have both my sons at their mercy.

"We will wait until my man returns to tell us what is happening." Joanna decides. She turns to me. "Stay here in Castle Nuovo where you will be safe." She looks to Louis, her face relaxing when he nods approval.

I bow my head. Her grandfather, King Robert, would never have sat here allowing a mob of commoners to attack his men, to torture the seneschal of his court. But then, King Robert's brothers did not challenge his rule as Joanna's cousins are doing. When his nephew Carobert of Hungary did so, his brothers all stood by him to defend Naples. If King Robert were still here… I feel the familiar clench in my gut, the ache in my chest, that have been with me since his death. King Robert had the wisdom of a great ruler as well as the iron fist of a warrior to back up his decrees.

Naples is a kingdom divided. Joanna has the wisdom to rule, but not the fighting force. Her cousins, the grandsons of those same brothers who supported her grandfather King Robert, have the courage and appetite to lead armies, but lack the wisdom to rule judiciously. Naples flounders like a man whose emotions and appetites have overcome his reason, bestial and stupid, without discipline or judgment. And my family is trapped in its madness, clinging to Joanna, who has barely the strength to save herself, let alone us. I wonder, not for the first time, which of Joanna's cousins and courtiers were so stupid as to kill Prince Andrew so publicly and bring this calamity down on all of us.

Louis must win. Louis' hired army must defeat his brother Robert of Taranto's forces, or we are all doomed. We, my family, will be destroyed if he does not succeed in time.

"Philippa?"

Joanna has asked me something. Advice. But I, who have advised her and her parents and grandparents, have little to give her now. *Send every man you have to rescue my Raymond*, I want to say. Want to scream. But it is bad advice. It would leave the castle unguarded and even then there might not be enough to fight Robert of Taranto's and Charles of Durazzo's joined armies, along with the crazed mob of citizens crying for blood. And that would be the end. I will not undermine a lifetime of good advice with very bad advice at a desperate time. Wisdom and calm are needed now, however useless they may be to save my son.

Raymond! I feel a pain so sharp I close my eyes unable to breathe until it passes. It does not pass. *Advice,* I think, groping for something else to cling to. Joanna is watching me, a worried frown creasing her lovely brow.

A stout knock on the door saves me from answering. "Enter," Joanna calls.

The guard ushers in Joanna's man. He bows to the queen and Louis of Taranto, but hesitates to speak, his eyes darting from me to Robert.

"Speak," Joanna commands. "You are in the presence of the grand seneschal of the kingdom and my most trusted adviser."

"Speak up!" Louis growls.

The young man bows three times, like flotsam on the sea, his Adam's apple keeping time. "Your Majesty, I followed the noise of the people to the public square and made my way through a large crowd to stand near the front. There I saw the Duke of Taranto and the Duke of Durazzo surrounded by their men, and with them the seneschal of the court, bound in chains." The man glances at me and hesitates. I hold myself straight in my chair and meet his gaze until he continues.

"He was bound in chains, without his surcote, his shirt torn and bloodied from the lash. His arms and body were cut with sword wounds, though none fatal—" He chokes to a stop.

"Tell us everything," Joanna orders. The man is trembling, his face damp. Raymond has ever been good to those he commands, careful of their lives when possible. He is liked and respected among the men.

"His mouth was full of blood. He kept coughing it out, and the sounds he made... Your Majesty, I believe they have cut out his tongue."

A choked noise escapes me before I can stop myself. My own throat has tightened as if I am strangling. My mouth fills with vomit. I turn and rush from the room for the privy. I am shamed by my weakness but it is beyond my control, a primal reaction: what happens to my son happens to me. Behind me the others resume talking as if my response is to be expected, for which I am grateful.

When I return, holding my handkerchief to my mouth, Joanna's man is telling them the violent performance is over, that the Dukes of Taranto and Durazzo have taken Raymond to the Taranto castle for further questioning.

"Public questioning?" My voice is raw but steady.

"Yes, my Lady," the knight says, his eyes downcast.

"You have done well to bring us this news," Louis says.

The man wipes his face. "Thank you, my Lord," he mumbles. He looks up, his eyes pleading, as though he wants forgiveness just for watching the atrocities of others.

"There is nothing we can do," Louis says when the man has left. "They have a right to question him."

"Raymond will maintain his innocence and we will soon have him back in our care," Joanna says. Neither of them mentions the lashing, the mutilation of his tongue. Raymond is not being questioned, he is being sacrificed. I despise their platitudes. Joanna, at least, is pale and shaken, with a vulnerable, wounded look in her eyes. I beg her indulgence to lie down.

"You will not be disturbed," she says, not quite meeting my eyes.

"Thank you, Your Majesty."

As I rise to leave she leans forward and clasps my hands. "His innocence will be proved. He will return to us."

I look at her steadily for a long moment. Then, because I raised her also, I allow her this. "God willing," I murmur, the lie nearly choking me.

Her blue eyes fill with tears.

"Your Majesty." I curtsey and leave, unwilling to see this. What right has she to weep? My Raymond is suffering because of her.

Not fair. We have also risen higher than we had any right to expect because of her, and her royal grandparents before her, and I made no complaint then. The wheel of fortune spins and we spin upon it. I remember my great-grandmother's prophecy then, but it is not my fate that concerns me now; it is my son's.

Sancia comes toward me as I cross through the queen's presence chamber. "I must lie down. See that I am not disturbed," I tell her. I do not have the heart to answer the questions in her eyes. What all of Naples knows will reach the palace soon enough.

Approaching the door to the bedchamber I am sharing with Sancia and another lady-in-waiting, I bend my back into an aged stoop and slow my steps, pulling a few strands of grey hair from under my headdress. I have lost some of my height but I am still a tall woman, able to hide the assault of age. I do not hide it now as I signal a passing chamber girl. "I am tired," I tell her. "I feel the cold these days. If you bring me your cape to cover me while I sleep, I will give you this to buy a new one." I fumble to unclasp the silver brooch from my bodice.

Her eyes widen. "Of...of course, my Lady. I will fetch it at once." She curtseys, already stumbling backward, my brooch clutched in her hand to prevent my changing my mind.

"See that it has a hood, to shield the light from my eyes so I may sleep."

She curtsies again, almost tripping herself in her backward flight.

It is a weak invention, especially as I have not asked for a fire to be built up. I hope her greed offsets her suspicions. To ensure this, I hesitate when she returns with her cloak, a dark, well-worn thing, as though I am reconsidering.

"Is it warm?" I ask, letting a whine creep into my voice.

"It is very warm," she assures me with the false earnestness of one who knows she is taking advantage. "And see, it has a dark hood, to keep out the light. You will sleep soundly." She holds it out eagerly.

"You would not take advantage of the queen's old nurse?" I ask plaintively.

"No, never!" she cries. She is in too far to back out now, but I see in her eyes the look I have been waiting for. No one will hear from her about this transaction.

"Do not let me be disturbed," I tell her, letting my voice tremble. "It is so difficult to return to sleep after being disturbed."

"No one will come near this chamber," she assures me.

And no one does, so I am not seen creeping down the stairs and outside, cloaked in the servant girl's dark rag.

They have resumed torturing my son when I arrive. I stand back, apart from the crowd, the hood of my cape covering my head and pulled forward to shield my face. There is a cool wind and I am not the only woman with her hood raised to shield her from it. No one gives me a second glance. Their attention is all focused on the second-floor balcony.

Raymond stands there, slumped forward, his head lolling from side to side, eyes closed. His shirt has been stripped off and his torso is covered in angry red welts. His lips and chin are black with dried blood. They have tied a rope around his chest under his arms and attached it to the upper balcony to keep him standing. Robert of Taranto stands on one side of my son, calling out questions loudly enough to be heard by the people below. Hugo del Balzo is seated behind a small table on the other side of the balcony.

"Were you a part of the conspiracy to murder Prince Andrew, Duke of Calabria?" Robert of Taranto shouts.

One of his men, standing close to Raymond, raises a pair of pincers, no doubt pulled from a bucket of burning coals. He holds them up so we can see the red-hot iron tips. I cover my mouth, choking back a scream as he fastens them to Raymond's chest, just below the bared nipple. Raymond's head jerks up, his eyes open. He gives a mangled cry that is drowned in a drum roll. Hugo del Balzo effects to write something down.

I moan under my breath, reaching a hand to steady myself on the wall of the building behind me as the pincers are released and plunged back into the metal bucket of hot coals, leaving another ugly welt on my son's chest. The torturer is working his way up, I realize, staring at the row of red marks rising from Raymond's abdomen. Around me faces are staring at Raymond's burned chest, at the red line of agony reaching toward his exposed nipples. Their eyes are hungry, titillated, their mouths open, some of them panting or licking their lips.

I want to be ill. If I had not already brought forth everything in my stomach, I would do so now. I want to leave but I cannot, nor even look aside. This is my son. I will stay here with him, one face that loves him and suffers with him, in this merciless crowd.

The process is repeated, Robert of Taranto calling out his questions—Who was with you? Who else? Who placed the noose around Prince Andrew's royal neck? Who hanged him from the balcony?—and then the pincers, Raymond's tortured screams muffled by the deafening drum rolls, del Balzo writing studiously as though he were hearing answers from my son's mutilated mouth. On and on until Raymond faints. Then they bring forward a second bucket, this one filled with cold water to revive him.

I close my eyes and see Raymond as a baby, with his chubby cheeks and wide, intelligent eyes and curly black hair. He toddled around our house holding onto walls and chairs and table legs, trying to follow his older brother. When he fell he would struggle up again without complaint, disdaining my help—if Robert did not need help neither would he—and toddle on his plump little legs after his brother again. He never cried or begged Robert to wait. He wanted no concessions, made no excuses, but took what came and pushed himself to meet it. He will tell them nothing, no matter what they do to him. Anything they write down is a lie. When he loses consciousness again I find myself hoping he will not revive but find at least a temporary release.

Or a permanent one. Even if he should be freed, cleared of their false accusations, how could he survive what they have done to him? The thought horrifies me; I will not pray for my son's death, not even deep in my wounded heart, not even for his own sake.

The gory spectacle reaches and passes its pinnacle. The crowd's frenzy begins to abate. They shuffle and look around, restless. Raymond no longer has the strength to scream, and even del Balzo cannot pretend to hear answers from a slack mouth.

"Enough!" Robert of Taranto calls. "We have the information we need. Take him away and have a public notary document what we have learned! Then we will force this worthless regicide to affirm the names he has given us in public."

Another drum roll accompanies the crowd's roar of approval as a notary steps onto the balcony to receive del Balzo's notes, and carries them inside. The rope is untied and Raymond is dragged away, down to Robert of Taranto's dungeon most likely, where he and the Duke of Durazzo and del Balzo can continue their torture, saving only that they keep him alive for the next demonstration of their merciless justice. And after that, when they no longer have any use for him?

Slowly I sink down the wall I have been leaning against, as though the rope binding Raymond was all that held me up as well. I sit shuddering in the dirt, an old woman in a shabby, worn cloak, who tempted Fortune and whose son must now pay the price.

Chapter 8

Autumn, 1298
Court of King Charles II, Naples

*Y*ou are an interesting girl. The words reverberated in my head. No one had said such a thing to me before, let alone a royal prince. I had hoped Prince Robert would notice me; I had never imagined he would think me interesting. Was it because he thought I was a seer? His face had given nothing away when I made my prediction, a calculated guess on my part. Did he believe I could prophesy? Or was he humoring me, thinking I believed so? Did he know I lied? He might be the kind of man who would find that interesting.

He did not speak to me again while we were aboard ship, although I caught him looking my way once. It gave me a delicious, plunging sensation in my stomach, both thrilling and terrifying. I told myself sternly that when a nobleman looked at a village girl, it did not end well for the village girl, and I did not return his glances. Glance. One glance. Most likely at the sea behind me, searching for land. (I did not believe that for an instant!)

We sailed into the port of Naples at dawn on the third day. People swarmed the quay and its adjoining streets, walking, running, riding horses, driving carts of all sizes, leading donkeys laden with goods or bending under the weight of their own parcels and panniers. They shouted and pointed and laughed and argued in a multitude of languages, competing with the shrieks of the sea gulls and the neighing and braying and clucking and crowing of their livestock. The streets and buildings continued inland as far as I could see – a huge city larger than I had ever imagined. I could not believe we would soon leave the ship and struggle through that chaos—I would have felt safer leaping into the sea.

A castle only a short way inland towered over the city, visible from the sea. "Castle Nuovo," one of the soldiers told me, pointing out the castle Prince Robert's father had built, where we would be going. Where I would be living! I gaped at its high walls and pointed turrets rising above us on the crest of a steep hill. A web of cobbled streets rose uphill from the port toward the castle grounds.

"Come this way," Violante's maid snapped as she passed me on the deck with Charles in my arms. It was fortunate I had already bundled up the nurse's belongings and my mother's herbs, for that was all the notice I received that we were disembarking.

I followed her down the gangplank, holding Charles tightly to me. She paused at the bottom. As I stepped off beside her she gave me a look of such ill will it shocked me. She leaned close and hissed into my ear, "Do not imagine the men here will look at you as those on the ship did. They had no other female to look at!"

"They had you," I said. "If they had wanted to."

Her hand lifted as though to slap me, but she satisfied herself with a glare and flounced off after Princess Violante and the two guards escorting her.

We had barely stepped off the ship and already we were engulfed by a sea of people. Where did they all come from? They were of every size and complexion, some pushing purposefully forward while others stood in conversation, though how they could hear each other I did not know. They accompanied every word with large gestures—perhaps that was how they understood one another? I stuck close to Violante and her maid, terrified that if I lost them I would be swallowed up in the crowd and vanish forever. The palace guards ordered people aside, breaking a path for the princess, but it was up to her maid and me to follow close enough to make our way through before they closed in again. Shops and houses lined the streets in unbroken rows, more than I could count. Mountains covered in trees stood in the distance, and over all the bright sunlight streamed from a clear blue sky. I could not decide whether Naples was the most beautiful of cities or the most appalling, but it was certainly astounding and I was surprised to realize that I loved it on sight. What other surprises would this city unfold for me?

A carriage waited for us as soon as we had crossed the pier. Violante and her maid preceded me and sat on the seat facing front. I bent my head and put my foot on the step, watching anxiously not to bump Charles' head in the narrow doorway—I had never got into a carriage before—and clambered in behind them.

From the protection of the carriage I peered out at this teeming city that would be my home. The closer we came to the castle the smaller I felt as the sheer mass of it rose before us. Its thick stone walls towered above our carriage, climbing into the sky, each corner rounded by a tall tower topped with a spire that pierced the clouds. We clattered over the wide drawbridge in our little carriage and passed through enormous gates into a large open courtyard. The inside walls rose around us, forming a huge rectangle and shutting the city out.

I had never been inside a castle. If I had ever imagined being in one, I would have pictured luxurious rooms and decorations, not this solid, overwhelming weight of stone enclosing me. I had lived all my life outside in the woods and fields near my village. Even the nursery tent in the encampment offered only a light shelter from the elements, not a solid barrier from the surrounding countryside. I had never thought what it would feel like to be confined inside stone. I climbed out of the carriage and stopped, unable to make myself follow Violante into the castle.

The guard holding the carriage door open coughed softly. I threw him a terrified glance. To my astonishment, he winked at me. It was so incongruous with the solemn formality of his expression that I nearly giggled. At that moment baby Charles yawned as if the entire drama bored him, and my immobility left me. I walked forward into the new texture of my life as though I had never hesitated.

Inside the entrance hall Violante left Charles and me in the care of a manservant instructed to take us to the nursery. I gaped at everything as we walked through the castle, stunned by the beauty and wealth displayed in the painted and gilded murals, the rich tapestries, and the intricate mosaics of colored marble on floors and ceilings.

We climbed a wide stairway past two levels of rooms and walked down a long hall before stopping outside a door manned by a weaponed guard. The manservant whispered something to the guard, who laughed. I blushed, certain they were talking about me in their foreign French language. Holding my back straight and my chin high, I entered the nursery.

The walls were covered with paintings of animals and flowers. Brilliantly-painted birds fluttering across a blue ceiling. A cradle and a little child's cot were set against one wall, with three beds for the nursemaids against the other. In the middle of the room was a small table with two little chairs, and beside it a larger one for the adult caretakers. Near the back wall, under the window, was an intricately-carved wooden rocking horse. A small boy, perhaps twenty months, sat astride the horse, rocking it wildly and laughing. He looked much like Charles, but older, the youthful image of their father. A nurse stood by scolding him in French, no doubt telling him to slow down, to be careful or he would tumble, but he paid her no attention. She looked up as I walked in.

The scolding frown on her face did not diminish as she straightened, taking me in. She said something to me but I shook my head. "So you are the Sicilian wet nurse," she said, this time in the formal Neapolitan Italian I had practiced on the ship. She crossed the room and reached for Charles.

I held him closer to me. "He will be hungry after the journey here."

Her frown deepened. "You may change his clout and feed him after I have examined him."

I opened my mouth to tell her he was perfect, but she might take that as a challenge to find fault with him, and with me as his wet-nurse. "As you wish," I said, handing him over.

While she unwrapped his swaddling cloths I went to see his brother. "You must be Louis," I said, bending down. "You have a fine mount." The little boy rocked faster, ignoring me.

"He has a mind of his own," I observed to the head nurse, rising again.

"He does not speak Sicilian. Come and change the prince's clout."

"I have not got his clean ones with me."

She pointed to a table beside the child's cot, where a stack of square cloths lay folded. "The older prince is not trained, then," I observed, trying not to sound smug. In my village a child was trained by the time he could walk.

"Prince Louis has missed his mother."

I glanced at her with the barest hint of a smile. "She is overly devoted to Charles, as well."

"Hm." She did not look up from watching me wrap the folded clout around Charles' bottom and tie it in place, but her frown eased.

"My name is Philippa." I settled into the chair beside the cradle and began unlacing my kirtle to feed Charles.

"Cover yourself!" She sounded shocked as she handed me a shawl. I blushed, although I had never been self-conscious about breast-feeding before.

"You are in a royal castle! Anyone might walk in—the nursery guard, a kitchen servant, Princess Violante and Prince Robert…"

Why ever would they care? Everyone knew why I was here. But I flushed hotter, remembering the princess's reaction when she found me breastfeeding Charles on the cabin floor. I pulled the shawl up over Charles' head on my breast.

The nurse nodded.

"Have I tied him tightly enough to his swaddling board?" I asked when I had changed and swaddled Charles again. "I have much to learn from you."

She was flattered as I intended, but I was also sincere. My knowledge of herb lore surely could not rival the healing power of the court physics. If I wanted to stay at the castle after Charles was weaned, I had to become a proper nurse, and that meant learning the French way of raising a royal child.

"Put him in his cradle. He must learn to nap when his brother does."

Louis was already in his little cot, complaining in lisping French between wide yawns.

I smiled over his head at the nurse. "It is good the baby is here with you. I could not train him in a noisy soldier's camp. And with his mother's tent beside us…"

"It makes for a badly-trained child when the mother interferes."

I nodded solemnly. Perhaps in this world I had entered, she was right. Perhaps the parents of little princes, themselves spoiled by luxury and servants, indulged their children too much. I could not agree that a mother's presence harmed a child, not while I missed my Antonio so desperately. But I had found a common ground with this woman, and was not about to lose it.

"Matriona."

I looked up from placing Charles in his cradle, and realized she had told me her name.

In the next few weeks I was more homesick than I could ever have imagined. I rarely saw a friendly face. Most were suspicious or, at best, uninterested. I was "the Sicilian", a representative of the kingdom that should have submitted to their King Charles but had not, that had beaten their crown prince and chased him out. My smiles and pleasantries earned me no friends, and even when men looked after me they did not stop to speak. I might make them laugh, might make them desire me in my bright yellow Neapolitan gown, but I was still "the Sicilian". I served their royals but I was not a loyal subject like them; I was only a traitor to the foreign king who was their enemy.

I seldom left the nursery. When the children were awake I was kept busy, but while they napped I sat alone, indulging myself in self-pity. I had tempted Fortune and Fortune had ceased to smile on me, just as our village saying warned.

But I was here and there was no going back; I had no choice but to make the best of it. Nor would I have gone back if that were possible. In Sicily I had belonged among my villagers, where I was poor and beaten. If I never belonged among the Neapolitans, at least I would do what I could to make sure I was never again poor or beaten. I recalled my great-grandmother's words: *She will rise high above her station.* I straightened my back and raised my chin. Wheels do not turn of themselves.

My greatest obstacle was my appalling ignorance, which I became more deeply aware of each day. Try as I might to speak Italian as it was spoken here, some small mispronunciation, a difference in emphasis or rhythm, always gave me away. And I soon realized it would not be enough to speak Italian well; the Neapolitan court spoke French. I set myself to learn French as quickly as possible, but there was no one to teach me and I was embarrassed to practice in front of anyone. Almost as bad, I was illiterate. It had never occurred to me that everyone at court would be able to read and write; at least, the important people, those who mattered. I hid my illiteracy as painstakingly as I hid my ignorance of Latin and French. Hidden in the nursery most of the time, I was seldom in a position to demonstrate my lack of knowledge, but I was determined to climb above the nursery.

As I learned her ways Matriona trusted me more and more with the care of the boys. I was not only breastfeeding Charles, but playing with both of them and putting them to bed. Unaware of my background and my ignorance, they accepted me happily as their playmate. They gave me the uncomplicated affection of children and accepted mine in return. I was comfortable with them. Too comfortable. One evening I was singing Charles and Louis to sleep, a little song my mother had sung to me, when the nursery door opened and the guard announced Prince Robert and Princess Violante. I stopped singing as soon as I saw them and slipped into a hasty curtsey with Charles still in my arms.

"No, please continue," the prince said, smiling.

I flushed, the words to the song forgotten. Nor could I have sung them if I had remembered. I knew I had a pretty voice, I had been told so often back at home, but Violante's face clearly told me her husband's compliments should be reserved for her.

"It is nothing, Your Majesty," I stammered, having learned enough French by now to understand his request. "Just a petit chanson I learned back—" I broke off, but it was too late.

"You are teaching them a Sicilian song?" Violante cried. "Are you mocking us?"

I stared at her, still bent in my curtsey, my mouth gaping open. Matriona, horrified at my error of judgment, and hers in not preventing it, snatched Charles from me. He began to wail. Louis, disturbed by the commotion, started crying also in his little cot.

"It appears they like Sicilian songs," Prince Robert said, looking at me coolly. He bent down to Louis and asked whether he wanted to hear a French song. Louis, pleased by his father's attention, announced that he already knew a good song. He began lustily singing the song I had just sung, complete with its rough peasant vernacular.

"How dare you teach my son to speak like a Sicilian peasant!" Violante glared at me. Louis clapped his hands and repeated "Sicy'an peasant!"

"I… I did not mean…"

"What did you mean?" Prince Robert asked.

Nothing. It is just a song to lull them to sleep. I bent my head and held my tongue, thinking fast. The obvious answer, the true answer, would show me a fool, a thoughtless young girl not equipped for the responsibility of raising royal children. I remembered the "prophecy" I had made on the ship: that Charles would be King of Sicily one day. Had Prince Robert believed me? I dared not test it too far. If he had not, he would not want a charlatan caring for his sons. Nor could I deny what I had said, and prove myself false when I said it. Something in between…

I raised my head and looked straight at the prince. "Do not despise Sicily, Your Highness. You are its rightful prince."

There is a certain type of smile that only reaches the mouth; another that lights both the eyes and the mouth; and last is the smile that gleams in the eyes while the mouth remains firm. That was the look Robert gave me. I could almost hear him thinking, *an interesting girl.* I looked back at him gravely.

Princess Violante frowned. Her mouth opened, then closed, clearly wanting to criticize but unable to find fault with what I had said. "I do not like the song," she said at last. Prince Robert laughed softly.

"I will not sing it again, Your Majesty," I promised.

When they had left and the boys had been calmed again to sleep, Matriona turned to me. "Go downstairs to the kitchen and fetch us some dinner," she commanded. "And take your time about it. I need to sit awhile in peace without your clever tongue wagging."

I had never been to the kitchen. Matriona must have known I would not know the way, but I left without objection. Aware that the kitchen would be on the ground floor I took the servant's stairs, and when I got close enough my nose guided me.

The kitchen was huge, with four separate fires all burning at once. The vapors from them made me sweat as soon as I stepped inside the room. An entire pig was being roasted on a spit over one fireplace, and a great pot of fish boiled above another. The smells of warm bread and mulled wine, sausage and several kinds of cheese all assailed my nose at once, making my mouth water. On a huge table were platters of grapes and pomegranates and tortes topped with marzipan, ready to be carried up to the dining room after the meat courses. Cooks and sauciers stood around each fireplace, pastry cooks pounded and chopped at long tables, molding their pastry creations around sweetmeats and nuts and fruits. Servers rushed about filling platters with food to take upstairs and porters ran back and forth from the fireplaces carrying wood and pails of water. Everywhere there was movement and people shouting instructions or calling for something at once, before their dish was ruined! I was pushed inside from where I had stopped in the doorway by a server carrying an empty platter. He quickly filled it with the next course and hurried out past me again.

Supervising everything was a tall man who looked like no human being I had ever seen. He was dressed in the clothes of a chef with the insignia of the Angevins on his tunic. By the way the others listened to him it was clear he was in charge, but I could hardly credit that he was the head of the kitchen. For out of the bottom of his white sleeves and the top of his white collar his hands and head were black, as black as charred meat. The whites of his eyes flashed in the blackness of his face and when he opened his mouth wide the rows of his teeth shone like two half-moons in the night sky, with his pink tongue between them. *Was he covered in soot from the fires? But then, why were his cuffs and collar so clean?* I stood and stared, wondering what kind of creature I was looking at, until I remembered hearing there were men in a distant country, Ethiopia, who were black-skinned. I had not believed it at the time, thinking they meant the deepest sun-browned shade of a few of the more weathered fishermen I knew. They meant black I realized now as I stared stupidly at this strange black man who towered above the others as though they were only half-grown. He ordered them about the kitchen in a mixture of French and Italian so strongly accented I could barely understand him. And they rushed to do his bidding!

"What are you doing here, girl?"

A stern voice startled me out of my stunned fascination. "I... I have been sent to fetch dinner for us in the nursery," I stammered, shaken out of any attempt to maintain my dignity.

The assistant cook chuckled. "A queer sight, is it not?" He shook his head. "But he can cook, mind you; his pastry melts on your tongue and his puddings are as light and creamy as the thick white clouds in a summer sky." He shook his head again. "I'll fix you a platter to carry upstairs."

As he went to do so the black man looked across the room and saw me. We stared at each other a moment, then his eyes roved up and down my person like a hungry wolf considering its next meal. I stepped back before I could stop myself. His wide mouth split into a grin that showed his gleaming white teeth. I blushed furiously, which made him laugh aloud before he turned away to check the pot over one of the fireplaces.

I fled upstairs with a well-laden platter and blurted out, as soon as I got inside the nursery, "There is a man as tall as a giant and as black as the night downstairs in the kitchen!"

"Ahh," Matriona said. "You have met Raymond of Campagno." She took the platter from me and placed it on the table.

"Campagno?" I set the jug of ale beside it, trying to subdue the tremble in my arms. There were giants like this as near as Campagno?

Matriona laughed. "He is not from Campagno himself. He was captured by pirates as a boy in Africa and sold for a slave. The prefect of cooks for King Charles, at the time one Raymond of Campagno, purchased him from them and gave the boy his name, since his Ethiopian chatter was completely unintelligible." She speared a slice of cheese from the platter and chewed it appreciatively.

"He is a kitchen slave, then." I felt a great relief though I could not say why.

"Not at all!" Matriona laughed again. "He learned the skills of cookery so well that soon he was managing all the royal banquets, and doing an excellent job of it. In that way he caught King Charles' notice. The king had him freed and baptized—by then he spoke French and Italian both—and when his first master went away to war, this "Black Raymond" as he was then called to distinguish the two, was chosen to take his namesake's place as master of the king's royal kitchen."

"Master," I repeated faintly. He had the look of a master. I shivered.

"He is fortunate to have landed in Naples. King Charles values natural ability and rewards it, regardless of a man's appearance. Not many are so open-minded." She looked at me pointedly. "As for bloodline, he claims he was a prince in his village in Ethiopia, before the pirates took him."

A prince? I shook my head, feeling dizzy. My great-grandmother's prophecy came back to me. "Never!" I whispered in horror.

"Well, since he has been freed one would think he would return to Africa if he is indeed a prince, but so he claims." She took a deep gulp of the ale. "Sit down, Philippa, or Charles will wake for his feeding before you have eaten."

I sank into a chair and selected an olive from the tray. Its bitter taste filled my mouth. From now on I would call a kitchen servant to fetch our meals, no matter if Matriona complained about the delay.

That night I dreamed of black men creeping through the castle with only the whites of their eyes visible. I woke up in a terror and stared wildly about the room, wondering how I would even see one if he were standing at my bedside. My heart pounded so hard I thought I would faint. But as my eyes adjusted to the moonlight through the window, the darkness became mere shadows. The room was empty except for Matriona snoring under her blanket, and the two little princes, and me sitting up in my bed too frightened over a dream to sleep.

I woke again to Matriona shaking me. Charles was already awake, wailing for his morning feeding. I rose blearily and put him to my breast.

"Is something ailing you?" Matriona asked, looking me over warily.

"How long have I been in this room?"

Her eyebrows rose. "All night, I trust."

"I need some air! I need to walk outside!" In Sicily I used to run to the woods or sit beside the river whenever I was disturbed. I would watch the clouds sail overhead and listen to the wind singing among the leaves until whatever bothered me was soothed. How long ago and far away that felt. I ached with homesickness and turned my face aside, blinking rapidly.

"Do you need to buy something at the market?"

I hesitated. I had walked through the city twice, gawking like the village girl I was at all the shops and merchants selling everything imaginable, and many things that were not, from food and spices and herbs to precious jewels and soaps and silks and linens and all manner of amusements. But it was not the glamour and noise and teeming streets of Naples that I wanted today.

"I could take Louis into the palace gardens to play while Charles naps," I offered. I looked at Matriona hopefully. Except for the gardeners, servants were not allowed in the palace gardens, but perhaps if I had little Prince Louis with me?

Matriona frowned, beginning to shake her head.

"Louis, would you like to play in the garden?" I asked.

"Louis play!" he cried, jumping up from his stacking blocks.

"In the garden?" I prompted.

"Jardin, jardin!"

"I do not think—"

"Jardin!" Louis yelled over Matriona's objections.

"After you eat your mid-day meal we will go," I promised him.

"If you are reprimanded again—" Matriona began.

"—I will say it was all my idea. That you find me headstrong and foolish and disobedient and can do nothing to change me!" I finished her sentence for her. I laughed happily at the thought of walking among trees and flowers and hearing birdsong for a little while instead of voices speaking a language I barely understood.

The nursery guard accompanied us down to the garden. Louis crowed with delight when he saw it and squirmed to be set down. I held him a moment, staring around in delight at the profusion of colors and scents: sunlight on rosemary bushes and neat plots of fragrant herbs intermingled with lilies, roses, and gourdon flowers, all carefully tended and blooming abundantly. A stone pathway, accented by a wall of shrubbery on either side, wound through the garden, widening in areas where stone or wooden benches invited visitors to rest amid the beauty. The fat, smooth trunks of palmetto trees bordered these interludes, their wide leaves overhead offering a cooling shade to those who sat there.

Louis wriggled more insistently. I set him on his feet and took his hand. He pulled me down the path, eager to see everything, stopping to examine a brilliant flower or charging after a butterfly until it rose beyond his reach. I laughed, enjoying his delight, and finally released him with a strict warning to stay on the path and not run too far ahead. A few steps behind me the guard cleared his throat but I ignored him. Children needed some freedom to explore, even precious royal princes.

The day was hot and bright. When we reached the first shaded bench I sat down and called Louis to me, lifting him up to sit beside me. I felt his cheeks and forehead: warm and slightly moist but not over-heated.

"We must sit in the shade every so often," I told him. His little lips protruded in a pout as he looked back at the stone path that wound its way into the garden so invitingly. Remembering how I had loved to watch the clouds I pointed them out to him, drawing pictures from their lazy shapes. I had not felt such peace since the day my mother called to me from the river shore.

Louis slid down from the bench and ran behind it crying, "Find Louis!"

This was a game we often played in the nursery. "Where is Prince Louis?" I called, standing up and walking to a bed of roses. "He is not here in the roses."

"Here he is!" Louis cried from behind the bench.

I walked to the nearest palmetto and looked behind the wide trunk. "He is not behind the tree."

"Here he is! Here he is!" A burst of chuckles shook the foliage behind the bench.

I smiled at the guard waiting by the path. He rolled his eyes, looking bored. I preferred the younger guard who had a sense of humor, even though he eyed my breasts longer than I cared for. I looked down the pathway. "He is not on the path through the garden. Where can Prince Louis be?"

"Here he is!" Louis shrieked. "Behind bench!"

Holding back my laughter I rustled the bushes beside the path. "He is not hiding in the bushes. Perhaps he is behind the bench?"

"He is! He is!"

"Why, here he is! Here is Prince Louis!" I exclaimed, coming around the side of the bench. He launched himself into my arms. I blushed, glancing over my shoulder at the guard. He was looking back the way we had come, paying no attention to us. I gave the prince a quick hug and let him go. "Again!" he cried.

"Once more," I agreed, as willing as he was to prolong our time here. I sat on the bench and closed my eyes. "Find a good hiding place, Prince Louis." I heard the bushes near the stone path rustle and smiled to myself. "This time do not tell me where you are. I will find you."

I looked behind the bench and in the rose bed and behind a tree, each time announcing where I was seeking him and the surprising fact that he was not there. The shrubbery beside the pathway shook with excitement.

"He is not behind this tree, either," I said. Hearing no response, I decided to end the game before his interest waned. I walked to the hedge where I had heard him giggling earlier. "Is he in the bushes?"

I said loudly. Getting no response, I parted them to look behind, but there was no sign of Louis.

"Who exactly are you looking for?"

I jumped and spun around. Prince Robert stood behind me, his eyebrow arched and his mouth quirked in an expression somewhere between amusement and annoyance. I caught my breath, dizzy to find him so near. If I reached out I could touch him. I dropped into a curtsey so quickly I lost my balance and landed on my bottom.

"Have you had too much ale?"

"No! No, Your Majesty." I scrambled up, realized I was standing in his presence and began another curtsey.

"Be careful," he advised. "Perhaps you should just stand with your head bowed." The wry tone left his voice as he added, "Who are you playing with in my royal garden?" He glanced back at the nursery guard standing as rigid as death.

"Prince Louis," I whispered, staring at my feet. My face and neck were so hot I knew they were scarlet. What a fool I was making of myself. Then, *Oh God, where is Louis?*

"With Louis?"

I risked a quick glance through my lashes.

The coldness in Robert's face had disappeared. "You are here with my son?" He smiled and looked around. "Prince Louis?" he called.

Receiving no answer, he turned back to me. "Where is he?"

Even if I had had an answer, I could not have spoken. I looked frantically at the bushes, praying the little prince would magically appear.

"Where is my son?"

I opened my mouth but nothing came out. Prince Robert turned impatiently to the guard who stared straight ahead, beads of sweat visible on his forehead.

"He is hiding, Your Majesty!" I gasped, before Robert could imagine worse. "We were playing hide and find. We play it in the nursery. He... he is hiding," I finished lamely.

"But you know where he is?"

I looked down at my feet.

"Prince Louis," Robert called. "Come out!"

"Where…where is Prince Louis?" I added hopefully. "Where can he be?"

Prince Robert gave me a shocked look, then turned furiously on the guard. "You let the prince out of your sight?" he roared. The guard shook as though buffeted by a strong wind. Robert whirled on me. "And you—"

"Here he is," a little voice said tentatively.

We froze in a silent tableau, dumbfounded with relief.

I caught my breath. "Prince Louis, come out now," I called gently, trying to keep my voice from shaking. "The game has ended."

A little sob that broke my heart came from the garden beyond the hedge. "L…Louis is lost."

With a roar Robert charged toward the sound. I raced after him. When I reached them Robert had scooped Louis into his arms. He held the little boy tightly, stroking his golden curls as Louis clung to him, weeping against his chest. "Father has found you, Louis," Robert murmured into his son's ear. "Father will always find you. I will never leave you lost and frightened."

Louis raised his tear-streaked face to his father. "Where is Prince Louis," he explained sadly.

Catching sight of me he reached out his arms. "Here he is, Phippa."

Chapter 9

March 7, 1346
Queen Joanna's Court, Naples

He told them nothing."

"He gave them our names! Hugo del Balzo was seen writing down his answers when they questioned him. They got all of our names from him!"

"They lie."

"Of course they are lying," my son Robert interrupts, frowning at the Count of Terlizzi. "None of us were there. My brother was asleep in his room when Andrew was murdered, that was established months ago, so how could he give up the names of anyone who *was* there?"

"He gave them our names to save himself!" Nicholas of Melizzano joins in, his voice a squeak of panic. Heads nod around the table in Joanna's privy chamber.

"He did not." I say again.

"How could you know that?" the Count of Terlizzi demands, glaring at me.

I stand up and lean over the table toward him and all my son's accusers. "Because I was there!"

The room is silent, every face gaping at me.

"You were there when he was questioned?" Robert and Joanna ask at the same time.

"I went, of course I went! Raymond is my son! I wore a servant's cape and kept to myself. No one recognized me." *Not even Raymond.* It might have given him some comfort to see me there, but I could not risk drawing his attention. He was too far gone when I arrived at any rate.

Robert looks furious.

"You will not leave Castle Nuovo again until all this has blown over," Joanna says. "I command it."

"Tomorrow they will have a notary read his confession in public, with him there. We will hear then whether he has accused us," Melizzano says.

"What does it matter?" Charles of Artois's face wears an expression of weariness. "Del Balzo, Durazzo, and Taranto, they have already decided who stands in their way. Our names will be read, whether Raymond named us or not." He glances at me. "I now believe he did not, but it will be the same as if he had."

"You will all be safe here," Joanna says, rising to her feet at the head of the table. "Castle Nuovo will protect you, and Pope Clement VI will send his emissary soon to quell this... this..."

"Bloodlust?" I suggest. "Insurrection?"

She looks at me in horror. But it has come to that in her kingdom, outside the very gates of her castle. If we are to survive this, any of us, we must face it for what it is.

"Unrest," Joanna says. She turns her back on us stiffly. By the time she has reached the chamber door her guard has it open for her.

Unrest. I get to my feet slowly. Will this 'unrest' send my son to his permanent rest? My eyes fill with tears. I can do nothing for Raymond but pray. Meanwhile, I must consider the others in my family. I take a breath and blink away the momentary weakness. The young queen may be right that we are safe in Castle Nuovo, but we are also helpless here. And I have never been one to sit and wait for rescue.

When you are most vulnerable, that is when you most need to appear confident. Another saying of my husband's. A good one. I raise my chin and walk with a show of confidence from the room.

When dusk falls I receive a message to dine with Queen Joanna. Dressing quickly with the help of a maid—I miss my own maid at my home—I make my way to the small hall. The room is full of faces I know, waiting for the queen to lead us to table. My son Robert is there with his wife, and Sancia with her husband the Count of Marcone, and Charles of Artois and his son Bertrand with their wives. All of Joanna's supporters and favorites. All but my son Raymond. Where is his wife this evening, I wonder? I hope she has left Naples, gone to one of their country estates where she will be safe, and taken her sons and their wives and children with her.

But I know they have not gone. Raymond's wife is a stalwart woman, and she cares for my son. She will be thinking: what if they release him and he is brought home, and I am not here to see he is cared for properly? Nevertheless I will send a message tonight begging her to leave, or at least to send her family to safety. I will suggest it to Robert's wife as well tonight when I have a chance to speak to her alone. There is one who will heed me and think of herself.

Joanna arrives with Louis beside her. I am startled to see him here, and even more startled to see Joanna lead us into dinner on his arm. I hide my surprise and curtsey as they pass. So she is ready to make her choice public, against my advice. Well, she has learned the art of power since the cradle. This will certainly bind Louis and his army to her. I only fear she is overestimating the love her people bear her. They do love her, but not as much as they love a royal scandal.

Joanna is radiant. She has been fond of Louis since she was a girl; more than fond, now. Her happiness cuts me deeply. Has she already forgotten the events of this afternoon? She loved Raymond as an uncle, and he loved her as a man loves his rightful monarch. I remind myself how young she is, barely twenty. This is a terrible time to have a young monarch.

Louis walks Joanna to the head of the table. He waits for her to be seated before gracefully taking the chair beside her. She looks at him as if there is no one else in the room. As if he is her savior. Indeed I hope he will be savior to us all, and quickly, for we are in desperate need of one. I look around for Catherine of Valois. How she will love to see her favorite son's triumph; but she is not here. We have grown old together, she and I, mostly sparring with one another through the years, but on occasion frosty allies, as we are now.

Conversation resumes as the rest of us take our places at the table. Robert escorts me on one arm and his wife on the other to our seats. How formal we are, how civilized, while my son lies moaning in agony on a dirty dungeon floor. But I must look calm and untroubled. We must all look like we are the confirmed seat of power in the celebrated Kingdom of Naples.

The room is hot and smells of sweat. Servants run up and down the table filling wine goblets and ale mugs, too busy answering demands for more drink to bring in the dinner. Men down their ale and swipe at their damp faces as if they are merely wiping their mouths before calling for a refill. Women dab at the sheen on their foreheads with little handkerchiefs and fan themselves, complaining of the heat, although it is barely spring and there are no hot dishes on the table yet, warming the room with their steam. Eyes dart round the room to discover if anyone else feels it, this nervous edginess, this hot coal of anxiety in the chest. But no one's eyes meet. The talk is too loud, the jokes too quickly repeated, the laughter too brittle. I make trivial conversation, smile, and pretend to be amused like everyone else, with the image of my son's bleeding body and mutilated face always before me.

The food arrives and is devoured with the same nervous energy applied to the drink. Joanna and Louis laugh and flirt and clap for the minstrels to sing gay songs and signal for more wine, like everyone else. There is no talk of the war being fought between Louis and his brother Robert, Duke of Taranto, of the angry mobs filling the streets, of today's attack on the seneschal of the court and by extension, against the crown of Naples.

I quell my resentment. Joanna learned how to reign from me as well as from her grandparents, King Robert and Queen Sancia. I should be pleased to see her apply her lessons so well. When dinner is over everyone has been cheered and fortified. We look at one another a little blurrily, united in our bold defiance of the threat that lies over every head in this room.

Joanna and Louis leave the table early. Louis must get back to his hired troops. The food and silver plates will be cleared away at once; no one is served after the queen leaves. But Joanna orders the servants to continue pouring wine and ale until dawn, to a dutiful cheer from the company. Ah, how well we all play our part.

The noblewomen—wives and ladies-in-waiting—leave as well, and I with them. On the way out I speak quietly to Robert's wife, who says she will leave Naples tomorrow, and to Sancia and her husband, who will not.

"You have been named a conspirator in Prince Andrew's murder," I tell my granddaughter harshly.

"I will be safe beside Queen Joanna."

It is what I am counting on as well, but these are uncertain times. Who knows where safety lies? I accept her decision and ask her husband, the count, to send a message to Raymond's wife, imploring her to take her family away from Naples. He promises to do so.

Sancia and I walk to the bedchambers assigned to the ladies of Joanna's court, but before we reach ours Robert meets us. I take one look at his face and tell Sancia to go ahead.

"What is it? Father, what has happened?" Sancia asks.

"Council business," I tell her before he can answer. "Go to bed, child, it need not concern you."

"I have been accused as well. My name has been linked with the estrangement between the queen and Prince Andrew." She shivers. "However bad the news may be, I would rather know."

Robert kisses his daughter's forehead. "Nothing has happened that I know of, darling. Go to bed. My grandson needs his sleep." He pats her swelling womb affectionately.

When she still balks he adds, "As soon as I have news of your uncle, I promise to tell you."

"The queen is leaving us," he tells me quietly when we are alone. "She is going to Castle dell'Ovo."

"Tonight?"

"At once. Louis is waiting with his men to escort her there. She told me of her decision when we left the dining hall."

"Where is she now?"

"In her bedchamber. Marguerite is with her."

Marguerite of Taranto. The Duke of Taranto's sister, and Louis' as well. Why Marguerite? Sancia is the first of Joanna's ladies-in-waiting, she has been Joanna's closest friend since they were children.

"Mother—"

"I am going," I tell him, already hurrying toward Joanna's rooms.

Joanna looks up as her guard admits me. "Philippa," she says, as though she is glad to see me. I note the strain on her face beneath her smile.

I curtsey stiffly. "I hear you are leaving us, Your Majesty."

"I am going to Castle dell'Ovo to be with Charles Martel."

"We need you here, Your Majesty," I murmur, still sunk in my curtsey, my head bowed.

"My son needs me now. You may get up," she adds.

"How will we make any decisions with you gone from your court?" I rise from my curtsey because my legs are shaking treacherously, but I keep my head bowed to mitigate the reprimand behind my words. She knows her place is here during this crisis, and she knows how running to Castle dell'Ovo will look.

Castle dell'Ovo is built on land jutting out into the sea, a short narrow causeway joining it to Naples. It is impregnable, the refuge of the Angevins in times of greatest danger. She will appear to be fleeing in fear, perhaps even to be deserting her office. She will also appear to be deserting us, leaving us to our fate. Washing her hands of us, as Pilate did to Our Lord. I raise my eyes—is this what she intends?—but she looks away before I can read her.

"I have placed Robert in charge, as grand seneschal of my kingdom. And Castle dell'Ovo is not far."

It is a short ride away when the city is safe to travel through. I do not point out that she now needs Louis and his guards to accompany her there.

"It is not safe for my son to leave this castle to consult you."

She flushes at the oblique reminder of my Raymond's ordeal. "I have given Robert complete authority to act on my behalf," she says.

"Your Majesty—" my voice trembles, taking on a pleading tone she has never heard from me.

"Leave us a moment, Marguerite," she interrupts.

"Philippa," she says, clasping my shoulders when we are alone. "You know I would not leave you if I thought you were in danger. You know I love you as my—"

"Then do not leave us!" I cry, desperate enough to beg. Robert of Taranto and Charles of Durazzo will not dare attack the castle with their rightful monarch inside. I want to shake her for her cowardice, I cannot understand it. She has never lacked courage before.

"I must! Louis has heard of a plot to take Charles Martel. The Hungarians are planning to take my son from me!"

"Pope Clement would never—" It is true he has requested that Charles Martel be brought to him in Avignon until all this is settled. But the Pope does not plot, he commands. At the back of my mind I am thinking, *Louis told her this?*

"Pope Clement VI has already shown he can be swayed by Elizabeth of Hungary's gold," Joanna says bitterly. "And my son's nurse…"

Charles Martel is in the care of Prince Andrew's old nurse, Isabelle the Hungarian, who would defend him with her life against any other enemy. But she cannot be trusted to resist a plot to unite him with his Hungarian relatives. She might even be part of it.

But would they do this? The unsubtle Hungarians? They bribe, they threaten, they attack, they are loud and cruel and violent, but they are not stealthy. And all the while I am still thinking, *She is leaving us because Louis told her this?*

"You are more dear to me than any person alive." Joanna's blue eyes fill with tears. "Except my son. You would not abandon your son, Philippa! I know you would not allow a child of yours to be taken from you in his infancy, to be raised by others! And your enemies at that! I must go to him. You have to understand!" She holds my forearms, shaking them in her extremity.

My mouth opens but I cannot speak. What can I say? What can I possibly say?

"Take Sancia with you," I beg her.

She turns her face aside, unable to look at me. "I cannot. Louis says it must be Marguerite."

Chapter 10

Winter, 1299
Court of King Charles II, Naples

I will be turned out of the castle in disgrace. If I am not hanged. Who would even know what happened to me in this huge, terrifying city? I carried Louis numbly back to the nursery and set him down. Matriona was sewing. She nodded without looking up from her work as he told her of the garden, of seeing flowers and butterflies and playing hide and find.

"Papa found Louis," he finished proudly.

Matriona looked up.

She saw my face and demanded to know what had happened.

"It is as Prince Louis told you. We went to the royal garden. Prince Louis wanted to play hide and find. His father came upon us while he was hiding and found him."

"And?" she asked, squinting at me suspiciously.

"And we have come back." I looked away, knowing I betrayed myself by not meeting her eyes. She would learn of my disgrace soon enough; I could not bear to talk about it yet. As though attuned to my need, Charles awoke and loudly demanded his milk. I changed his clout and put him to my breast, wondering if it would be the last time I did so.

Surely Prince Robert would not have me hanged? I remembered the look on his face when he yelled: *And you—*! I closed my eyes to shut it out. As if I could. No more than I could unknot the pain that had lodged in my breast ever since. Prince Robert was the love of my life. I had known it the moment I saw him. And now he hated me and he was right to do so. He hated me as much as I would hate anyone who hurt or endangered Charles or Louis.

I caught myself in that thought. *As much as I would hate anyone who harmed Antonio,* I quickly amended.

At the very least he would send me away so he would never have to see me again. Would I be given any money, or turned out penniless with no way to get home? The very word, *home*, made my eyes fill. I squeezed them tight and bent my head over Charles, kissing the soft little crown of his head. It bobbed slightly as he sucked and swallowed hungrily. *Home!* I wanted to go home! I was so far away and all alone and sixteen did not feel so very grown up any more. I wanted my mother!

I bit my lip to keep from sobbing. I could never go home. It made me want to weep all the more, but I took a shaky breath and forced myself to smile down at baby Charles as though I was as carefree as a girl who has just enjoyed a walk in the royal gardens. I could feel Matriona's scrutiny across the room. She had warned me not to go. But I was headstrong. I wanted to walk in the garden and I did. Mother always said I was stubborn, that it was bound to get me into trouble. And now I must face that trouble, and somehow survive it.

What would my mother tell me to do? She would know; she always had advice for me. I would follow it this time, by all the saints in heaven I would, if only she was here to give it!

"What troubles you, child?" Matriona asked, with a gentleness that nearly broke me. I wanted to tell her. I wanted to weep against her breast like little Prince Louis did when he was over-fatigued. I wanted to tell her everything and have her tell me what to do.

But she was not my mother. She would be shocked and furious as Prince Robert had been, and she would wonder how my negligence would reflect on her. I shrugged and smiled carelessly—or so I hoped—and said, "I am a little homesick at times, but I am very fortunate to be here." I nearly choked on the last, for my good fortune was nearly over, but it was something she had told me many times and sure to satisfy her.

The afternoon passed slowly. When the door opened I jumped, but it was only a kitchen servant with our dinner.

"Oh ho!" Matriona said, gloating over a swan-shaped pastry steaming with the rich scent of venison, and a large pudding topped with sprinkled sugar, as well as the usual fish and cheeses. "We dine like royalty tonight. Come and see, Prince Louis." She looked at the servant. "Is there a feast in the castle tonight?"

"Not that I know of," he mumbled, bobbing his head and glancing back at the door. "I'm wanted in the kitchen, Madame."

When he left I saw a new man outside our door, guarding the nursery. Not the young guard who came in the evening, but a new day guard.

"Come and eat," Matriona urged. I forced a few bites down but I was filled with a sick dread and could not do justice to the delicacies.

It was late in the evening when the door opened again. A man in royal livery walked in.

"What? What is it?" Matriona spluttered, half-undressed for bed behind the dressing screen.

"Madame Philippa," the man said smartly. "Come with me."

"Shall... could I bring something?" Surely they would let me gather my clothes and my cape before putting me outside the castle gates, or locking me in a cold prison?

The man frowned, then he sighed. "If you need to freshen your face or fix your hair, do so quickly."

I shook my head sadly. What did I care what my hair looked like in prison? "May I at least bring my cape?"

He looked at me as though I was simple. "Get it then."

I ran to take it from the peg and followed him out of the room. Matriona, her head sticking out the side of the screen, stared after us open-mouthed.

With every step we took I became more confused. Instead of taking me to the stairs he led me down a back hallway in the

direction of the royal chambers. Unless I was mistaken and there
was a smaller stairway leading directly to the dungeon? Was there
a dungeon in Castle Nuovo? It was the royal residence, would they
not put criminals somewhere else? Perhaps they were going to lock
me in a room until they could transport me to Castle Capuano, where
I had been told the worst villains were locked. I clutched my cloak
to my chest as though it could protect me.

"Where are you taking me?" I finally found the courage to ask.

"Prince Robert has summoned you."

I stopped abruptly. "Summoned me? Summoned me where?"

"To his chambers."

"To his chambers? At this hour?"

The man looked back, his face twisted in a scornful grimace.
Seeing me standing still he stopped also.

"Why?"

"He does not confide in me, Madame." His frown turned into an
unpleasant leer. "If you have no idea, I am sure I do not."

When I made no response he scowled again. A servant in the
nursery does not keep the Crown Prince waiting. He continued
walking and I had no choice but to follow.

Not prison, then, although I might be going to hear my dismissal.
But in person, from the Crown Prince of Naples? In his own
chambers? I pictured his face again: *And you—!* Would he have me
beaten in front of him? No, that was a foolish thought. If I were to
be beaten it would be in the city square in mid-day, in front of
everyone, with my crime read out first: Endangering the life of the
eldest son of the Crown Prince, third in line to the throne.

I stumbled, managed to catch myself before falling. Enough! My
mother would not waste her time trying to determine someone else's
plan. She would be using this time to form her own.

Should I throw myself on his mercy?

That would never be my mother's advice. "Do not let him see you
are afraid," she told me when my father had been drinking and came
into our hut and closed the door and untied the thick rope around the

waist of his tunic. I stood as straight as her and looked him in the eye scornfully, and she was right: I was beaten far less than my sister Anya, who cowered and pleaded with him.

No pleading, then. Although whatever happens, I do not think I can look at Prince Robert scornfully. But I can stand straight and look him in the eye. After I curtsey, of course, and he gives me leave to rise.

The man stopped before a plain wooden door. He knocked once and opened it. I peeked in to see a small alcove that led into a larger chamber. A fire roared in the fireplace warming the room against the night chill, and two large chairs sat before it, with a small, ornate table between them on which sat a carafe and two mugs.

"Well? Go in!" the man hissed, giving me a push. I stumbled into the narrow alcove and heard the door shut behind me.

"Come forward."

I moved toward the chamber slowly and dropped into a curtsey as soon as I saw Prince Robert standing beside the fireplace. No one else was visible in the room.

"You may rise."

I stood tall and straight and held my head high, as I had promised myself I would. With only a moment's hesitation, I looked him in the eye. At the back of my thoughts, as steady as the beat of my heart, was the certain knowledge that I must not be turned out of this castle, for I had no where to go.

"How is my son?"

I blinked. He looked at me with an anxious frown. "Charles or Louis?" was all I could think to say.

"Louis, of course. Wait, is something wrong with Charles?"

"There is nothing wrong with either of them, Your Majesty. They are soundly asleep in their beds."

"Louis was not afraid to go to bed? Did he startle at sudden noises, or cry out in his sleep?"

"No, Your Majesty. He was quite happy and ate a good dinner. He went to bed cheerfully as he always does."

"Good." Robert nodded to himself. "Good," he repeated, smiling at me. "He did not mention this afternoon, then?"

Suddenly I understood. "He told his nurse his Papa had found him," I said, tentatively returning his smile. "He seemed to feel she should be impressed. I am not certain whether in his mind the accomplishment was his or yours."

Robert chuckled. "In this case I would call it his." He dropped into one of the chairs by the fireplace. "Sit down, sit down. Would you like some wine?"

"Thank you, Your Majesty," I murmured. My legs were shaking so much I sank rather than sat down in the chair. I realized a moment late that I was expected to pour the wine, and did so with some embarrassment at the delay, but he appeared not to have noticed. He was staring gloomily into the fire.

'I am sorry for this afternoon." He lifted his mug and took a large swallow of the wine without looking at me.

Sorry? Sorry because of what he must now do? I took a gulp from my own mug and started coughing. I had never drunk unwatered wine before and had not expected it to be so much stronger than ale. Its clear, fruity smell fooled me until it hit my throat, sharp and warming. I took a small second sip to stop my coughing and put the mug down so I could wipe my eyes.

"I have upset you. I was unreasonably angry." He leaned toward me.

I wanted another drink but dared not touch the wine. "Please, Your Majesty…"

"No, I shall say this." He sat back and looked into the fire. "I myself was lost and frightened once. As a child…" He took another sip of the wine still gazing at the fireplace. "I do not ever want my son to feel that way."

I remembered the rumor of his imprisonment in Aragon. "Your father could not find you," I said softly.

He looked at me, his face hard. "My father knew exactly where I was. It was he who put me there."

I reached for my wine and took a gulp. Another fit of coughing, but I subdued it.

He gave a little shake of his head. "And now he has made me heir to the Kingdom of Naples." He smiled indifferently. "As you so boldly pointed out to me, Fortune's Wheel must turn and I am rising with it."

"Your Majesty, I did not mean——"

"Of course you did. You cast your fortune with me. You told me that, as well. So now, what shall I do with you? If our fortunes are entwined, as you claim?"

It was my turn to look into the fire, hoping its flames would justify my rosy cheeks. "Forbid me to take Louis to the royal gardens?"

He laughed. "Well that, of course. But is it enough? I was unreasonably angry, but you were unreasonably careless." He held up his hand to stop my protest, as if I would dare. "I know, you were in the royal gardens. There is little that can harm even a child there, and you were guarded. Still, my son was frightened."

"He acted very bravely."

Prince Robert observed me coolly. *Wrong thing to say.*

"Before I decide what to do I would like to know, are you a fortune-teller or a fortune-hunter?"

I took another quick drink. This time I only coughed once. I felt a pleasant buzz in my head that overrode my fear. What would my mother say? A fortune-teller was valuable, but some would call her a witch and burn her. A fortune-hunter was acceptable in a man, a man was supposed to be ambitious, but in a low-born girl?

"Both, Your Majesty," I said. "And neither. I simply recognize what I am seeing, and act on what I know. How could you rise on Fortune's Wheel without taking everyone who cleaves to you with you? I deeply regret that you now doubt me, but I cannot regret what happened. Prince Louis is sleeping soundly in his cot more fearless than ever, for he knows his father will always be there." I bowed my head, trying to look both submissive and wise.

Prince Robert took my chin and turned my face to him.

111

How long we sat there staring at one another I do not know. I could have sat staring at him forever. Suddenly a log in the fire snapped, expelling a burst of sparks that made me jump.

"It is late," the prince observed with a lazy smile. "Good night, Philippa of Catania. Take better care of my sons from now on."

I curtseyed and made my way back through the door in the little alcove. My legs were shaking under my skirts and my chin burned where he had held it. I imagined that strong hand touching me again… I forced a neutral expression onto my hot face. The same man was waiting to take me to the nursery. He smiled at me unpleasantly. I gave him a sharp look until he realized that if what he was thinking was true, he would do best to keep on my good side.

"What happened?" Matriona demanded as soon as I stepped into the nursery.

"Nothing. He asked about his sons."

She snorted. "If that was what he wanted, he would have sent for me."

"It is the truth. Believe what you want."

"I see that disappointment has made you irritable," she said. "Perhaps you are not as pretty as you thought."

I undressed in silence, thinking up a dozen angry retorts and biting them back. They would only convince her she was right. But when I hopped into bed and lay in the darkness under the blanket, the thought that filled my mind was of that long silent look Prince Robert gave me and I gave back in the intimate warmth of his fire.

I was so relieved at not being dismissed I could not hide it. Over the next few days I caught myself singing as I cared for the boys. Matriona sent me knowing glances which made me try to damp down my high spirits but any attempt to do so did not last. *What shall I do with you?* Prince Robert had asked. I began to daydream of a few things to suggest if he asked again.

Our dinner and evening meals continued to delight Matriona with cheeses formed in the shapes of flowers and the choicest cuts of meat, whole pigeons cooked into the breasts of hens and marzipan confections fashioned into cunning little animals. New marvels arrived on each platter.

"Someone in the kitchen likes you," she began to tease me. I smiled and said I could not think who, which convinced her she had guessed my secret, and effectively diverted her suspicions from Prince Robert. He had met me walking in the courtyard with Louis (his little hand held tight in mine) and stopped to talk. On his suggestion the next day I took Louis to the palace menagerie. Prince Robert was there with Violante and her ladies and several young men in his court. They stopped to make a fuss over Louis. Prince Robert complimented me on my new green kirtle. His eyes had the same deep look we had shared at his fireside. There was something between us, I could feel it. I was certain he had given the order for the special creations sent from the kitchen for my pleasure.

As Charles grew he napped longer, which gave me more free time. Inside the castle I had to keep to the servants' halls, but I was allowed to walk in the courtyard and visit the stables. I was not much interested in horses, but I soon learned when Prince Robert and his young noblemen left for the hunt, and when they returned.

Violante came to the nursery every day to play with the little princes. I made sure she would find me singing French songs to the boys, and whispered to them to go to her the instant I heard her voice at the door. Charles, at nearly one year old, would toddle after Louis who ran with a two-year-old's exuberance, stopping just before his mother, suddenly shy, as she bent down to him. Meanwhile I would pick up my embroidery—Matriona was teaching me to do ladies' needlework—and sit in the nursery like one of her ladies-in-waiting. I had taught the little princes that I would not play when I was at my needlework so they had learned not to approach me then. Violante had no cause to be jealous of their affection for me while she was visiting.

I was one of the first to notice the tiny swell of her belly, and after that made sure to compliment her health and appearance, for women are anxious when they are with child. As she neared her time, I noticed her paleness, the way her eyes darted restlessly about, like one of the sleek animals trapped in the royal menagerie.

"Do not distress yourself, Your Majesty. All will be well," I murmured to her at the end of one visit, hoping to reassure her. She gripped my hands. "Will I be well, Philippa? Do you see it?" she asked urgently. She kept her voice low so as not to frighten the little princes standing nearby, but there was genuine terror in her eyes.

A chill went through me. She thought I was prophesying. I could tell by the shape of her womb and her gait that the infant was growing and healthy, I meant only that. But seeing the dread that filled her I could not correct her error. She would take that, too, as a prophecy. *The prophecy comes true in the telling, because of the telling,* my mother had told me. Praying that she was right, I nodded: "You will be well."

Her look of gratitude and relief shamed me, but the words she said next were worse: "You shall come into confinement with me and deliver this child!"

"I... I would be honored to see you through your confinement, Your Majesty," I stammered. "But I am not a midwife. There are better women for that than I, in Naples."

"You will be my personal maid, then. And they will be told to obey you if... if..." Unable to finish she bent and kissed her sons and hurried out.

I stared at Matriona, astonished. Charles was nearly weaned and I had been hoping to stay in the nursery as a second nurse now that there would be three children. But lady's maid to the Princess Violante? And not the least, but her personal maid? I could hardly believe it.

The next day a court seamstress came in to measure me— Violante's personal maid needed a better wardrobe than a wet-nurse, and I had little time to acquire it. As I stood being measured I remembered my mother altering the hem of my first court dress, the yellow linen one I still treasured. I wished she could see me now.

I had two new kirtles and three under-shifts as soft and white as clouds by the time I accompanied Princess Violante into her confinement.

No matter how many children a woman may have borne, no matter how young and healthy or mature and experienced she may be, she always enters her confinement with fear in her heart and a prayer on her lips. Men never expect to die in battle, I am told. Filled with visions of glory and flanked by their comrades-in-arms, they think only of the enemies they will kill. But a woman goes into childbirth alone, no matter how many companions sit by her bed, and the enemy she must overcome is her own frail body.

When the day came for the princess to enter her confinement, Violante gripped my arm so tightly her fingers would leave bruises. As we walked together into the darkened room, I could not blame her. I would have liked someone to lean on too, for I was as terrified as she, having promised her safety. Whether she had told anyone or not, I felt the weight of that promise. Death had attended her bedside when Charles was born and only my mother had kept him at bay. I wished I could ask about Louis' birth, but what if his, also, had been perilous? Why had I not simply told Princess Violante the truth? Even my great-grandmother could not *always* see the future. Surely sometimes she had been wrong?

And if she was never wrong?

This girl will travel far from home and rise high above her station. She will be mother to a queen—

If Violante died in her confinement, Prince Robert would be free to marry again.

My heart pounded in my ears, hot and dizzying. I stumbled.

Violante's hand on my arm caught me. She gave me a sad, apologetic smile and loosened her grip, as though she thought she had caused my misstep.

I did not want Violante to die! My great-grandmother was wrong about me!

Besides, even if Violante died, Louis, and after him Charles, would inherit the throne before any child of mine. Which proved the prophecy was false.

As if Prince Robert would ever be allowed to marry me! His wife must bring with her an alliance for Naples. A royal lady's maid, however exalted my sudden new position might seem to me, was no more suitable a bride for a crown prince than a Sicilian laundress.

And yet I had been dreaming... Childish things! Wicked things! I saw that now, faced with the possibility of Princess Violante's death.

The princess moaned, holding her enlarged belly. I gently helped her onto her bed and plumped the pillows for her to lean against. She looked around at her ladies-in-waiting and the three mid-wives who had accompanied us into this room. She smiled graciously as though she was holding court. She was not a strong woman, but she was never a coward.

I laid the little bag of herbs I had brought with me on a table in the corner. I thought no one had noticed, I did not want to worry the princess, but when I returned to her side she nodded at them and murmured, "Thank you, Philippa. Whatever happens, you have been good to me."

I flushed. I had not been good to her. I had flirted with her husband, and tricked her into thinking Charles had a fever so I could cure it, and lied to her about seeing her future. I had imagined she might die, and I had been secretly glad for just a moment, thinking Prince Robert might turn to me. That moment of gladness shamed me more than anything I have ever done.

I straightened my back and raised my chin and swore to myself that I would do whatever I had to, to bring Princess Violante safely out of this room.

Chapter 11

March 8, 1346
Queen Joanna's Court, Naples

We have chosen to sit in the queen's council chamber, my son Robert and I, Charles of Artois with his son Bertrand, and all of Joanna's councilors who are still here in Castle Nuovo. I would prefer to stand in the courtyard and hear more quickly the news from the messengers dashing through the city to keep us updated, but it would make us appear weak and frightened to stand so desperately waiting for news.

We *are* weak and frightened. These councilors, who once looked to me for wisdom and leadership, now listen to no one but argue endlessly among themselves. And I, who so often brought them to order for Joanna, and could still do so, instead sit numb with dread.

Queen Joanna's absence has been kept secret—she left in the night, her face hidden by the hood of her cape—but secrets have a way of being found out. I suspect the guards are already wondering why they have not seen Queen Joanna in her presence chamber. Her lack of visible presence here could be enough to embolden her citizens to revolt.

We hear boots bounding up the stairway, a rattle at the outer door. All argument ends abruptly. We wait, frozen in our seats, for the latest news. When the door of the council chamber bursts open the messenger sees twelve of the highest-ranking men and women in the kingdom, saving only the queen, all turned toward him, white-faced and silent.

Momentum has already carried him inside the room and down into a bow, but there he stays, immobilized. The queen's top advisors stare round at each other, barely breathing in fear of what he will tell us. The young soldier's face, pale with whatever he has just witnessed and must recount, grows paler still at the sight of our terror. His eyes dart round the room.

"The queen is resting," I say, forcing a calm tone of authority into my voice. "We will pass on your report when she returns. Rise and tell us what you have seen and heard. Spare nothing."

Robert nods at the two guards. With a casual gesture of his hand he bids them close the door and resume their stations, one outside, the other just inside the room. *The kingdom is safe, its rightful government in control,* our words and motions proclaim. The rest of the councilors straighten, breathe, take a gulp of wine, but no one speaks, no one's eyes move from the young man whose message is all we care about right now.

"The citizens have been incited to a frenzy. I have heard they intend to storm the castle."

The young man's words are greeted with gasps and exclamations of dismay around our table. Robert snaps his fingers at the guard just inside the room. "Tell the master of the guards to take up the drawbridge, to close the outer doors and bar them at once! And double the guards on the walls. Tell him just to watch for now, but to put his men on alert. And inform the mercenaries to be ready." He turns back to the messenger as the guard hurries out. "Now, tell us exactly what you saw and heard."

I regain my courage in that moment. My son's command, his steady self-control, his leadership all fill me with pride. *This is what he must be like in battle,* I tell myself. And then the soldier begins his report.

"When I arrived, they had dragged Lord Raymond up onto a platform in front of Santa Chiara."

I nod to myself. So everyone will see the cathedral behind them, a silent ally to their evil acts.

"A notary stood beside him, reading his testimony aloud for everyone to hear—"

"Who else was on the platform?" Robert interrupts. The Count of Terlizzi frowns at my son, impatient to hear the testimony, the names Raymond gave them. But Charles of Artois nods. We need these names too, the names of our enemies.

"Robert, Duke of Taranto, Hugo del Balzo, Charles, Duke of Durazzo and his two brothers—"

"The Duke of Taranto's brother, Philip?" Charles of Artois interrupts.

"No, Lord Philip was not with them."

Charles glances at my son. Louis of Taranto has told us his younger brother sides with him, and his mother also, Catherine of Valois, the matriarch of the Taranto family. Robert catches Charles of Artois' look. His chin dips, a tiny gesture of agreement over these allies.

"The testimony," Terlizzi says in a tight voice.

"He confessed to participating in the murder of Prince Andrew, and gave the names of the others involved."

I press my lips together, disgusted. Everyone knows Raymond was in bed at the time. Everyone with eyes must know his tongue had been cut out when he gave this false testimony. The councilors ignore my silent protest. It does not matter what is known, it only matters what is believed. "How many were in the square?" I ask.

"Hundreds. Perhaps thousands. They spilled out into every adjoining street."

And they all believed this charade? I do not ask it aloud. The look on his face, horror and pity and fear as he stammers out his story makes it unnecessary. And guilt? Is it guilt that tints his cheeks and turns the corners of his mouth down? Did he, too, find the spectacle so persuasive that even now, in front of us, he finds himself wondering and cannot meet our eyes?

"The notary read the seneschal of the court's testimony?" Robert asks.

"Yes, my Lord." The young man nods.

"And who confirmed its accuracy?" the marshal of the realm asks, following my son's lead.

"The prisoner."

Robert looks at the young soldier coolly.

"The seneschal of the court, Lord Raymond," the soldier quickly corrects himself. "He nodded after each name was called, for all to see."

Terlizzi and Melizanno and a few others around the table groan.

Rubbish! I am filled with rage. *Never!* Never in this life would Raymond convict the innocent. And never would he convict his own family, innocent or not.

"He was being tortured," Robert says.

"Yes, my Lord. They had a pail of hot coals and a pincer on the platform. After each name was called..." the young man trails off, possibly remembering Robert and I are this "prisoner's" family.

"They applied the burning pincers to his body," I finish grimly. "And when they did, his head jerked up, and fell back to his chest."

"Yes!" the soldier nods. His eyes widen. "He...he was not nodding."

"No." I let my scorn be heard in my voice.

"The names," Nicholas of Melizanno says. "Whose names did he give?" There is an edge of panic to his voice. I have no doubt that he, at least, is guilty of the crime my sons have been accused of.

The young soldier glances at my son. Robert nods. He swallows, his Adam's apple bobbing, and takes a breath before continuing: "Lord Robert, Count of Eboli and grand seneschal of the kingdom." His eyes flick toward me and quickly away. "Lady Philippa, advisor to Her Majesty the Queen. Lord Charles of Artois. Lord Bertrand of Artois..."

I look around the room. Charles of Artois left a short while ago, after the messenger told us the names of those involved in this heinous inquisition. Now his son Bertrand quietly leaves.

"Lady Sancia, Countess of Marcone..."

Sancia? What is Sancia to them? A young mother, one of Joanna's ladies-in-waiting. How can she be in their way, she has no power at court! I am sick with anger. It is her background they despise, her rise from what they see as the basest of breeding to Countess of Marcone and friend of the queen. That someone of her origins should be greeted at court as their equal infuriates them. She puts on no airs, her parents have taught her the need for humility, but she is what she is. I have fought them all my life, these and others like them, with the subtle power of the courtier. They care only for appearance and bloodline, not intelligence and ability. Oh, give me a sword and a strong male body and I would cut them down myself!

I should have ordered Joanna to take Sancia with her! I should have confronted Louis! I did not know Sancia had been named an accomplice. *Did he?*

"The Count of Terlizzi, Marshal of the Realm," the soldier continues, "Nicholas of Melizanno..."

Everyone in this room is named, and several others elsewhere in the castle. Robert of Taranto wants Joanna friendless and alone when he marries her, with no one to support or advise her but him. Charles of Durazzo would add her name to the list if he could, and thus make way for his wife, Joanna's younger sister Maria, to take the throne. And Hugo del Balzo? That one simply enjoys torture and murder for its own sake, and the more bodies the better. He is enjoying his role of investigating Andrew's murderers. God keep us from falling into his hands.

As Raymond has. I shudder with grief.

Robert sends the young soldier to the kitchen to eat and rest, and tells him to have the cook send platters of food to us.

When the door opens we hear a distant clamor outside the castle. It rises as we listen, cries and shouts and chanting. We hear the sound of pounding boots below as guards rush to reinforce the walls. In no time there is a crowd of furious citizens raging right outside the castle walls!

"Stop!" Roberts cries when a number of councilors leap up. "Do not let them see you at the windows. Our soldiers will take care of them, along with Lord Louis' mercenaries. We are well-defended. Castle Nuovo cannot be breached."

The assault continues into the night. We eat little, huddled and frightened in our absent queen's chambers while our own citizens, crazed with bloodlust and lies, battle against foreign mercenaries for the privilege of butchering us. The messengers who bring us reports look haunted—civil war is an ugly thing, painting hideous grimaces onto familiar faces—but they do not look afraid. Spears and daggers in the hands of shopkeepers are no match for trained soldiers shooting crossbows and pouring rocks, tiles, boiling oil, and whatever other ballistics come to hand down on them from the castle walls. Inevitably a messenger comes to tell us the throng has withdrawn.

Withdrawn but not dispersed. They surround Castle Nuovo and there they stay, out of range of our soldiers' arrows, waiting for hunger and thirst to do what they cannot.

"We are at siege!" Nicholas of Melizzano gasps when we are informed of this development. He flops back into his chair panting, his face so pale I expect him to faint like a woman.

Robert stands, motioning to the marshal of the realm to come with him.

"Where are you going?" Nicholas cries, his voice sharp with fear. As if my son would desert us.

"Wait here," Robert says.

I glance at him and receive a barely perceptible nod. While he is gone I rise stiffly and go into Joanna's presence chamber. There is nothing to be done. No amount of discussion will solve this, and the chairs are more comfortable here. Sancia comes to sit beside me.

"You have heard?"

She nods.

"It was all show. He told them nothing."

"I know he would never name me. Name any of us." She wipes her eyes, takes a deep breath. "Maybe Melizanno."

I chuckle. It comes out forced and we fall silent. I am so weary with worry my eyes close.

When Robert returns, his face is grim. "Louis' mercenaries were already there, looting the kitchen supplies and getting drunk. I have locked up as much as I could."

"They are looting the castle." I have been hearing noises outside the queen's rooms for a while now, drunken voices, the crash of things breaking.

"I cannot stop them. There are too many." His face looks anguished. "The queen's guard, at least, is loyal. They will not let them in here, or in the wardrobe room. And the royal jewels are well-guarded…"

"You have done all you could. Queen Joanna should be here. Or Louis."

"We can last several days. It is an undisciplined mob of citizens, not a well-trained army. They will come to their senses soon."

Louis' mercenaries roam the castle like pirates looking for plunder. How long will their interest in protecting us last when supplies become scarce? They are not defending their own castle against a foreign invader. Their lives are not in danger if the walls are breached. This enemy does not want the castle or its defenders; they only want us.

We wait to see which undisciplined mob will tire of the game first.

Chapter 12

Autumn, 1299
Court of King Charles II, Naples

Princess Violante's infant, a tiny girl, died at birth. Violante nearly followed her but I would not allow it. I had the midwives pack her opening with a poultice of sage leaves to staunch the bleeding. I fed her teas of comfrey root and motherwort to close her womb, valerian and yarrow to help her rest, fennel to prevent jaundice and burdock and vervain to lower her fever. I ordered hot broths and organ meats from the kitchen and forced her to swallow them. I would have made her eat the afterbirth, my mother did that once with a woman who was dying, but at court I would be branded a witch for something so bizarre. The court physicians watched my every move for something they could object to, but who could protest against teas and broth?

When she asked for her baby I told her the infant was sleeping, that she could hold her when she was stronger. I knew she would hate me later for this lie, but I also knew she would die without it. I made her ladies-in-waiting leave the room with their tear-stained faces, and ordered the court physicians to maintain my falsehood or I would tell Prince Robert they had let his wife die. Outraged, they demanded I leave the room. But I am my mother's daughter; I drew myself up to my full height and looked them straight in the eyes and said nothing. And that put an end to that.

When Violante was strong enough to learn the truth, I was the one who told her. I also told her that Louis and Charles needed their mother, Prince Robert needed a wife, and Naples needed its future queen—in that order. Prince Robert might find another wife and Naples another queen, but no one else could ever be Louis' and Charles' mother. I told her that bluntly, in all its harsh kindness, and she nodded because I spoke true. She asked me about my son and I told her everything I remembered, speaking about him as though he were dead, for dead to me he was. We mourned her daughter and my Antonio together in that dark room while she waited for her bleeding to stop. Then we walked out, her holding my arm as tightly as when we walked in, as full of sorrow as she had then been full of fear. I brought her out as I had promised myself I would, but it was a different woman who left that room with me.

After that she would have no other maid. I slept in the servants' rooms but during the day I sat in her presence chamber with her and her ladies-in-waiting. I combed out her hair and chose her outfits and dressed her in them. I brought her jewels to her and helped her select which ones to wear and adorned her with them myself. I fetched her boys from the nursery to visit her every day, sitting little Charles on her knee. She listened to their sweet prattle and now and then at my encouragement she told them stories of her girlhood. Slowly she came back to life.

It shamed me, how she mourned. I had not grieved so for Antonio. But he was not dead. I would never see him again but I had the comfort of knowing he was alive and well-cared-for and happy, doted on by his father and his grandparents who had got rich because of my sacrifice.

I was thinking of this, justifying myself with these bitter thoughts, when Prince Robert entered the princess's presence chamber with his young lords. My heart leapt up at the sight of him. He strolled into the room, beautiful and powerful and manly, and I watched his every movement as one spellbound. I had not made a sacrifice; I had made a choice. And even now, even though I had faced and accepted that I would never be his wife—that the prophecy would come true another way or else my great-grandmother was simply wrong—despite all that, I would make the same choice again, just to be able to look on him. And have him occasionally look at me, and smile at me, as he was doing now.

I flushed and looked down, hoping he could not read my thoughts. I had forsaken everything to follow him, like the worst of camp followers, a strumpet who pretended she was not and thought herself better than those who were honest with themselves. My flush grew hotter. I turned to go to the window and hide myself till I regained my composure. As I turned I looked up. Princess Violante was staring at me, a frown creasing her brow. She glanced at Prince Robert then back to my burning face. Slowly her face drained of color. I stood frozen, my mouth open—but what could I say? She turned away and began a conversation with one of her ladies. I walked in what seemed like slowed time toward my window refuge, and I heard her laugh, a brittle, fabricated bark without any amusement in it. A false, angry laugh.

I left soon after. I did not ask the princess' leave; she would be as unwilling to speak to me as I was to face her. At last, in the empty servant's passage, I allowed myself to weep. Everything was ruined. Violante had seen us looking at each other, her husband and I, my feelings as clear as though I had spoken them out loud and Prince Robert's interest evident in his smile. She was a jealous woman. She would find some reason to dismiss me, or have me assigned to a lower position. And all over nothing: a smile, a breathless glance, a shameless thought swelling my breast...

Well, several, actually, and a few very detailed dreams. But nothing, really! Prince Robert had his dalliances, what royal lord did not, especially when his wife was so often with child? But I had never given him a word to indicate that I might be willing. I had foolishly hoped for more. I bitterly regretted it now. If I was to be punished, I wished I had sinned!

I wept all the harder thinking of what I had missed, unaware that I was no longer alone until two hands grasped my shoulders. Enormous hands, their grip followed by a deep, accented voice: "What has happened? Has someone hurt you? Tell me, and I will beat the cur until he wishes he had never touched you!"

I looked up with a gasp that stopped my tears, then gasped again to see a scowling, pitch-black face staring down at me. I wrenched myself loose and backed away, panting with fear. "You threaten to beat the crown prince of Naples?" I cried, meaning to frighten him away. I recognized him now, the Ethiopian cook.

"The crown prince? Prince Robert has done this?" Far from being frightened, he looked furious.

He thinks— Oh Mary, Mother of God, if he should spread such a rumor and attribute it to me—! "Nothing! Prince Robert has done nothing! How dare you suggest—"

His face changed before me, enlarged, intensified. If before he was furious, now he was enraged. His huge hands curled into fists, the knuckles whitening under his black skin. Such hands could kill an ox! "If he has threatened you—!"

"No! You have it wrong!" I cried, backing up until the wall stopped me. "No one has threatened me, no one has hurt me! I have just... I thought... Prince Robert smiled at me and Princess Violante saw!" I blurted out. Immediately I thought: *Mother Mary help me! What have I told him?*

I had not mollified or reassured him or accomplished whatever was needed to tame this wild man. Instead, I saw his fury turn to comprehension and then into an equally intense expression of disgust. "You are a fool! You would be the prince's whore when you have the ability to be so much more? I thought you were intelligent as well as beautiful! But you are just another silly maid!"

Stung by the truth—as if he had any right to fling it at me—I drew myself up and glared at him. "I will be the mother to a queen!" I spat out.

"Mother to a queen?" His eyebrows rose mockingly. "Your bastard will never be—"

"How dare you! How dare you imagine—" I raised my hand to slap him, but he caught it easily and held it despite my struggle to free myself.

"So, my congratulations are too early." He laughed sarcastically. "This is only your dream?"

"It is not a dream! It is a prophecy!"

He looked at me, the laugh gone now. "A prophecy? Why do you say that? What sort of prophecy?"

Why, indeed, was I telling him this? I yanked my arm back again and this time he let it go. "You are right," I said haughtily. "I am just a foolish maid." I tried to brush past him but he put out his arm. I stopped short of his touch.

"Perhaps I was wrong. On several counts."

His accent, now that he was speaking civilly, had a lilting quality that was strangely appealing. I looked up, ready to accept his apology if it would allow me to escape. He smiled, his teeth a startling white in the blackness of his face, like the gleaming fangs of a wolf in the night. I shuddered and drew back. Immediately I wished I could take it back. His smile froze and disappeared. He bowed to me stiffly and left.

I looked after him with regret. I did not think myself a cruel person. He was alone, a stranger in this foreign court, like me. It was just his appearance, his blackness, so like the figure of Death my father had frightened me with as a child. I could not endure it.

Well, I would seldom have to. He and I moved in different areas of this huge castle. What was he doing here, outside his kitchen, anyway?

I rubbed my face to erase any lingering sign of tears and headed for the nursery. Playing with Louis and Charles always lightened my mood and Matriona, if not quite a friend, was the closest I had to one here.

Princess Violante no longer asked my advice on what she should wear. She would not look directly at me, but when I was not beside her I could feel her watching me, especially if Prince Robert was in the room.

Those were the only differences between us. I combed and braided up her hair, helped her in and out of her shifts and kirtles and nightdresses, cleaned and cared for her jewelry and clasped the pieces she chose around her neck or wrist or slid them onto her fingers and into her hair. And removed them again and buffed them, and put them into their cases for the master of the princess's jewels to take to the wardrobe room, where they would be locked up and guarded. I ordered the princess's meals and brought her rose water to wash her face and hands with, and saw that her fire was lit and her bed turned down in the evenings. And through it all we barely spoke, other than her instructions and my quiet: "Yes, Your Majesty."

Prince Robert noticed. I saw him talking quietly to her once while glancing over at me. Afterwards she made an effort to address me more cordially. He must have told her I was not his mistress, but she had seen the way he smiled at me that day. She had seen the longing in my eyes and the flush on my face as I returned his smile. I had betrayed her in my heart. We had been through the loss of a child together, and she had given me her trust as she had done no other, and I had broken it.

I no longer took any pleasure in my position. I had climbed higher than even my mother could have imagined, but every moment in Violante's presence was a reproach to me and an unpleasant reminder of her husband's infidelities for her.

I saw the Ethiopian slave—freed man, I had to remind myself each time—in the halls occasionally. Matriona informed me he had been promoted from the kitchen to Guard of the King's Wardrobe, a position of great honor. He nodded to me when we passed and I nodded back, a small quick motion, for I was embarrassed to remember our prior exchange.

Autumn passed and winter came and the feasts of Yuletide drew near.

One morning when I brought Violante mulled wine to warm her while she was being dressed, she sent the other women out of her bedchamber, save only me. "I have good news for you, Philippa," she said. She smiled at me for the first time since that day she had caught Prince Robert and I looking at each other. It was not the kind of smile I had hoped to see again on her face. I dreaded what might come, and raised her nightdress over her head with trembling hands. She let me worry, waiting until I had finished dressing her and stood behind her combing her hair.

"I have arranged a marriage for you," she said.

I dropped her braid, catching it again as it began to unravel. "I…I was not expecting to remarry, Your Majesty."

"Then this will be a pleasant surprise," she answered. "And he is a wealthy man, with horses and a fine, big house for you to live in together. Did I not promise you on the boat trip here that you would be rewarded for your loyalty?" There was an edge to her voice that made me sweat.

"Yes, I remember. You promised I need never fear for my future."

"And you need not, for when you marry you will be a wealthy woman."

I took a deep breath, soundlessly, never pausing as I pinned up her braids, the model of self-control. "May I know who I am to marry, Your Majesty?"

"A man whose position is higher even than yours." She paused with a little smile on her face that set my heart hammering. "King Charles himself proposed the marriage. You have been honored indeed, Philippa. You are to marry the Guard of King Charles' Wardrobe."

"The Guard of the King's Wardrobe." I could barely get the words out.

"Yes. Do you know him? His name is Raymond of Campagno."

"Raymond of Campagno." I pinned her headdress in place slowly. My hands and limbs felt numb. My heart was numb. Even my mind was numb. I could not think except to repeat his name. This was my punishment. This was her chance to mock me. Instead of the golden-haired, blue-eyed prince I had dreamed of for two years, I was to marry an African slave. Freed man. What difference? A man I could hardly bear to look at.

"King Charles has favored him above all other servants," she reminded me coolly.

I commanded myself to think, to break through this numbing stupor. This could not be happening! But it was happening, would happen. I had this moment; if I did nothing I would be lost forever. "I am honored," I murmured, searching desperately for some way out. "It is only…" *What? What could I say?*

I dropped to my knees at her side. "Your Majesty, I swore an oath in Sicily, on the ship, when we were leaving," I spoke quickly, urgently, thinking even faster, "…that if I ever married again it would be to a soldier, one who could come back and help…" I had been about to say 'your husband' but she would not care for me making an oath to help him. "…help King Charles of Naples to win Sicily back for its rightful… king." I finished a little awkwardly, the best I could think of with such short notice. I bowed my head and waited for her response, whispering *Hail Mary's* while I waited.

"A soldier," Princess Violante said slowly. "What a noble sentiment. How loyal you are."

When I told her of my predicament, Matriona gave a delighted hoot. "Oh-ho! So that is who was sending us all those extravagant meals while you were Charles' wet-nurse. And you did not even know you were being courted!"

"Being courted?" I shook my head. "I thought it was…" I closed my mouth. What a fool I had been, a blind fool! I should have been batting my eyes at the young knights who turned to watch me as I walked by swinging my hips, instead of dreaming of Prince Robert and counting on a dead woman's prophecy. I should have found myself a husband if I did not want one found for me. But I knew I was married! I had forgotten that to everyone else I was a young widow.

I *am* married! Married to Guilio! What if they learned—? No, even if Prince Robert returned to Sicily, Guilio would never reveal my secret. He could have let it be known when I became Charles' wet-nurse, but he accepted the term "uncle." He benefited from it. He is as committed as I am to the silence we both kept then.

"I told her I could not marry him."

Matriona stopped laughing. She looked at me, her eyes narrowing. "What did she say?"

"Nothing." She left me on my knees beside her chair reciting even more desperately my silent *Hail Mary's*.

Matriona shook her head.

I lay awake all night. The servant's chamber was cold but I sweated in my sheet. I could ask Princess Violante to find me a position elsewhere. But no ladies' maid would leave the service of the future queen of Naples without a reason, and neither Violante nor I wanted people to speculate about that reason. What if I found another suitor? I would have to do so quickly, and it would have to be someone they would approve of. Princess Violante wanted me gone from Castle Nuovo in a way that would not break her promise to me; but she might break that promise if I refused to marry. I must reconcile myself to the sin of bigamy unless I wished to defy the King of Naples and run away penniless.

Princess Violante did not mention the previous day's conversation when I dressed her and braided up her hair the next day. I was nervous and jumpy all morning. When she went for her mid-day dinner I wandered through the halls and down to the outer courtyard, looking over my prospects. I glanced sideways at a number of handsome young knights, and lowered my lashes when they looked back at me. A few of them bowed and I gave them a lazy smile, which brought several over to bid me good morning. I returned to the princess's chambers having made my availability known. If only I would have the time to snare someone suitable!

As the afternoon waned I began to relax. Princess Violante had accepted my condition, or at least must be considering it. King Charles's interest in my prospective nuptials was more problematic. This was a man who had sent his young sons into captivity in Aragon. What would he care for the oath of a Sicilian woman? No doubt Violante had brought me to his attention, but now that I had it, would I be able to escape it?

The Princess returned to her presence room after the evening meal with a smile on her face.

"You are happy, Princess," one of her ladies-in-waiting said. "Do you have pleasant news?"

"I do," Violante replied, "and you shall all hear it while we do our sewing." Violante and her ladies were busy sewing shirts and handkerchiefs and other yuletide gifts for their husbands or families. "Philippa, you must not serve us tonight," she added. "You may sew with us."

"My sewing is in my room, Your Highness," I said, curtseying. "I could fetch it..." I was sewing a new shift and was embarrassed to bring it out, for it was obviously meant for me, and equally obvious that I had no one for whom to make a Yuletide gift.

Violante shook her head and waved me into a chair. She clapped her hands for the court musician to begin playing for us. "Something gay and romantic," she instructed him.

I was not the only one in the room waiting to hear her next words, but I was surely the only one who wished they would never come.

"...in honor of my maid, Philippa, who will be married as soon as Yuletide is over!"

The ladies as well as the maids and servants in the room all clapped and smiled at me, a sea of smiling mouths and envious eyes trapping me in their insincere congratulations, the foreigner being favored over Naples' own. I straightened my back and smiled back at them, including Princess Violante. The musician began a joyous tune.

"But I did not know she was being courted," trilled one of the younger ladies-in-waiting who had recently arrived at court. "Who is she marrying?"

"A soldier," Violante said, looking straight at me with that cool smile on her face. "After the wedding he will leave for his first military command."

"Oh dear!" the naïve young lady cried. "How sad! How romantic!"

How fortunate, I thought. Especially if he dies in combat.

"Tell us his name," someone said.

I did not need to hear it; the smile on Violante's face had already told me.

"Raymond of Campagno," she said.

The room went quiet. Even the musician stopped playing. All eyes were now averted, the maids' to their duties, the ladies' to their sewing. Only the young lady still stared at me, her mouth a little round "0".

I turned away from her horrified stare. I will run away tomorrow morning. In a city as large and wealthy as this, I will surely find a way to make a living.

As if she had divined my thoughts, Princess Violante looked directly at me. "King Charles is taking a *personal* interest in our Philippa's nuptials. Raymond is a favorite of his," she announced to the roomful of averted faces. "The bride will be given the use of one of the royal carriages to take her to her groom on their wedding day." Someone giggled nervously. I flushed, aware of the image of Raymond and me in their minds.

Violante's smile widened. "And to show my love for Philippa, I have decided to send my court musician to entertain them at their wedding feast."

She nodded to the musician whose jaw had fallen open. "Play," she commanded.

Chapter 13

March 11, 1346
Queen Joanna's Court, Naples

On the second day of the siege we awaken to see the mob outside our castle walls has dwindled. Those who remain stand there sullenly, their enthusiasm waning. But at mid-morning they suddenly recover, renewing the vigor of their jeers and curses as more and more people join them. We gather at the windows to see why. My son Raymond is being half-dragged, half-carried through the crowd. I wince at the sight of the good citizens of Naples hurtling mud, stones, and spittle at him as he passes.

He is thrown to the ground in front of the gate, just beyond reach of the arrows of our guards stationed in the castle turrets and along the walls. In a loud voice del Balzo proclaims Raymond guilty of regicide by his own confession. My son is laid out on a rack of hot coals. He is prodded with red-tipped iron spikes. He screams in anguish while I watch helplessly. The terrible smell of my son's roasting flesh fills the air.

I run to the privy and am violently ill. When I emerge Sancia is weeping in the chair where her Uncle Robert thrust her after pulling her away from the window. "Is he dead?" she sobs.

"Pray God he is free of this world," I cry.

Robert shudders. "He was still… moving when they carried him away." He presses his lips tightly together.

They do not want him dead yet. A swell of dizziness overtakes me. I may be ill again. I clench my teeth and sink onto the chair beside Sancia's. "You did not see?"

She shakes her head.

"Good." I thank God I am old and do not have many years left, for I will see my Raymond's burning body as long as I may live. I close my eyes. Without intending to, I rock in my chair. The weight of an arm around my shoulder stops me. I look up at Robert, standing beside my chair. His cheeks are damp. The little brother who followed him everywhere, who wanted to be just like him, is beyond his protection now. I stand and fold him into my arms, this hardened soldier, this skillful royal advisor, this grand seneschal of the Kingdom of Naples—my weeping son.

If they did not mean to kill Raymond, why do this? A threat? A show of power? If so, it has backfired, for the councilors' expressions are grim. They will be more determined than ever not to be captured.

"It was not meant for us," Robert murmurs, divining my thoughts. He gently moves against my embrace. I let him go reluctantly.

"For the queen?" I ask. But the queen has not been seen. They torture her man in front of her castle, the seneschal of her court, and she does nothing, says nothing? Does not even appear? They will guess now that she is not here. They will believe she has abandoned us to them. I glance at Robert. He is watching the royal guards stationed with us. They look around, frowning and uncertain, avoiding our eyes. Fear grips me. "If they abandon us…"

"Not for the queen," Robert says. "They did this for the people of Naples."

I look out the window from where I stand, loath to move any closer. "Ah…" I nod.

A siege is long and dull. The common people will not remain vigilant for days while nothing happens. They have stores to mind, farms to tend, children to provide for, wives demanding they return home. They want to put their feet up in the evening. A righteous anger, however hot, cannot compete with a hot dinner. Not day after day.

Now, with the scent of fresh blood in their nostrils, they are passionate again. The siege has revived. No food or drink will get into this castle. My son was tortured because the mob had thinned; a piece of fresh meat to keep the dogs attentive.

I clench my hands until my nails dig into my fists. This is no spontaneous uprising of the citizens of Naples. It has all been staged by Robert of Taranto and Charles of Durazzo. Most of these "honest citizens" are their vassals, pressed into service for their lords. During the day their numbers swell as the townspeople join them, hoping for another show to break the routine of their lives, convinced the cause is noble. After all, it has been sanctioned by the church.

I am certain I will never sleep again, and do not go to my bed, but when the day finally wanes and the shadows lengthen across the room my eyelids close, my head lolls against the back of the armchair.

I am standing in the market when the church bells begin to ring. Every church bell in all of Naples. I look up, alarmed. On every face I see the same expression. Someone has died. People begin to cross themselves. They drop whatever purchase they were considering and hurry toward the Basilica San Lorenzo Maggiore. I see them whispering Holy Mary's name and praying for King Charles as I run to the church with them. "Not Prince Robert!" I whisper. "Holy Mary Mother of God, anyone but Prince Robert."

All around me people are weeping, "He is dead! The prince is dead!"

But it is not Prince Robert. It is ten-year-old Prince Louis, dead of a hunting accident. I fall to my knees on the steps of the church at the priest's words. Louis! Dear little golden-haired boy who played hide-and-find in the garden with me!

"Papa will always find you, Louis," Robert had promised him. No one will find him now; he is lost to us all forever. I weep on my knees on the steps of the Basilica.

"Louis," I sob...

"Louis!" My own voice startles me. I struggle half-way between sleep and waking.

"Death to all traitors!"

Traitors? My eyes fly open.

Loud shouts and the clash of weapons can be heard through our window as Louis of Taranto's mercenaries engage in skirmishes with Robert's and Charles' men.

"They are coming to rescue us, Grandmother!" Sancia cries, standing at the window. "Louis of Taranto is coming for us!"

I try to collect my thoughts, to understand who has died. It cannot be little Prince Louis. He died years ago, in the summer of 1310...

"No! Do not leave! Keep fighting!" Nicholas of Melizzano shouts at the window. The others in the room slowly grow quiet.

My son Robert comes over to me. "They have deserted us," he says bitterly.

I nod, having returned to the present. It is not little Prince Louis who is dying now, but my own son. And we are all in danger of sharing his fate. Our would-be rescuers have withdrawn. Joanna is not inside the castle waiting for rescue; Louis of Taranto has nothing to gain by expending his forces for us. And now our enemies know it, for he would never withdraw otherwise.

"Have extra guards placed on all of our chambers at night," I tell him. "The queen's guards, not the mercenaries."

"I have already given the order." He smiles grimly.

"Who is tasting our food? Did the queen's taster go with her?"

Robert nods. "A good thought," he says. "I will see to it."

I slump back into my chair when he has left, closing my eyes. I am weary from my sleep being broken by nightmares, current ones and those from the past, and by my fellow councilors' constant need for reassurance. But I am not dozing. I am alert, listening to everyone in the room. They are still a little intimidated by me, even my own son. I have been a powerful royal adviser since before most of them were born. They speak more freely when they think I will not hear. I listen to every voice, to its timbre and tone, judging the steadfastness of those here with me.

All that stands between us and the bloodthirsty mob outside is the loyalty of the queen's guard and Louis' mercenaries. And all that holds them at their post is the fact that we are the queen's council.

Are we the queen's councilors still, when she has left us to the wolves at her gate and sought counsel elsewhere? Sooner or later they will ask themselves this, and it will be sooner if they see any doubt in us.

How can we not doubt? How can we not wonder if she has forgotten us? I see it in the haunted eyes and drawn faces of those around me. I wonder myself at her silence. But I know my Joanna. She is torn up about us and full of indecision. She will not abandon us. But she has no council now, save Louis, and Louis will not be counseling her to save us. He has a war to win, a war that is going badly. And we are not an asset.

I do not say any of this, not even to my son Robert. I straighten my back and hold my head high as though I know something they do not. I will not allow a word to be said against Queen Joanna. I listen to the voices of her council for any hint of doubt creeping in. I listen to hear who are still strong in the confidence of their position, and who might be near to breaking. I note who needs a quiet reminder that we will prevail because we are the head of the queen's court, and who needs a sharp reminder to maintain the dignity of their position. I listen to what they say when their voices tremble, to what they particularly fear, so I can dispel it with logic or scorn, whichever will work, when we talk together in the council room. Robert follows my lead. He is counting on me to give him direction in this as I count on him to emphasize my messages. The act must continue as long as necessary. No, I will not fool myself: *as long as possible*. Until we have another choice to make.

Between us we keep the councilors steadfast, or at least maintaining the appearance of being so, and the palace troops stand by their queen's councilors. But Louis' mercenaries are another thing. They are not loyal to the queen of Naples or to her council. They are loyal to the man who pays them, and he is not here. Even if he were, they are loyal when it suits them. This dreary, inactive, soul-destroying siege does not suit them. By the third day the mercenaries, realizing they are expendable and having looted as much from the castle as they can, announce that they cannot fight without food and ale. After three days of their gorging, both of these are growing sparse.

On the afternoon of the third day Robert calls Joanna's councilors into the privy chamber and closes the door. He slumps in his chair looking weary, defeated. I have never seen him this way before. He looks around the room slowly. There are fourteen of us now. Charles of Artois and his son Bertrand have not been seen for days; they must have slipped away before the mob arrived. I wish them well. At Robert's and my insistence we have admitted to our meetings the four other people accused with us of Andrew's murder. Sancia perches at the edge of her seat beside me, unconsciously holding her swelling abdomen as if her little hand could protect the infant she is carrying from what will come.

"It is time to negotiate terms of surrender," he tells us.

"They will kill us all!" Nicolas of Melizzano cries shrilly.

"The palace guards will continue to defend the castle even without the help of the mercenaries," the Count of Terlizzi argues stoutly.

"And die for their loyalty," Robert replies. "And then we will be in no position to negotiate and they will certainly kill us all." His statement is greeted first with silence, then a storm of argument.

Prepare yourself!

My great-grandmother's prophetic voice rings in my head, a gale shaking the very foundations of the castle. I grab the table to steady myself. No one else appears physically shaken. Sancia alone notices my distress. "Are you dizzy, Grandmother Philippa?" she murmurs, her eyebrows puckered with concern.

"Only tired," I answer. She nods. None of us has slept much these three days.

The prophecy is still echoing in my head. Surely my end is coming. How do I prepare myself for that? Joanna, or whoever will rule the Kingdom of Naples when all this has passed, will distribute my goods and property as she sees fit. The only decision left to me is how many others will face their end with me.

"It is time to negotiate our surrender," I say firmly, over the voices of those who are arguing that the guards have a duty to defend us, the castle is impregnable, that somehow, something will happen to rescue us if we can hold out. "Any other course of action will only enrage them further."

The room goes silent.

"The master of the guard has offered to negotiate on our behalf," Robert says. The others look at me. I nod. The master of the guard is a good man, he will do his best for us. At any rate, we have no choice but to trust him. Hugo del Balzo is a proud man, a self-righteous, arrogant man. He would not bargain with anyone accused of Andrew's murder. Does a dog converse with the rabbit it intends to devour?

Robert signals to the guard who opens the council room door. The master of the royal guard has been waiting outside for our decision. He enters with a crisp walk that is at odds with his troubled expression.

"My Lords and Ladies." He bows low. When he rises his face is flushed. I have known him since he was a youth. He is taking it to heart that he has failed to protect us, and failed to prevent the looting of his queen's castle. This must be the worst day of his life. I hope it is, that there is nothing worse waiting for him, or any of us.

142

I feel Sancia trembling beside me. She is not yet twenty, a half year younger than the queen. A child still, though she considers herself a woman. At the corner of my eye I see her straighten in her seat and raise her head. My heart twists at her youth and her innocent courage. *Oh, let me bear the burden of the prophecy, let Fortune's Wheel crush me, only me!*

"Do not release us to the mob outside," Robert instructs our negotiator. "We will face trial before the chief justice of the kingdom, not before that rabble. We must be assured safe conduct to a prison befitting our rank—"

"Castle dell'Ovo," I interrupt. The master of the guard bows his head in agreement. Castle dell'Ovo is suitably provided with locked cells for noble prisoners. If he knows Joanna is at Castle dell'Ovo, making it the safest place in all Naples for us, he shows no sign of it.

"I want their assurance that you and the palace guards," Robert hesitates briefly, "and all the soldiers and servants within the castle will remain safe. We will leave, but none of their men may enter the castle and they will disperse the crowd when they have us."

"Thank you, my Lord. I assure you, I will do my best for you." He bows himself out, wiping away the beads of sweat on his forehead.

We watch from behind the curtains of the upper windows as the Dukes of Taranto and Durazzo, in company with del Balzo, ride up to the gates. The gates open to admit them, the master of the guard waiting just inside. I watch them dismount, their movements unhurried and confident. I cannot hear their words from here, and although I once could understand a conversation by watching the speakers' lips, my eyesight is no longer what it was. I can only note the gestures, the appearance of argument, the arrogance in the movements and postures of these hard men, soldiers all, for whom death is a duty they owe the devil.

Finally I see the master of the royal guard's stance relax. His right hand, resting on the hilt of his sword, reaches forward to shake the hands of our enemies. In all, it has taken less than an hour, perhaps half an hour. He has not come up to discuss any counter offers with us. I frown, moving the drapes aside until I can clearly see the three men below me, poised like venomous spiders at the edge of the courtyard. What are they planning? They will not be satisfied until they have sucked us dry.

Del Balzo looks up and sees me at the window. He smiles slowly, as patient as a spider waiting for the fly to land in its web.

Chapter 14

November, 1300
Court of King Charles II, Naples

I had been looking forward to my third Yuletide at the Neapolitan court. This time I would not be sitting in the nursery breast-feeding an infant. Even if I had no-one to give a present to, or who cared to give me one, there would be feasts and dances and music, archery and jousting tournaments, decorated ships taking elegantly-dressed nobles up and down the coast, troubadours and perhaps even a masque! I would not be a guest at these events, but I hoped I would be able to watch some of them while serving Princess Violante. Now I dreaded the festivities, for the nearer they got, the closer the time came for me to be married.

Had I risked so much and travelled so far only to end up once again married to a man I despised? I would have been happier if I had stayed with Guilio! At least in Trapini I would not be endangering my immortal soul. Would it be bigamy if I married an infidel?

Or something worse?

I searched for Raymond in the hallways, determined to convince him to stop this, but he now served in the King's court while I stayed in the princess's court. At last I ran into him on the servant's stairs.

He grinned broadly when he saw me, as if he imagined I would be happy to see me. I waved him urgently over to a landing where we could talk with some measure of privacy. As soon as we stopped there, he pulled me against him and kissed me!

I shoved him away with a gasp and wiped my face, crying, "What are you doing?"

"Kissing my affianced wife." He grinned as though he had every right to do so.

"I cannot marry you!" I had intended to use more diplomacy, but his astounding intimacy shocked me into bluntness. I glared up at him. I am a tall woman, used to looking men in the eye; he was the only man who had ever made me feel small.

"Cannot? That is a hard word," he said in his lilting accent. "I thought I could not survive the burning of my village. I thought I could not endure the galley prison on the pirate ship. I thought I could never be anything more than a kitchen slave for my first master," he paused. "But he is dead, and I am here, Guard of the King's Wardrobe, and soon to be a soldier proven in battle. As you see, I did everything I thought I could not."

"I *will not* marry you," I hissed, unmoved by his tale of woe. I could tell one just as pitiable if I chose.

"But you will. My master and your mistress have agreed."

"Keep your voice down!" I looked around. No one else was in the hall. "You must tell King Charles you do not want to marry me. Ask him to choose someone else for your wife."

"But I do want to marry you." He looked me straight in the eye with a pleased smile. "I want to very much."

"You…" I choked on the sudden realization. "You *asked* for me!" I backed away from him.

"I did." His smile widened.

"How dare you! I am not a prize!"

"Oh, but you are. The best prize I have won so far."

Quick as lightening I whipped my hand up to slap him, but he was quicker and caught my wrist a hand's length from his face. He laughed and caught my other hand, already rising to do what the first had failed, and pulled me against him. "What a prize you are!" he repeated, bending his head down. His breath tickled my ear as he said it. I shivered involuntarily, at which he laughed and released me. I jumped back, trembling.

"You are exactly the woman I want. And I am exactly the man for you, whether you know it or not."

"You are an infidel!" I cried, not caring if someone heard us as I backed further away.

"I have been baptized," he said. "I am as much a Christian as you are." His face remained serious but his eyes mocked me.

"You are... You are too bold!" I itched to slap him.

He caught the slight movement of my hand before I stilled it, and shook his head. "Do not try that again," he advised me. "I will not have it. In my own country I would be a king."

A king? I laughed in contempt. But my great-grandmother's prophecy came to me once again, shocking me into silence. *She will be mother to a queen...*

I narrowed my eyes as if it was he who mocked me, not my own foolish thoughts. "If you imagine I will follow you into the jungles of Africa to set up a squalid little court of black-faced, half-dressed heathens in a mud village, and have your children there, you should think again!"

He threw back his head and laughed. "It is a lion I am marrying!" he said, wiping tears from his eyes, unperturbed by my furious glare. When he had laughed his fill, he said more seriously, "Do not worry yourself. My village was destroyed; there is no one left for me to go back to." He looked at me thoughtfully. "And you? Have you anyone to return to?"

For a moment I considered telling him I was married. That would put an end to this farce. But I remained cool-headed enough to resist the temptation.

"No," I said. "My mother has other children to care for her when she is old."

"Ahh. You are a tender woman, as well as a fierce one. I am a lucky man." He drew his finger gently down the curve of my cheek.

I grabbed my skirts and ran up the stairs so he would not see the tears in my eyes. I expected him to laugh at me for fleeing from him, but he did not. When I glanced back before leaving the stairwell he was still watching me, his expression unreadable.

I did not see him again during Yuletide. I smiled and pretended to enjoy the festivities but as often as I could I crept away to lie on my bed in the servants' chamber. I was constantly tired and yet unable to sleep, no matter how early or late I went to my bed. I dared not reveal the lie I had maintained for so long, even to avoid the sin of bigamy. Instead I prayed in advance for forgiveness. But how could I be forgiven a transgression I intended to commit? I prayed for strength, for I had already once married an arrogant man older than me and I knew what I could expect. Raymond was strong and sure of himself in a way Guilio had not been, and clever enough to see through me if I tried to manage him as I had Guilio. I remembered his strength when he grabbed my wrists and pulled me hard against him, and shivered in my bed and told myself it was fear.

Christmas came, and the feast of the Epiphany, and then there was nothing else but the wedding to think about. Princess Violante had her own dressmaker sew my wedding gown, in whatever color I chose. I would have chosen white for mourning, but I would not give Violante the satisfaction of seeing me distressed. I smiled and laughed and appeared utterly carefree in her presence, as though I believed she was rewarding me by finding me a wealthy husband. I rejected the usual wedding colors—green for new life or blue for purity—instead I chose red. It was the most expensive color I was allowed to wear, and since Violante was paying, let it be an expensive dress!

The week before our nuptials Raymond came to Violante's presence room. He bowed to Violante and turned to me. "I have been given permission to walk with you in the royal gardens."

"I have work here."

He raised his eyebrows. Violante had already risen to depart to her bed chamber for her mid-day rest. She waved her hand at me. "I can spare Philippa," she said in a tone that made me flush.

There was nothing I could say. I rose ungraciously and reached for my cape. Raymond took it from the peg at once and draped it over my shoulders with a flourish as though I was a countess. I flushed again as the ladies-in-waiting hid their smiles.

When we entered the royal gardens the colors and scents of the flowers mollified me somewhat. Raymond could not have chosen a better enticement to walk with him—except for none at all. "I was told you have a love of flowers," he said as I looked around with a smile I could not hide.

"Matriona talks too much."

He chuckled and tucked my hand under his arm, strolling in a leisurely manner along the path. I pulled my hand away and set a faster pace, making it clear that I would accept no liberties. Then I had to stop as a butterfly fluttered across the path in front of us. Raymond stood beside me quietly.

"Where I come from, the butterflies are as large as my hands." He held up his broad hands, his thumbs locked together and his fingers spread to show the span of two wings. As though a butterfly could possibly grow so large. What a monster it would be!

"They are so brightly colored they look like church windows," he said, watching the pale little butterfly float toward a red flower.

I snorted with derision and continued walking.

He guided me down the path that led to the menagerie. I was content with his direction, for the exotic animals were a singular sight and I had only been there a few times. But when we stopped before the cages of these strange creatures from distant lands I stared at them with an intense awareness of Raymond's lost childhood. What did he see when he looked at the funny striped zebra, the chattering monkeys? Did he see home? I glanced briefly sideways and saw him smiling as though he and these dumb beasts shared a secret.

I had overheard Raymond called a "black monkey" once. I was inexplicably angry now at the young lord who had said it, and at the same time embarrassed to think someone might see me standing here with him before the monkeys' cage. I was ashamed of my thoughts but still I moved quickly on, away from the monkeys that had amused me the last time I was here, toward the cages of the great felines.

The lion turned its massive hooded head to watch us approaching. Raymond put out his hand to stop me several feet from the bars, but I had stopped already. The huge beast lay still on a rock slab. Only its tail twitched, but there was something in its eye that belied its stillness. I felt small and vulnerable standing before it, and looked around. Now I would be happy to see a guard nearby.

"It is wrong to cage him." Raymond's voice was so low the words came out almost a growl. The lion's eyes shifted a fraction to focus on Raymond. They stared at each other a long time, as though in silent understanding. Slowly my fear left me, replaced by a sense of profound safety in the presence, or under the protection, of these two fearless beings.

Raymond broke the spell first, turning abruptly to leave without a glance at the cage beside the lion's, where a large panther paced silently from side to side. A restless power rippled under its fur, as black as Raymond's skin. Its malevolent yellow glare reminded me of a mural portraying the angel of death. Suddenly I was filled with dread at the thought of those menacing gold eyes noticing me. Why ever had I found the lion frightening, I wondered, as I hurried after Raymond.

When we had left the menagerie far enough behind us to find calm in the swaying flowers and the twitter of birdsong, Raymond directed me to a bench beside the path. Enough of the strangeness of our journey through this garden still held me that I went to it unquestioningly and sat down, letting him sit beside me.

He pulled from under his tunic a small cloth bundle and handed it to me. I unfolded the layers of linen as though in a dream, revealing a golden brooch with a brilliant black stone and two topaz gems shining on it. An engagement brooch.

"This is what I see in you." He pointed to the black stone. "The color of your hair," he said, "and of all the nights I hope to spend stroking it." He smiled at my blush. Then he touched the topaz gems. "And the eyes of a lion, because of the strength I sense in you."

"I am not strong."

"You are." He nodded. "You will know it some day."

But all I could see was the black fur and the yellow glare of the restless, hungering panther. I shivered, looking away from the brooch. "I have nothing for you."

"Oh, but you have. What a gift you have given me!"

He laughed at my confused expression. "You insisted on marrying a soldier!" He shook his head. "What courage you have, what power! To stand up to the King of France and demand the right to marry a warrior! To turn a palace guard into a leader—a commander—of men!" He gave me such a look of admiration I flushed with pleasure despite the fact that he had it all wrong. He took my hand. "There is no limit to how far we will climb together," he said in a tone as solemn and binding as any prophecy of my great-grandmother's. Enthralled, I forgot to pull my hand away and sat staring at him as though there could be some truth in such a wild claim.

Until I heard approaching footsteps and the music of a laugh I knew well. Prince Robert and his friends! I leaped up, horrified that he, of all people, should catch me sitting here with this... this Raymond! Without a word of farewell I fled out of the garden.

On the morning of my wedding Violante's maid, the one who had travelled with her to Sicily and whom I had deposed after Violante's stillbirth, dressed me in my new red gown. It was a bold color and suited my dark hair and eyes. She braided up my hair and arranged it under my red headdress, silent the whole time. Her resentment at having to attend me was one of the few pleasures I expected from this day.

"I am sorry you are so old and will likely never have a husband," I said.

"I am greatly comforted by the thought of you leaving court for good," she said, jabbing the last hair pin into my scalp.

"As I will be comforted by my husband's great wealth. When you are too old for service and kneel begging in the streets, I will throw you a coin for your service today." I gave no sign that her vicious jab had hurt me as I drew my wedding veil down over my face, letting her see the seed pearls Raymond had sent to be sewn onto the lace.

I had never worn anything as beautiful and expensive as this, nor ever dreamed I would. I was afraid to breathe on the veil, afraid to walk for fear the lovely gown would catch on something. I was beautiful enough to marry Prince Robert in this outfit, but he would never see me in it. When I walked down the stairs and out of Castle Nuovo I would not come back, Violante's maid was right about that. I hesitated at the door, but feeling the maid's eyes on my back I pretended to shift my skirts and walked on firmly. The carriage was waiting to take me to my new home which I had not seen, and to a new husband I wished had never seen me.

I asked no one to stand with me, invited no guests to the feast. I stepped into the carriage alone and brought nothing with me to my new life except the clothes I wore. I had used all my mother's herbs. I knew a woman in the market who would get me more if I should need them, but I brought none with me. I gave the yellow dress I had loved when I wore it in Trapani to a kitchen maid who had spoken kindly to me, and all the clothes I had received or made for myself while I lived in the castle I bundled into a basket for the poor and left on the steps of Santa Chiara. King Charles had given me to Raymond, delivered me to him in a royal carriage. Let him have his prize, and nothing more. If I could, I would not even bring this dress, but would go to him wearing the "ugly rag" as Violante had called it, that I had worn when I came to the soldiers' encampment to help my mother midwife her.

My father sold me to Guilio, Guilio sold me to Violante, and now Violante and King Charles were handing me to Raymond. I was a thing. A beautiful thing in this red dress and pearl-strewn veil, but still a thing to be passed around by others and given no say in the matter.

The day was overcast and chilly. The carriage clipped through the narrow, twisting streets of Naples, winding uphill away from the sea. As we climbed higher the smells of the city diminished—horse and donkey dung in the streets, butchered meat and over-ripe vegetables mingled with perfumes and spices from the market, cooking and baking and sewage from all the tightly-packed houses and businesses, and the tangy salt-water smell of the sea—all the familiar scents I had become accustomed to. From time to time the carriage slowed as carts or people crossed our path. Each time my hand fell onto the door latch as if by its own volition. As if I could simply open the door and flee. As if I had anywhere to flee to.

Higher we climbed, reaching the larger houses overlooking the city. The air here smelled of green shrubs and flowers and yes, some of the smells of people and livestock, but even more the smell of the land. I leaned out the carriage window, remembering the country smells of my childhood home.

Many of the houses had walls around them. I gaped as the carriage stopped in front of a fine mansion, rising three stories high behind its stone wall. A servant standing at the gate swung it open. The horses pulled us into a small courtyard. To one side was a stable, but the magnificent house commanded my attention. It was built of stone with a short outer stairway leading up to the carved wooden doors above the undercroft. There were at least a dozen chimneys that I could see, with smoke rising from four of them at once.

A servant hurried toward the carriage and opened the door for me. I let him hand me down, glad now that I was wearing such an expensive dress. Could this really be Raymond's house? My future house? I climbed the steps and followed the man through the doors into a huge hall.

The walls were decorated with a forest scene, very green and lush, with extraordinary bright-colored birds and huge butterflies like the ones Raymond had described to me in the king's garden. The ceiling high above was painted blue with stars and a sun so brilliant it must be done in gold leaf.

I had little time to look around, for Raymond stood there, waiting for me. He was dressed in a rich red tunic embroidered with gold and silver thread. Had he known the color I chose for my gown? It fit him perfectly, showing off his wide shoulders and brawny arms, flowing down his muscular body and narrow hips. I caught myself staring and quickly looked away.

When I looked back I expected his expression to be mocking, or at least to wear a possessive leer, the kind of look I had often received. He was staring at me as I expected, but he looked... a little breathless, and for the first time that I had seen, unsure of himself. I frowned, wondering at his expression, and it vanished. He raised his hand and beckoned me. I had no choice but to go to him.

When I reached him I noticed his palm was pale, only a shade darker than mine. I lay my hand on his calmly, determined he would not see I was afraid, and let him lead me where he would.

I thought we would be married in the main hall, but he led me to a door which was opened for us—another servant, how many did he have?—to reveal a household chapel. Nor was it a tiny personal chapel, but a room large enough for a family and their household to worship in, with a painting on one wall of Saint Thomas with his hand in Christ's wound and a tapestry on the other wall of Mary weeping over her crucified son. An altar stood at the far end, with a narrow window of colored glass behind it, a mosaic depicting Peter cutting off the soldier's ear. I frowned at the odd choices for the

154

illustrations but was more surprised to see several dozen people dressed in the current court fashions standing about the room. They turned as we entered. I recognized a few faces from the castle, and several wealthy Neapolitan merchants with what I assumed were their wives and families. There were other faces I did not know, all dressed in expensive silks and brocades that proclaimed their wealth. But I saw no faces like Raymond's, nor for that matter like mine. We were without family, we two, having drifted into this cosmopolitan city like flotsam washed to the shore.

The door closed behind us. I glanced back to see a huge man, bigger even than Raymond, holding his sword at the ready. The best man, standing guard at the door to ensure no one interrupted the ceremony. As though any man was going to rush in and steal a disgraced lady's maid. But the gesture touched me. If I was a prize, at least I was a prize worth guarding. I looked back to the front. A priest had come forward and stood ready behind the altar.

This was real. I was about to take a second husband in the sight of God. I considered for a moment lifting my skirts and running. I even glanced behind me to the door. The best man caught my eye and held it a brief moment. Raymond's hand tightened on mine. I turned back to the altar.

The priest began. I saw his mouth moving, but could not make out his words for the ringing in my ears and the pounding in my chest. I felt a drop of sweat run down my face beneath the veil, and then another, and I could not tell if they came from my forehead or my eyes. I blinked hard several times, for I would not be weeping when Raymond lifted my veil. I drew a slow, deep breath. Soon I would have to give my consent. I tried to hear the priest's cue.

"...Any reason this man and woman should not be joined, speak now or forever hold your peace."

The ringing stopped suddenly, and my heart as well. I could not breathe. Now! Say it now! *I am already married before God.* Say it! For the sake of my immortal soul, say it!

The priest's voice resumed, asking Raymond if he would have me. Over the tiny gasps for air that I hid behind my veil, I heard Raymond's firm voice confirming his will. The priest turned to me. It was my turn, my chance to confess gone, my soul damned. I saw his mouth working, but the hammering had returned, the ringing had become a roar. And then his mouth was still, his brows drawn into a frown as he stared at me.

I could not breathe. The silence in the room bore down on me. I opened my mouth but could not make a sound. The priest's frown deepened. His lips moved, repeating his question as I struggled for air.

Behind us the best man cleared his throat. Raymond frowned, his eyes slightly narrowed as if in warning. He would keep me imprisoned here, married or not. These were his friends, here to see his will done. To see King Charles' will done. This was none of my doing, surely God would know. With that thought my breath returned. I nodded.

"Speak up," the priest hissed.

"I consent."

I sat silently beside my husband at the head table, hidden behind my veil. Raymond's seed pearls fell over my face like teardrops. Would that *I* could weep. Would that I could mourn. Whether or not the choice was mine, I had sold my soul this day.

Despite the delicacies of pastry and meats offered to me, I ate nothing. I stared at the morsels Raymond had placed on my trencher, resisting the urge to hurl them in his face. I had imagined a life at court free of any master but those I served. If I had to marry, may God forgive my sin, why not a wealthy, well-connected merchant or the third son of a Duke, instead of this shameful marriage that made me a mockery to those who had recently envied my rise. Despite its fickle nature, Fortune was not a woman. Fortune was a man, a blind, arrogant man playing with the lives of others, ignorant of the damage he does. I had never had a choice. The decisions had been made for me. Let the blame rest on their immortal souls!

But I chose to come here. For the sake of a yellow dress and the golden hair of a prince, I chose to leave my home where I had no choices left. I had had a choice today—a choice between my soul and my body. Had I confessed, it would have meant death. Whether from a swift punishment for lying to the prince and princess, and in effect to King Charles himself, or from being banished and left to starve on the streets. Swift or slow, it would have been death to admit to my lie.

I was no saint. A woman who abandons her child is not a saint. I had already chosen this life over the next; how many more times would I be called to do so? Was God thick?

My hand shifted involuntarily to cross myself at this sacrilegious thought, but perversely I held it still.

Raymond leaned toward me and said something. I heard his voice, I turned and saw his eyes anticipating my response, but I could not make meaning of the words. A jumble of sounds, indistinguishable from the babble of noise around me.

The musician had come forward—Violante's musician. He bowed to Raymond and then to me. His eyes were courteously lowered, but his lips twisted slightly, the corners turned down. He put his bow to his instrument and began to sing a song I had not heard before. I realized, with disbelief, that he had composed it for our wedding. I listened in outrage as he extolled Raymond's virtues and manly vigor, and predicted great victories in battle with Raymond leading the charge! But it was all exaggerated, verging on the ridiculous despite his solemn expression as he sang. Nor was I pleased when his verses turned on me, claiming for me a preposterous degree of modesty, patience, and tenderness, qualities I had never possessed. Then he sang of my Christian virtue.

The sardonic manner underlying his praise stirred something deep in me. I felt it as a dark pressure behind my eyes, a tightness in my chest, a fist gripping my throat. I pressed my lips together for fear it would spew out like vomit if I let it. I dared not speak, even to order him silent, for if I spoke I would scream. I gripped the side of the table, imagining myself rising from my seat and throwing the table over. I saw myself grabbing my chair and bringing it down on my new husband's head, gripping a broken wooden leg and attacking the smirking priest who had asked whether anyone—whether *I*—dared raise an objection to this marriage, and then carrying on as though he did not see my soul on fire before him.

I found myself shaking. My husband's eyebrows rose. He lay his hand on mine. I pulled my hand away and clasped both hands in my lap, gripping my skirts until at last the song ended. A burst of applause broke out. Did no one else hear the jongleur's mockery? Perhaps only I, for I knew him from Violante's court and had heard him sing sincerely. With an effort I steadied myself and governed my thoughts. He was right. I had chosen life, not virtue.

I had chosen life!

I reached for a meat pasty lying on my trencher and raised it to my mouth. It melted on my tongue, but to me it was as dry and tasteless as church bread. I forced myself to swallow it, a small communion to the wicked deity who made us love this life.

Raymond smiled. I caught it at the corner of my eye, but I had smiled and laughed and pretended to happiness for months now; there was no false happiness left in me. I tried to watch the jester juggling knives and cups, but it was all I could do to sit in my chair and hold my head up. I longed to leave, yet I dreaded the fall of night. Raymond would lead me to his bed… I shuddered and took up my wine cup to stop my thoughts, but the taste of the wine in my mouth revolted me. I swallowed with difficulty and set my cup down.

When the women—wives and daughters of Raymond's guests—came to accompany me upstairs, I let them lead me away. I had no strength to resist, no will to object. The anger had burned out of me. We entered the bedroom. The walls were painted a light blue adorned with yellow flowers and fluttering birds. Blue for purity and yellow… yellow for the dress and the yellow hair that had seduced me to come to this land. Yellow birds and flowers to remind me of the sin that stained my soul. I stood silent and cold while they undressed me. They opened a trunk at the bottom of the bed and lifted from it a long lacey night dress. I barely looked as they exclaimed over it, admiring the fine lacework, the threads of silver, like moonbeams embroidered onto it. I felt only the shifting of air as it floated over my head and down around me. I wanted the women gone. I wanted silence, not the awkward falling away of their voices as I failed to respond. Raymond would come when they left, but for a few moments between their exit and his arrival, I would be alone. How I longed to be alone.

At last they withdrew. I closed my eyes, waiting until I heard the door close before I got out of the bed they had tucked me into. I walked, stiff and straight with the last of my willpower, to a chair by the fire. Falling into it, I pulled up my knees and curled into a ball and held myself there, silent and still. Alone and silent and still.

I did not look up when the door opened. I heard the raucous noise of revelers making bawdy suggestions for our wedding night, and then the door closed again. I heard Raymond walk across the room, felt him stop beside me. He spoke, he sat in the chair beside mine, he offered me wine from the jug on the table between our chairs, and spoke again. I ignored him, not even looking up. But I had made my choice. When he rose and put his arms around me, I made no protest. He lifted me as though I was a child and lay me on the bed and pulled a cover over me. I shivered under the warmth of it, only now feeling the coldness of the room. I heard him walk around the bed, felt it shift as he climbed onto the other side. I held myself still, waiting for him to demand his rights.

I felt his hand on my forehead, stroking the hair back from my face, as gentle as my mother's touch. Then the hand withdrew, the bed moved as he rolled over. I heard a soft exhale of air and the lamp flame flickered out.

I waited in the darkness for him to turn to me. I trembled, for I had not been with a man in many years, and Guilio was old and quickly satisfied. It had hurt, the first time Guilio took me. Raymond was a much bigger man than Guilio.

I waited in the dark for him to turn over again, thinking of all the times I had been hurt, reminding myself how quickly the hurt faded. Raymond would not intentionally hurt me, not tonight. He was not angry with me. He had been laughing at our wedding feast. He had a huge laugh. For all that he had been through since he was stolen from his home, and all the slights he bore because of his skin color, he had a laugh that was pure happiness.

I waited in the darkness for him, and realized I was no longer shivering. How long did it take for two people lying absolutely still to warm a bed in a cold room? Was he waiting for me to do something? Say something? I turned my head a little to look at him. He lay very still.

If I was going to be hurt, I might as well get it over with and leave myself some time to sleep. Did he expect me to stay up all night until he was ready? How long did it take for a man to get ready? Guilio certainly had not put this much time into it.

"Raymond?" I whispered, somewhat sharply. I was not ready to call him 'husband' yet.

I waited in the darkness for him to answer, and he did, with a low, deep snore.

Chapter 15

March 13, 1346
Queen Joanna's Court, Naples

No one talks as we descend the castle stairway. I am filled with a sense of dread that increases with every step I take. I am an old woman. I have lived long and well. The thought of death does not frighten me as it did when I was young. It is the thought of all the slow and dreadful ways I might die that fills me with terror. Each step downward feels like a descent into hell.

And yet I would walk toward it willingly if only I could find a way to deliver my sons and my granddaughter into safety. Why did I not insist that Sancia leave when I sent my sons' wives and families out of the city?

I thought we would all be safe here. Castle Nuovo is impregnable. And where in Christendom would Robert and Sancia find safety after their names had been written on del Balzo's hideous list? Pope Clement VI has already condemned our family once.

Some of the councilors tremble as they walk. Nicholas of Melizzano moans under his breath, I hear the terrified sound just behind me. I glance at Robert, walking with Sancia on his arm, their backs straight despite Sancia's extended belly, their eyes steady, staring straight ahead. I am filled with a fierce pride, followed by a tenderness that almost makes me weep. I look away, blinking, and continue downward with the cool dignity that has marked my life.

Let those who would harm us tremble, for they endanger their souls with the sin of envy.

The master of the guard awaits us in the front hall at the base of the stairway. A half-dozen palace guards stand by him, ready to escort us outside to where del Balzo is waiting. They look anywhere but at us.

Louis' mercenaries lounge about the room. Their insolence is a show; they are fully armed, waiting here to make sure the Dukes of Taranto and Durazzo keep their word and do not order their men to storm the castle when the doors open to cast us out. We are all aware that Louis and the bulk of his mercenaries have been taking a beating while we have been locked in the castle. The men he left here can expect no help from them if these disloyal dukes renege on their agreement. Nor can we, the hostages to del Balzo's dubious honor. It is one of the reasons I have found the terms of our surrender disturbingly generous.

I descend the last step to stand beside the master of the guard. His eyes are troubled, his mouth turned downward. Perhaps he, too, is having second thoughts about the speed of the negotiations. When he came to us, his face wide with relief, to tell us the terms of our surrender, he accepted our praise humbly, satisfied with himself. Del Balzo, Charles of Durazzo, and Robert of Taranto had all pledged that we would be taken to Castle dell'Ovo directly, and remain there in safety for the chief justice of the kingdom to examine. He would investigate the charges against each of us, not these three false men.

"You have done well by us," I murmur. "Whatever follows is not on you." He nods, his Adam's apple bobbing as he swallows his emotion. I remember when he came to court as a boy, his older cousin's page.

The castle doors open slowly. We stand in their shadow, unmoving, until my son draws in his breath and leads us out. It is a dull day, the sun hidden behind gray clouds. A cold wind blows off the sea, making me shiver. This is the third time I have been cast out of Castle Nuovo. Will I ever enter it again? The wind on my face tastes of salt and grief. I am reminded of Lot's wife, looking over her shoulder as she fled her home for an uncertain future. I do not look back.

The throng surrounding Castle Nuovo has doubled in number. It seems all of Naples has come to watch our surrender. Their shouts of condemnation and brutal suggestions for our punishment assault our ears as we walk out through the castle doors.

"We will never reach Castle dell'Ovo alive!" Nicholas hisses, giving voice to all our fears.

"That foul mob will not touch you," the master of the guard assures us. "You will be taken down the coast to Castle dell'Ovo by sea, in Hugo del Balzo's own galley."

There are murmurs and sighs of relief from the others, but I do not share them. I have never trusted del Balzo. Queen Joanna's presence was all that kept him in line. Robert of Taranto was arrogant and cruel even as a boy, and Charles of Durazzo... I would have trusted him once despite his ambition, but years of frustration as Joanna overlooked him, promoting and rewarding others instead, have made him bitter and angry. Together these three men have goaded each other and all of Naples into this thinly-disguised rebellion against their rightful monarch.

And we are caught in the middle of it. They dare not touch a queen anointed by God and the Pope, but we, her closest advisors and councilors, whom she has trusted and rewarded over them time and again, we have become the objects of their envy and spite. Especially my son and granddaughter, their dark skin standing out amid the olive complexions around them, proclaiming them base-born intruders in this royal court.

The master of the guard, a brave man, steps ahead of us to where del Balzo and the two dukes wait with their men. "I entrust these noblemen and ladies to your care under the terms of our agreement for their surrender," he says firmly. Robert of Taranto inclines his head, stone-faced. Del Balzo smiles.

The threats and jeers of the crowd have increased in volume. We walk without speaking to the sea, huddled together for protection, glad of del Balzo's armed soldiers surrounding us. As we board the rowboats that will take us to his galley, waiting as close as it can come to the rocky shoreline, I see my companions' shoulders slump with relief. Del Balzo and the Dukes of Taranto and Durazzo have kept their word: we have not been turned over to the mob despite their shouts for immediate justice. Castle dell'Ovo is only a half-mile up the coast, we will soon be there and at least temporarily safe.

We set sail, passing beyond the grounds of Castle Nuovo toward Castle dell'Ovo. The crowd, seeing us escaping on the galley, becomes more enraged. They rush to the shore where those in front hurtle rocks and shells at us, but we are beyond their reach. Nicholas of Melizzano smiles at the Count of Terlizzi as the sun breaks through the clouds. I put my arm around my granddaughter and look away from the raging faces of my fellow citizens, into the sinister whisper of the wind and the salt spray of the waves slapping at our ship.

Two of Hugo's men grab my son Robert's arms and haul him roughly toward the front of the ship. Before I can reach for him others grab my arms, and Sancia's, and drag us after him. The galley slows to a stop. An anchor is thrown overboard. I look for my son and cry out in horror. He is being strapped to a large rack at the front of the galley, in clear view of the shore and the watching crowd, who roar their approval.

"Is this the way you keep your word?" I demand of Hugo del Balzo. He says nothing, watching calmly as his men wind the lever extending the rack. Robert's face is beaded with sweat, his eyes closed in pain, but he presses his lips together, bearing it silently.

"It is," del Balzo answers me at last. "Did I not promise to prevent the citizens from storming Castle Nuovo in their righteous anger? I am drawing them away by providing an alternative." He looks at me, his eyes glittering. "They must be satisfied, one way or another."

"That is what you tell yourself you are doing? Satisfying them?"

"Not me," he says, with a smile that chills my blood. "You and your son and your granddaughter." He nods at one of the soldiers, who immediately pulls his knife from its sheath. Sancia screams as the sharp blade slices through the lacing of her kirtle. A second thrust cuts the neck of her undershift and tears down through the fabric. She grabs for the falling garments, holding them to her chest, but the men peel her hands away and tear the fine cloth off her. Weeping she stands naked and exposed, her pregnancy making her shame all the greater.

I glare at del Balzo but before I can speak the point of a blade cuts down my back and with a ripping of cloth my own garments are torn away.

A cheer rises from the beach at the sight of our humiliation. I feel the hot rush of shame, the urge to cover myself. Then I look at my beautiful granddaughter. I straighten my back and raise my head and stare silently at the crowd on the beach, daring them to look at us, an innocent young wife pregnant with her unborn child and an old woman the age of their grandmothers. The shame is theirs.

The frenzy on the beach decreases. Del Balzo frowns. My stalwart defiance and Robert's silence do not make a good show. No matter how they stretch the rack, my son will not scream.

"Take him off and flog him," del Balzo snaps. "Lash him to the mast where they will see him bleed."

His men untie Robert's arms and legs and lift him off the rack. As they carry him to the mast del Balzo points to Sancia: "Her next."

I promised myself no matter what they did to me, I would remain silent and stoic like my courageous son. Let our courage and endurance illuminate his baseness and spoil the pleasure of those watching. But when he points to Sancia and utters those words my resolve disappears.

"No!" I cry, struggling against my captors, my desperation so great I break free and lunge toward him screaming every invective I know, as vulgar as a peasant. His men grab me again before I can reach him. He stands there smiling as Sancia is dragged to the rack. Robert roars behind me, but his hands have already been tied to the mast. He swings his feet wildly and hits one of his guards in the knee, taking him down. Two others leap to secure his ankles to the mast.

"My baby!" Sancia shrieks, struggling as they heave her onto the vile contraption. "For the love of God have mercy on an unborn child!"

The younger of the pair holding her hesitates, looking to del Balzo. Receiving a glare from his master he pulls her arm upward and shackles her wrist to the top of the rack. Her other arm is already secured. Poor Sancia arches her back, kicking her feet in a vain attempt to prevent them from stretching her, crying all the time for mercy on her innocent babe.

I hate del Balzo more than I have ever hated any man. Oh, I am giving those on the shore a good show, and I do not care. I throw back my head and howl "God in heaven is watching you this foul day!"

Hugo del Balzo leans into my face with an ugly laugh. "God does not love black-skinned infidels any more than I do. I have killed uncounted numbers of them in Holy Crusades with His blessing. What are two more?"

I spit at him. It lands on his cheek. His derision turns to fury. He wipes away the mark of my contempt and snarls to his men, "What are you waiting for?"

The rack groans and creaks as it extends, and Sancia shrieks in agony. The lash whistles through the air, followed by a wet sound as it digs into Robert's bared back. He grunts, once again refusing to cry out. The sounds of my family's suffering surround me. I pray to God to strike this monster down, but my only answer is the hard brilliance of the faithless sun shining down on us.

When Robert passes out they throw salt water on his back. Still he will not scream, but moans and jerks convulsively against his bindings like a speared fish. Sancia is roused from fainting three times before her voice gives out. Then del Balzo motions toward me.

My heart pounds as they lead me to the rack. My breath comes in little gasps that leave me faint-headed, but I do not waste my energy in struggling. At least they must take my poor granddaughter off the rack to put me on it. I pray her child has not been harmed. A ripple across her abdomen reassures me it still lives. One of the men has seen it too; I give him a hard look. He turns his face away quickly.

The wood is cold against my back as I lie on it, and slick with sweat and salt spray. Two men pull my arms over my head as far as they will go and strap them there while others shackle my feet to the farthest reach of the boards. The stiffness in my joints complains already, before the ordeal has even begun. I tremble and sweat as I wait for them to turn the crank, closing my eyes so they will not see my terror. Dear God, let me bear this in silence. Every nerve in my body is on edge waiting for the pain to begin.

I hear the whistle of the lash. Sancia emits a raw, choking sound, no longer able to scream. I turn my head to see her tied to the mast, her naked young body on full display for those watching on shore. Are they not satisfied yet? Has she not suffered enough for them?

The crank beside me turns. My legs and arms begin to stretch, the pressure building to a burning pain as my joints protest. I hear the pop as my left shoulder dislocates, and then my right, and I cannot stop myself from screaming...

I gasp, choking on salt water, coughing my way back to consciousness and searing pain. Another turn and they will surely tear my arms and legs from my torso. But the wood groans, the lever turns, and I am not torn apart, although I wish to heaven I was, to put an end to this agony. I prepare to die, will myself to death. I am an old woman and ready to leave this world.

My great-grandmother's voice comes to me amid the inferno of my body. The final words of her prophecy, which my mother never wanted me to know: *She will die in misery and all that she has accomplished will come to nothing, crushed under Fortune's wheel.*

The prophecy, and Fortune's wheel, have come full circle. The sun fades to a dullness, and my agony recedes…

"Mother Mary, take me."

The broken whisper reaches me as from a great distance. Not my voice, though it is my prayer as well. Not my surrender, but Sancia's.

Sancia and her baby. Preparing to die.

No!

I reach toward the daylight, toward the pain. It is a long way and I do not want to return. I want peace, but I will not have it if I allow this. *Sancia,* I call in my mind. *Sancia!*

I cannot hear her. Am I too late? I struggle against the pull of darkness.

"Sancia…" My voice comes out, a strangled croak.

You cannot die. You cannot sacrifice your child's life.

I feel hands at my wrists and ankles. The release of pressure stretching my limbs is agonizing. For a moment I am lost in this new pain.

Beneath me the boat shudders into movement.

"Sancia!" I croak. Why is she silent? "Sancia, live. For the sake of your child, you must live."

A short distance away, Sancia moans.

Chapter 16

Spring, 1301
City of Naples

I lay still in the bed with my eyes closed, barely breathing, listening for any sounds in the room. Silence. I risked opening one eye enough to peer through my lashes. I had thick, dark lashes. They obscured my view annoyingly, but I was able to assure myself that I was alone in the bed this morning. I opened both eyes without moving my head. No one in sight, and still no sound in the chamber. I sat up and looked around, sighing with relief.

There was a small click as the latch was raised and the door began to open. Too late to lie down and feign sleep, so I drew a breath and called out, "Who is there?"

The door stopped moving. "It is only me, Madame," a female voice responded. "I have brought you mulled wine and come to dress you and do up your hair, if it please you."

Dress me? Do my hair? I almost laughed. But I had eaten very little dinner, and whoever it was had mentioned mulled wine. "Come in then. You cannot do it from there."

The door opened wider. A young girl slipped in, perhaps thirteen years old. She curtsied, nearly spilling the wine she carried. I motioned impatiently, half expecting her to trip as she hurried across the room. Surely as the owner of a manor like this, Raymond could afford to hire more experienced servants. I took the mulled wine while there was still some left in the cup and watched as she lit a fire in the fireplace. It was odd to drink my wine under the covers, watching someone else blow on the embers, a task that had been mine only a year ago.

"Where is…" I took a sip of wine to cover my hesitation, "…your master?"

"He rose at dawn, Madame. He has gone to look over his troops." She laid some twigs carefully upon the now-glowing embers.

His troops? Could he be leaving already? I considered how to ask the question without displaying my complete ignorance about my—about Raymond.

"He instructed me to tell you he will be back for supper."

"Yes," I said, as though I had assumed as much. As though I was not now faced with another host of questions. *Was there a cook? Did he or she know what Raymond liked to eat? Did I need to send someone shopping?* And then I realized: *Raymond will be gone all day.* If I left soon, I would be far away before he even knew I was gone. I could take a horse, if he had horses. I remembered my terrifying ride to Violante's tent back in Sicily and shuddered. No, I would not take a horse.

The girl sat back on her haunches, watching the little blaze she had achieved for a moment before she rose and curtsied, offering to bring a bowl of rosewater for me to wash in. The curtsey was not very low, a little bob. I noticed that and motioned her to leave without so much as inclining my head. Then I settled back in my covers to let the room warm while rosewater was being fetched for me. I permitted myself a laugh after the door closed behind her.

As quiet as it had been, the sound echoed in the large room, my own laughter mocking me. Did the servants here know they were waiting on an African slave and a fisherman's daughter? Well, they had to know about Raymond, and even if they did not know my origins, they would know I was little better than they or I would not have been married to him. I must be on guard here. They would resent me putting on airs, and resent me even more if I did not.

I leaned against the headboard and sipped my mulled wine. Perhaps it was a good thing the girl waiting on me was so young. Was she a general chamber maid, or was she intended as my personal maid? There was something familiar about her, something in her appearance or her voice. Had she been serving at the feast last night? I did not remember her. She was small and brown-eyed, with thick hair so dark it was nearly black, like so many girls from my village.

I sat up so quickly the wine sloshed in my cup. Like the girls in my village? And her familiar voice, with a touch of the Sicilian accent left in it—how had she gotten here? How had she gotten *here*, in Raymond's home? She was from Sicily, but was she from my village? *Did she know who I was?*

I stumbled out of bed. My hands were shaking, spilling wine onto the floor. I set the cup on a table before I dropped it and sank into the chair beside it. Had she told Raymond? Was that why he had not slept with me, because he knew our union was a sham? That I was already married to another?

I took a deep breath to calm myself. The girl might not even be from my village. She might know nothing. It might be a coincidence that she was a servant here.

If it was deliberate, if Raymond had hired the girl to—to what? To keep me here? To threaten me with exposure if I tried to leave? I *had* thought about leaving…

The door opened, admitting the girl again. It was all I could do not to demand *Who are you? What do you know?* But I had been well-trained in subtlety, first by my cunning father and then by two years at court.

"See that you do not spill it," I said as the girl carried the bowl to the table by my chair. A light mist rose from it, and petals floated on the water. *Warmed* rosewater. I sat back and closed my eyes, pretending to be relaxed as the girl washed my face with a cloth.

"What is your name?"

"Cicillia, Madame."

"Cicillia. That is not a common name in Naples." I knew full well it was a very common name in Sicily.

"I am from Catania, Madame. I came with my mother when the soldiers returned to Naples." She patted my face dry.

I opened my eyes. My throat had gone dry. At least she was not from Trapani. But the two towns were not far apart.

"Shall I comb your hair, Madame?" she asked, saving me from responding. But she would know I was from Sicily. My accent, for all that I have worked to lose it, would be as apparent to her as hers was to me. It would not be natural to let the comment go, if I had nothing to hide. I might even be pleased to meet someone from home. If I had nothing to hide.

"What a coincidence," I murmured, the words nearly choking me. "I am also from Sicily."

She said nothing, the comb stroking through my hair smoothly. I looked straight ahead into the fire and let her comb my hair in silence. She knew something. Did she know something?

"How does your mother like Naples?" I said at last. It was foolish to be talking like this to my servant, but the ominous silence was too much for me.

"My mother died last summer of the fever."

"I… I am sorry to hear it," I told her, trying to sound regretful.

"Thank you, Madame." She returned the comb to the little drawer in my table. "What would you like to wear, Madame?"

For a moment I sat there silent. I should have brought something with me. My mother had warned me often enough that my pride would lead me into trouble if my temper did not find the way first. I opened my mouth to tell her I would wear my wedding gown. I came in it, and I would leave in it.

But how could I leave until I knew what this girl knew? What she might tell about me? She was the bait with which Raymond had caught me—for now.

The girl was waiting. Reluctant to admit I had nothing but my wedding kirtle to wear, I said, "I will have something new for my new life here. Send for a dressmaker."

"Of course, Madame," the girl said. "But in the meantime, would you care to wear one of the kirtles your husband has had made for you?"

I looked at her sharply. Was that a hint of amusement in her eye?

"Well, your master has left me a pleasant surprise. You had better bring me one and dress me. Then I will go see the cook." A man who had a set of clothing made for his new wife would have a cook.

She brought me a fine linen undershift in a soft cream with a light green kirtle to go over it, made of silk. It was all I could do not to gasp when I saw the expensive silk cloth. Green for spring, for a new start, for the stirring of life. The symbolism was not lost on me.

"Your lord husband knows fine clothes," Cicillia murmured, stretching on tip-toe to lift the kirtle over my head while I obligingly bent.

He did indeed. He had always dressed exceedingly well at court, but I had not imagined he would be so generous with me. I found myself holding my breath as Cicillia slipped it over my head. The skirt was so full she had to straighten it at the hips, but for all the material, it was as light and comfortable as it was beautiful, and perfectly suited to my dark coloring. I was so delighted I turned in a circle just to watch it twirl and hear the rich rustle of the shimmering fabric.

"There is also a blue one," Cicillia said, moving behind me to pull the lacing tight up my back.

"Light blue?" I guessed. I looked over my shoulder and caught her blush. The color of true love. Well, I would leave that one for now.

"And a yellow one, as bright as the sun," she hurried on.

"Yellow?"

"It would not suit most women, but on you..." she trailed off. Yes, I knew what it would look like on me. When had Raymond seen me in my yellow dress? I did not doubt he had. Had he suspected I would not bring it, or had he feared I would? I shook my head. He was a complicated man.

"The undershift is white, bright white, to bring out the yellow." Cicillia stepped around to arrange the folds of my kirtle.

Three new silk kirtles, and an undershift to go with each gown. For a wife who did not even bring him a dowry. He was indeed a generous man. Or a proud one.

"Shall I do up your hair, Madame?"

I nodded and sat on the chair. "Where did you learn to be a lady's maid?"

"My mother taught me, Madame. She said I would need to make my way. But I think she only wanted me to serve her."

I laughed. The girl was entertaining in her odd way. "How old are you?"

"I do not know, Madame. My mother said I had ten summers in Sicily. Enough to remember our lives there and be grateful to her, she said."

"Are you still not grateful?" I asked, amused at the tone of her voice as she mimicked her mother.

"I miss the smell of the woods, and the feel of the earth under my feet. Of course, Naples is a majestic city," she added quickly. I nodded slightly, distracted by her words. They brought me the smell of green leaves unfolding in the sun and the coolness of the warm river mud between my toes and the soft breeze on my face. I felt a swell of homesickness. It was all I could do not to confess my feelings to this girl from my homeland. From my past.

God forbid she knew my past! Heaven help me if I let my guard down to her nostalgic enchantments. The past was past and I was no longer a simple maid. I had to protect my present and look to my future. Let this foolish child dream of a time past. I was overworked and hungry and beaten in that past, and no doubt she had experienced similar privations. What a bewitching fantasy the past was.

I said no more. I had asked enough questions and given away too much already. The girl was more intelligent than her years, but sooner or later she would not be able to keep what she knew from me.

It was pleasant, though, to have my hair combed and braided and pinned up for me. To have nothing to do but sit and wait while my maid went back to the wardrobe and returned with a light green headdress in the newest fashion. A headdress to match my gown! He had put much thought into my wardrobe, this new husband of mine. I considered that as Cicillia tucked my braids in under the beautiful headdress. When she was finished she held up a glass for me to see myself in. It was all I could do not to laugh out loud as I preened in my glorious outfit. If only my mother could see me now. The thought made me pause. If only there was a way I could let her know that I was well. Perhaps even send some money to her.

Was I well? Was a green dress and matching headwear and a maid to serve me all it took to content me? I stood up.

"Oh, I forgot!" Cicillia cried, laying the glass down. With a quick curtsey she ran from the room, returning a few moments later with a piece of the green cloth in her hands. "Master said to give this to you when you put on the green kirtle."

I reached for the kerchief, but it was heavier than I expected. When I drew back the folds of green silk I saw a stunning gold necklet with three large emeralds embedded in the center. I gasped with surprise and nearly dropped it.

"How beautiful!" Cicillia cried, clapping her hands with delight. "Let me put it on you, Madame."

I handed her the necklet and accepted the looking glass she offered me. She lay the brilliant stones against my breast and drew the gold chain round my neck to clasp it together.

"How beautiful it is on you!" Cicillia said. I gazed into the glass. The emeralds glowed against my skin, drawing me into their depths...

"Take it off!" I threw the glass clattering onto the table. "And the headdress, also! I will not wear them."

Her mouth was a round 'O' of surprise but she said nothing as I sat down again in the chair. I stared straight ahead refusing to watch as she unclasped the necklet and wrapped it in the piece of silk, and then unpinned the fashionable headdress.

"Take them away," I said when she hesitated. "When you return I will see the house, and the kitchen, and the stables, and learn what my…" I hesitated only a second, then looked her full in the face. "What my husband needs me to manage for him."

When Raymond returned I met him in the hall as a proper wife would. "When would you like your supper, my Lord?" I watched his face, trying to read there what he knew, what Cicillia might have told him of me.

"Good evening, Madame Wife," he said with a sweeping bow, mocking my own brusque greeting. He glanced at his man, standing a step behind me.

"Your basin and tunic are waiting for you, Master Raymond," the man said.

"Excellent. We will refresh ourselves before dinner." Raymond turned to me, holding his arm out. "Allow me to escort you."

I could hardly refuse in front of his man. I lay my hand lightly on his forearm, but he took it and tucked my arm under his elbow against his side, so that I had to walk close beside him, and thus we ascended the stairs, followed by his steward.

Raymond led me into the room we had shared the previous night. Instead of stopping, he escorted me through a small door at the other end, which led to an adjoining bed chamber. This second bed chamber was larger, the walls painted like those in the main hall with exotic birds and animals sporting in a green forest thick with ferns and vines, more lush and fertile than any woodland I had seen.

The furniture was massive and ornately decorated with embroidered cloth and cushions: a bed, a table with a large bowl of water on it and a drying cloth, three chairs by the fireplace, a writing table. This last surprised me. Was it for his steward, or could Raymond himself read and write?

"Have wine sent up. And figs." Raymond turned to me. "You like figs, do you not?"

I nodded. I had eaten them only a few times in the castle and afterwards sometimes dreamed of them. He smiled at my nod and I realized, blushing, that I had first tasted figs when Raymond began sending dinner trays up to the castle nursery.

When the man left, Raymond stripped off his tunic and linen shirt and began to wash his face and upper torso in the bowl of water. Embarrassed by the intimacy of observing his toilet, I walked over to the mural and examined it more closely. Some of the creatures depicted were purely imaginative—a yellow spotted horse with long, thin legs and a ridiculously elongated neck standing so tall it ate from the top of a tree; a grossly fat thing that looked like an oversized grey pig with a unicorn's horn stuck on its snout—while others were merely strange, like the black-and-white striped ponies and spotted felines I had seen in the king's menagerie.

The abundant foliage made sense when I realized I was looking at an African jungle, the landscape of Raymond's native home. I turned slowly, observing the jungle on every wall. It pressed in on me from every direction, this bizarre green world. Even the ceiling was covered in curling vines. What kind of human could call such a place home? In the corner beside the fireplace I saw a man depicted, black-faced and smiling, possibly a representation of Raymond himself. He wore what appeared to be a long narrow skirt tied about his waist, with a length of the same brightly-woven cloth draped over one shoulder, and stood poised to throw a long spear he held balanced above his bare shoulder. He was tall and muscular, intensely male, with a proud, fierce expression on his face. He was at once both primitive and majestic, a warrior and a king among men. I looked up, bemused, and caught the real Raymond watching me as he toweled himself dry. I turned back to the painting, confused by an unidentifiable emotion.

On the other side of the fireplace a woman had been painted. She was tall and willowy with skin as black as the man's—I found it necessary to refer to the first figure objectively as "the man"—and wore a similar multi-colored woven cloth wrapped loosely around her from neck to ankle. Her shapely bare feet showed beneath. Despite the blackness of her skin she was undeniably beautiful. I felt a stab of something I would have called jealousy if Violante had been this lovely. I turned and looked at Raymond.

He came across and stood beside me. Beads of moisture glistened on his chest. He smelled of soap and sweat, like any other man. I was tempted to touch him and tempted to run. I looked steadfastly at the painting.

"My mother," he said, "as I remember her."

"She is beautiful." I felt him look at me but I would not look up. He was too close in this wild, primitive landscape. Too large and too close in any world. Not trusting my voice I pointed to the other figure, the man.

"That is my father, the king of our tribe. The artist painted him to look like me." He chuckled disparagingly. "But he was much...larger than I am, much more..." he trailed off.

I nodded. My mother was also much more...more everything...than I will ever be.

The door opened. Raymond and I stepped apart as his man entered carrying a tray with wine and figs upon it. He set it on the table and poured the wine, handing a cup to each of us. He appeared not to notice his master's state of undress except for a brief glance at the foot of the bed where a clean linen shirt and a fresh tunic had been laid out.

"We will be down for dinner presently." Raymond said, offering me a fig. I accepted it and bit into the soft, sweet fruit, letting its sun-drenched flavor fill my mouth. "Send my wife's maid up,"

Raymond called to the retreating servant. "Tell her to wait in my wife's chamber while we drink our wine."

I swallowed the sticky treat with a gulp of wine. "Why have you sent for my maid?"

"To help you dress for dinner."

"I am quite well-dressed." I chose another fig from the platter although I had no appetite for it now.

"I would like to see you in the headdress and the necklet that matches your green kirtle. Did she not show them to you?"

I set my wine cup down. "She did. I chose not to wear them."

"I would like you to."

"Why did you have all these things made for me? The gowns, the headdress, the jewelled necklet...?"

"I like to see something pretty when I come home."

"You want to *see* something pretty?"

"Have I asked anything more of you?"

"I cannot be bought."

He smiled, amused. "I am your husband."

"I mean my affection, my loyalty," I stammered, furiously aware that I was making myself ridiculous.

"I am glad to hear it. I want a friend I can trust."

"You are my husband."

"We will get to that in time. For now, let us learn to be friends." He went to the bed and began to put on the linen shirt laid out for him. "Go prepare for dinner," he said, when I did not move. "I mean you to wear them."

"And if I refuse?"

He looked over at me. "Do not refuse. It would be disrespectful." There was something in his face, something I should heed. A warning look, such as my father wore before a rage took him. I straightened my shoulders and raised my head and gave him a level look, this man who spoke of disrespect. Let us have the truth between us, then.

"Why did you hire that girl?"

"My wife must have a maid."

"That *particular* girl?"

"I thought you would like to see someone from your homeland."

"If ever I do, I will have them painted on my chamber wall."

He stood very still for a long moment. Had I gone too far? Then he laughed. "Perhaps you are right. A painting can never betray you."

I gritted my teeth. "What does she know?"

"Everything."

Chapter 17

March 15, 1346
Castle Capuano, Naples

I awake in a haze of agony to find myself lying on the damp floor of a dungeon. I am naked except for my thin shift, which is stiff with blood and dirt and smells of vomit. I lie still. Even the slightest movement brings fresh waves of pain. The flesh on my back is ribboned with lashes, my chest and arms feel like they are on fire. I remember the red-hot iron, and push the memory away. My left eye will not open. Slowly I force the other open, blinking to clear my vision. The dungeon is dark with only a single narrow slit in the stone wall high above me letting in a meager shaft of light. I judge it to be shortly after dawn.

After the torment we endured on del Balzo's ship, we were not taken to Castle dell'Ovo as promised, but to the castle of Charles of Durazzo. Throughout the night he has had us tortured in turns.

I hear a low moan. Bracing myself against the pain, I turn my head. Three feet away I make out a lump in the darkness: Sancia. She moans again. She is alive, at least.

I grit my teeth and try to rise. My right arm will bear no weight and my left foot is in agony. I struggle to crawl toward my granddaughter, groaning despite my efforts not to.

"Sancia." My voice comes out raw and hoarse, unrecognizable. It is not kind to wake her. I would be more compassionate if I smothered her now, insensible in her anguished stupor. For the sake of her child, my great-grandchild, I cannot. "Sancia, you must try to live." I croak.

"I am trying, Grandmother."

Her voice is a broken whisper that brings tears to my eyes. I do not want to know what they did to her, nor think what they will do next to us both. "Joanna will get us out of here," I say. I think it is a lie, the queen has done nothing to prevent our torture, but I must give Sancia something to coax her to live. I lie down beside her and stroke her hair with my good hand, a small touch of kindness among so many brutal ones. She moans again and begins to weep quietly, hopelessly. I whisper, "Shh, child, courage," and smooth her hair from her face until her sobs subside.

When I hear the thud of men's boots descending the stone stairway to us my hand stills, lying on her head like a benediction. I close my eye, waiting for what will come.

A man's voice mutters something, lost in the grate of the iron cell door swinging open.

"Oh, she will be alive. She is too stubborn to die." Charles' voice, arrogant and cold, fills the dark cell.

I open my eye and see his boot in the muddy straw a few inches from my face. I am made of stern stuff, as he says, for I do not move a muscle although inside I feel myself cringe, expecting him to kick me.

"So you have come to this," I say, peering up at him with my one good eye.

He opens his mouth, closes it again with a glare, and gives a forced laugh. "Arrogant still! Are you expecting a rescue? Lord Louis of Taranto has been forced out of Naples. He has retreated as far north as Capua with all his troops. Naples is ours!"

It is my turn to say nothing.

He smiles. "You are not so clever after all. You have chosen the wrong side this time."

"Does your Lady Wife know what you are doing down here in your filthy dungeon?" My voice comes out a broken rasp but the disgust I feel is still audible.

I hear a harsh intake of breath followed by a hushed silence from the guard. Then Charles bends down. His face, just above mine, is cruel and hard. "Why would she care that I am punishing a woman who conspired to murder her prince?"

"You know I did not."

"You have confessed to it. I have witnesses."

"They are lying." But I have doubts. I was delirious with pain half the night, I cannot be certain what I said.

"You will die and all your accomplishments will come to nothing."

I stare at him through my good eye, horrified. He has used the very words of my great-grandmother's prophecy.

He laughs as though he has won, as though he personally engineered my downfall. It brings me back to myself. "Your Lady Wife is a princess, raised by a noble king and queen. She will remember that I supported your marriage when no one else would. That I spoke on your behalf, for her sake. She will be disgusted when she learns of this, and see you for the treacherous creature you are."

He stands up with a roar of outrage.

I raise my hand, pointing my finger up at him, and with my remaining strength I cry, not knowing where the words come from but certain of their truth, "You, too, will die by treachery. It will not be long, not long now, before you are betrayed!"

He does kick me then, hard enough that I feel my rib crack before darkness takes me.

I come to under the rough hands of soldiers pulling me upright. I stumble on my feet, gasping with pain, and fall when they let me go.

Two of them grab my arms and half-carry me out of the filthy cell and up the stone stairs, cold and rough under my bruised, swollen feet. Sancia follows behind me, leaning heavily on a third soldier.

I squint when we reach the main hall with its bright windows. Is that Princess Maria watching us? I would like to see her better, to learn whether she knew her husband was torturing us while she slept in her bed, but they pull me on, out through the door. The harsh sunshine completely blinds me.

"Climb up! Get in!" one of the men holding me growls, pushing me forward. My outstretched arms knock into the back of a wagon. I dimly make out the iron bars of a prison cage built onto the wagon bed.

"Lady Mother!" Robert cries. "You are alive!" His arms clasp mine and help me in beside him.

"I am too stubborn to die," I inform him, sinking down onto the clean straw and drawing in a shallow breath, careful of my broken rib. I squint at him through my one good eye as he helps Sancia up. He is covered in dirt and crusted blood, under which I note bruised flesh and burn marks. One of his ankles is twisted at an awkward angle. "Where are they taking us?"

"To Castle Capuano. Queen Joanna has rescued us."

I nod, hearing the irony in his voice. It is not much of a rescue. Castle Capuano is the prison where the worst criminals are interred, usually for decades unless they die, which they often do. But we are out of the hands of Joanna's enemies, and that is something.

Castle Capuano is dirty, cold, and damp. Sancia and I are locked together in a stone cell with a wooden cot and a plain wooden chair and table. I hobble over to the rough-hewn cot and sink onto the dirty straw mattress. Luxury!

Raymond's wife brings us our dinner, a fish stew with bread still warm from the oven and a jug of small ale. I am so hungry and weakened I nearly weep at the sight of it. She drapes a shawl over my shoulders and has her servant lay the two blankets she has brought us on the cot, along with two clean shifts. She has also brought a pail of fresh water and cloths, and they set to wiping our faces and gently washing away the dried blood from our bodies.

"Lord Robert's wife has left Naples for her family's estate in Provence," she tells me.

"You should leave also," I answer.

"My family will protect me." Her mouth forms a thin, tight line. I remember her brother has allied himself with Duke Robert. It will not help my son, but it will ensure her safety, at least for now.

"Tomorrow I will send over two chairs with arm rests and cushions, and more clothes. What else can I bring you? I have paid the guards well to supply your needs, make sure they do not cheat you," she fusses as she cleans me.

"Beatrice, you have done well," I murmur, clenching my jaw against the pain despite her gentleness. How pleased I am to be clean again. But when she reaches for my left foot I cry out and pull it back. She turns her face away, her shoulders heaving.

"Is it Raymond?" I have been afraid to ask for fear of what she might tell me.

"He is alive," she says, struggling for control.

My eyes well up. "Well then," I say. I swallow twice. "Well then, we are all alive, and we will heal." I take a breath. "Put that clean undershift on me, dear Beatrice, and wrap me in your warm shawl and let me have some of your good fish soup."

She looks at me in surprise, for I have never been one for endearments. A flush rises up her neck. "Cicillia will be here soon, Madame Mother-in-law. She is with my Lord Husband now."

I accept her gentle rebuff. She loves me, this one. She wants me to be well. She wants me to be *myself*. She needs my courage, not my kindness. They all do.

"My shift," I say, nodding at the clean garment. "Sancia will need Cicillia more than I." Sancia's baby is still alive despite her ill treatment, I have ascertained that, but I will be happy to have Cicillia confirm it. Cicillia, the daughter and namesake of my old maid, is a fine healer. I taught her mother everything I know, and she taught her only daughter. The girl's father taught her to read and under Queen Joanna's new laws permitting women a profession, she became a physic for women.

"Lord Robert is lodged with my Lord Husband," Beatrice says as she helps me out of my dirty shift and into the clean one. "He told Cicillia he did not need her care either, and to look to his brother."

I huff a snort of disgust at my prideful son.

"Do not worry, Madame. Cicillia would have none of it. And at least you will be examined in a clean shift." She turns, hiding her smile, to fill a bowl of soup for me from the pot.

That night I kneel and thank God for our lives. We have produced a line of survivors, my husband and I. I am relieved and grimly proud. I thank God also for the dismal prison that is Castle Capuano and pray that we may stay here out of sight until the turmoil in Naples subsides.

The next morning my old maid, Cicillia, visits. She brings fresh kirtles, fresh bread, and fresh news: "Queen Joanna has publicly renounced the Duke of Taranto's suit and made clear her preference for his brother Louis," she tells me while she examines my wounds.

"Pope Clement has given his permission? They are betrothed? Ahh!" I gasp as she winds the cloth around my ribs more tightly than I permitted her daughter to.

"He has not. And I doubt he is pleased with her public statement. We must wash that foot."

"You will not touch it. Is Louis of Taranto still at Capua?"

"He is fighting his way toward Naples, I have heard. And gaining supporters daily." She places a bowl of water on the floor beside my chair. "We cannot leave it like that. It will fester. I must wash it and draw out the poison with a poultice and then rebind it."

"Your daughter sent you here to torture me."

"She sent me here to heal you. Which she would be perfectly capable of doing herself if you were not so—" She catches my look. "—my Lady, you know it must be done."

"Is Queen Joanna still at Castle dell'Ovo?" I extend my left foot reluctantly toward the bowl.

"The toenails?" She unwinds the loose cloth her daughter tied there and examines the dirt- and blood-crusted foot.

I grunt a rough agreement, and grit my teeth.

"The queen has returned to Castle Nuovo. I understand she has set up a temporary council. Do not ask, I only know the Empress Catherine is her head advisor." She trails off, bending over my foot now submerged in the water bowl, gently dabbing with a cloth at the crust of dirt and dried blood. I distract myself from the pain with the strong poppy tea she brought and consider what she has told me.

Catherine of Valois, Empress of Constantinople and matriarch of the Taranto Duchy, is the last of Joanna's old council. They dare not touch a royal, these villains. Nor would Robert of Taranto permit it—for all that they hate each other, she is his mother. He cannot have any suspicion fall on his own family, or people might look at him. This is what has kept him from accusing his brother Louis of the conspiracy against Prince Andrew.

A groan escapes my clenched lips. The water is loosening the filth covering my exposed toes. I take several gulps of the bitter tea. Cicillia stops dabbing at my foot until I settle in my chair again.

Joanna will have discussed with her new council the decision to announce publicly her preference for Louis. Catherine of Valois has always preferred her second son. He listens to her while Robert of Taranto listens to no one. She is a powerful woman and skillful in court intrigues, but she is blinded by her family's interests—in this case; the interests of her favorite son. It is not the advice I would have given Joanna, had I been there. Louis' forces might gain a slight edge by her endorsement, but the absence of a formal betrothal has shown everyone the Pope opposes her choice, which is all the encouragement Robert needs. Moreover, her Hungarian in-laws will be incensed. They want a Hungarian prince on the throne of Naples, or none at all. Charles Martel may die in infancy. Even if he does not, it will be years before he takes the throne. Elizabeth of Hungary and her son, King Louis of Hungary, will be enraged to see the kingdom of Naples slipping from their grasp.

Joanna must know her Aunt Catherine's advice is tainted. She has been trained all her life to rule this fractured and highly-coveted kingdom by her grandfather, King Robert the Wise. But she needs a husband to lead her army and protect her realm, one who is fully committed to her, and she has been attracted to Louis since they were children. Did she not have him escort her in to dinner at Castle Nuovo? But to make a public declaration? Without Pope Clement's blessing?

"How have the people responded to their queen's choice?"

Cicillia shrugs. "They have returned to their business, although there is still uneasiness and discontent. I think they are waiting to see what will happen." Cicillia lifts my foot out of the water and rests it on a pillow. I make myself look at the mutilated toes, because I do not want to. Cicillia covers them with a light poultice. It stings excruciatingly. I have done this to others, I remind myself, as I drain the last of the poppy tea.

I should be there. I should be warning Queen Joanna to be more cautious, more subtle, to hold her cards close. To hint at much and promise nothing. She is a clever girl, a brilliant girl. Her grandparents trained her well in the art of kingship, in the careful balance of royal command and royal favor. But she is not a subtle girl. Her step-grandmother, Queen Sancia, imbibed her with too much piety to admit the calculating guile necessary to rule a court of hot-blooded, ambitious Neapolitan and Hungarian cousins. And she has never needed to depend on her wits for her very life.

Until now. Now, when everyone she could trust is either dead or locked up under the accusation of regicide. Not by chance. No, not at all by chance. Leaving her, a lamb among wolves. A clever lamb, though, and well-trained in royal politics—she will surprise them. Somehow, I must help her.

"Leave the poultice on until I return," Cicillia says.

"You think to instruct me in herb lore?" I say it lazily rather than sharply. The tea is having its effect. Cicillia rises, her joints creaking. At fifty-six, she is nearly a decade younger than I.

"Thank you."

She looks at me.

"It is the tea. It mellows."

"You are welcome, Madame." Cicillia's mouth quirks as she ties on her cape.

"Tell my daughter-in-law I need writing materials," I say as she leaves. Cicillia has known me since she was a child. She will understand what I need.

That afternoon our guard admits another visitor, one of Sancia's maidservants sent from the count of Marcone. She brings us a basket of pasties and figs, a bag of money which the guard confiscates at once to 'pay the debts we will incur while imprisoned', a warm cloak and a clean set of clothing for her mistress, and a message from her master.

"The Count will not visit. He cannot associate with you while you are under suspicion of conspiracy to murder a royal prince," she tells Sancia bluntly.

"Is he well? Is Maroccia—"

The servant's face softens now she has delivered the count's distasteful message. "Your daughter is very well, Countess. She walks more confidently every day. Soon she will be running. Your Lord Husband... I never saw a father so attached to a child. Rest assured, Madame, he will never allow harm to come to her."

"Tell her... tell her I love her. And tell my Lord Husband I believe he is right not to visit me, for Maroccia's sake. We must keep her safe, above all." She touches her abdomen. "Tell him that his son is well."

"It is a lie!" the servant says, suddenly fierce. "It is a wicked lie that you were involved in any conspiracy!"

"It is," Sancia says. "And I will be proved innocent. You will tell Maroccia I love her?"

"I will, my Lady. And I will pray for your release so you may tell her yourself." She bows and hurries out, leaving Sancia praying for her daughter.

I am not much of one for prayer. God gave us faith and wit, and in my experience wit is the more useful gift. It is time I put mine to use again. I wait impatiently for Beatrice to bring me writing materials.

She arrives the next day. "My maid, Blanche, has agreed to take your letter to her brother, Giovanni. He will see it reaches Queen Joanna," she murmurs as she passes a small package from beneath her bodice into my hands. I quickly slip it up my wide sleeve while thanking her for the soup, and the olive oil she has brought for our lamp. I know her maid; I once brought her an herbal drink when she had a fever, and my husband's recommendation secured Giovanni a position in the royal kitchen. Beatrice has anticipated my intent precisely.

When Sancia and I are alone again, I unwrap the writing materials and lay them out on the little table. I may not be able to sit at Joanna's council table, but I have influence yet.

My Most Magnificent Monarch, who as a babe I cradled in my arms and cared for above my own children, I begin. I am not above incurring a sense of indebtedness where warranted. I think a moment. If this missive should fall into my enemies' hands...

My greatest wish is that you are well and safe, and the crown prince also. I anxiously await your reassurance that you and our future king are strong and well-defended. Such an assurance cannot be measured in gold. It is priceless not only to your royal person, but to your entire kingdom.

I examine my letter. No one can object to my wishing the queen of Naples health and safety. Joanna will understand what I am saying: that she must cast her gold where she has cast her alliance. What she has done in announcing her preferred suitor cannot be undone, so it must not be half-done. It is more important than ever that Louis wins over his brother, and he will need her gold to do so. She will also know, when I ask for her reassurance, that I am awaiting a reply, and by that she will know the man who gives this to her can be trusted.

I seal my letter with the wax Beatrice provided along with the vellum, and press my ring into it. They took my necklet and my gold brooch but dared not steal my ring, given me by the queen herself.

Next day the letter leaves, pressed to my daughter-in-law's bosom under her shift while the guard at our door checks the empty basket in which she brought us bread and fruit and cheese. I watch him nod and wave her on her way. Now we shall see.

I wait anxiously for three days before Beatrice brings me a reply, and then must wait till we are alone and the guard has left to read it. I open it breathlessly.

Joanna, too, chooses her words carefully. We cannot be entirely certain of anyone. Her subjects, who so loved her for her beauty, piety, and justice, are now crying in the streets for blood. A monarch who brings war and the threat of privation to her people has no virtues.

She writes that she hopes I am well while I await my trial, and expresses her faith that God will protect the innocent and expose those guilty of treason who until now have hidden their falseness. (*Hah, she is furious over the betrayal of Hugo del Balzo, in whom she misplaced her trust*). She thanks me for my letter which brought her great relief, and tells me she will guard her and her son's safety with all possible means at her disposal.

So she will follow my advice and is eager for more. I am about to begin a reply when I hear the key in the lock at our door. I have barely time to hide everything before the door opens. I am shocked to see the master of the royal guard walk in.

"Leave us," he commands. Our prison guard looks about to object, but thinks better of it.

"Have you come to release us?"

"I wish I could, Madame Philippa." He looks around the little cell, avoiding our eyes.

"Is it bad news?" At his nod Sancia sinks into a chair, her hand on her belly. I stand beside her, my throat dry.

"Not that," he says quickly. "Forgive me, Madame." He pours Sancia some ale from the jug on the table, then, distracted by his thoughts, drinks it himself.

"Tell us." My voice is raw and strange to my ears.

"The Duke of Taranto has moved into Castle Nuovo."

"Moved in?" I stare at him open-mouthed. Of all the news I might have anticipated, this had not occurred to me. "Into Castle Nuovo with Queen Joanna? Surely she has not agreed to that!"

"Duke Robert of Taranto forced his way into the royal castle, and ordered my immediate departure, along with half of the queen's royal guard." He looks down miserably. Before I can speak, he says, "He was inside before we realized what was happening. We fought, but his men outnumbered us, and the queen ordered us to put down our swords. She said she would not sacrifice her men needlessly."

I grasp the back of the chair for support. The master of the royal guard stands with his head hanging, like a recalcitrant child.

"There is more?" I manage to get out.

"He has begun issuing royal proclamations."

"In whose name?"

"In his name, Madame."

"From Castle Nuovo in his own name? What sort of proclamations?"

"That all citizens of the Kingdom of Naples must resist Lord Louis and his forces, that none may join him or obey an order given by him."

"Has Queen Joanna not denied it?"

"The queen, in retaliation, has issued an edict naming Lord Louis her protector."

How desperate she must be. If Duke Robert has his way, she will be locked up the day after he forces her to wed him. Or worse. I forgive her for deserting us in Castle Nuovo, for not being able to prevent our torture, for putting herself and her kingdom first. But I cannot imagine Joanna frightened. Distraught over what to do, perhaps. And angry. Yes, she will be furious! She is God's anointed, the rightful queen of Naples. She cannot help us now while she is fighting for her life, but it is in her nature, as it was in her Grandfather's, to stand by those who are loyal to her. If I can help her save her crown, she will help me save my family.

"Can you get a letter to her?" It will be much more dangerous now. I dare not put Beatrice, Blanche, and Giovanni at risk.

"I can." He does not raise an eyebrow when I get my writing materials from their hiding place.

I smile to myself. I have lived up to expectations.

I write a second carefully-worded letter to Joanna, urging her to seek the blessing of the Holy Father in all things (I expect she has already sent an emissary to him) and above all to resist the devil (she will take my meaning) and to keep faith with those in whom she has put her trust.

Queen Joanna and Duke Robert of Taranto battle for power all spring, issuing edicts and counter-edicts. Meanwhile, Louis fights his way back to Naples, gaining supplies and soldiers as he comes. By the end of May he has reached the hill northwest of Naples, and sits there with a large army looking over the city.

We wait breathlessly for visitors to bring us the news each day, and even in our foul surroundings, find hope and healing. We will survive this, I and my sons and my granddaughter. Louis will free the queen and the kingdom from his brother's tyranny and protect us, I promise Sancia. Our family will be freed and reinstated in the top positions of Joanna's court. So I tell myself. And so I tell my great-grandmother when she whispers *prepare yourself!* into my mind in the dark of night.

We will survive.

If we can just hold on until Joanna regains her power, we will triumph once more over our enemies.

If we can just hold on.

Chapter 18

February, 1301
City of Naples

Everything?

How could Cicillia claim to know everything about me? And how would Raymond know whether he had been told everything about me? He could not know I had a husband, he would never have married me knowing that! I had hoped for a more specific answer; this veiled warning told me little except that whatever the girl knew, Raymond knew. How he had found her I could not guess, but she had given him at least some of my secrets. She was his, not mine. I would do well to remember that.

I went to my bedchamber, closing the adjoining door behind me, and bid Cicillia pin on the green headdress and clasp the emeralds around my neck. I itched to ask her what she knew of me, and how she knew anything at all, but I would not let her see my concern. What did it matter what a servant thought she knew? That attitude was my best defense, that I was too high for her reach. I sat proudly as she tucked my hair under the headdress, as though I had merely found a simple veil over my braids more convenient during the day and had always intended to dress for dinner with my husband.

We dined in the small hall at a table that only seated thirty. I was surprised to discover Raymond had invited several wealthy merchants of Naples to join us with their wives. I entertained those around me with the latest court gossip while I still could, earning

Raymond's smiling approval, and watched them, particularly the men, when Raymond spoke of drilling the soldiers he would lead on his first commission for King Charles, and how a victory would affect trade here in Naples. They leaned toward him smiling, interested. These were men who had earned their positions through intelligence, ambition, and careful business dealings. They admired their betters, but they also respected those who had climbed above their station as they had, through effort and competence. As did King Charles, I reminded myself, for Raymond's climb was by the King's grace and the tolerance of his cosmopolitan court, as was my own rise. What other ruler would have so amply rewarded two such base-born subjects? So I spoke generously of the king who had given me in marriage without my consent, and of his chosen heirs, Prince Robert and Princess Violante. Our guests added their praise to mine, and not only because they must extol their rightful rulers. I saw sincere enthusiasm in their faces and heard it in their words. A monarch who brings peace and prosperity to his people has no faults.

Would Prince Robert be such a king? Of course he would, he was in all things noble and wise. But peace and prosperity were not always easily secured. When a prince was in descent on Fortune's wheel, his people suffered with him, and those who had the least to lose, lost the most. I touched the necklet at my breast.

"Beautiful," the woman beside me commented. "A gift from your days at court?"

I lowered my hand, embarrassed. She wore a gold brooch with two rubies on it, both smaller than the emeralds in my necklet. She leaned toward me, her lips parted, as though waiting to hear some scandalous story.

"A gift from my husband," I said coolly, fully aware of what she had all but accused me of. She leaned back and looked at Raymond, surprised.

Then I understood my husband's generosity. He was proud, and he was laying claim, and I was wearing his credentials into this influential circle of successful merchants. All of that was true. But I remembered the pictures in his bedchamber of his mother and father, beautiful and regal despite being unadorned by any valuable possessions—and both dead in one violent night. I had climbed up from the river mud easily compared to him. So easily I had not stopped to think how much easier the slide back down would be.

That was the message on his walls. That was the reason behind the silks and gems, the elegant furnishings and lavish feasts. Raymond was building a wall of wealth around himself.

Around us both, now. I looked at him thoughtfully. He was laughing with one of the merchants as though he were utterly carefree. A carefree 'black monkey' within a white man's world.

Was that how they saw him underneath their worldly indulgence? I glanced around the table, looking for a false note in their cheer. There, in that one, a narrowing at the corner of his eyes: envy? And in another, a tightening of his lips beneath his smile: scorn?

In most I perceived a genuine respect, but there were small signs—a momentary withdrawal, the straightening of a back—when Raymond laughed too loud, when he indulged in subtle boasting. He was not one of them. I knew that look on their faces, however well-hidden; I had received it too often not to recognize it.

And now because I was listening and watching for what lay behind all their masks, I heard something in Raymond's voice: a note of triumph, a mocking glint nearly invisible beneath his smile. He knew. They thought they were better than him because of his origins. I had received the same veiled condescension from Violante's ladies, for a similar reason. But Raymond turned it back on them. He was laughing as much at them as with them, he was so confident in his future. It drew me, that confidence. It drew us all like a tide sweeping over us, pulling us into his swell. I blinked and sat back. But my brief insight changed me. I looked at Raymond and saw a man now, a man with greatness in him, rising on Fortune's wheel.

Raymond did not come to my bed that night. Although I rose soon after dawn, I did not see him leave. When he came home for supper I greeted him in the green dress—green for change, for a fresh beginning—holding my head high under the headdress, with the emerald necklet gleaming at my throat. He noticed my concession and smiled, but neither of us spoke of it.

So our days went. We conversed over dinner about the household, or what was happening around Naples, news I picked up at the market or he learned... he never said where or how he came by any information. He spent his days training the men who would serve under his command and I spent mine ordering our household. I saw the strain on his face when he arrived home day after day, but I did not ask how his days went and he did not offer anything on that topic. He kissed me chastely each evening before retiring to his bedchamber, and I to mine.

Then one day he walked in grim-faced with his lips pressed tight and roared to his steward for wine without a glance at me. The man scurried off.

"You are at home," I reminded him.

He turned his head as though he had not seen me till then. "I killed a man today," he said.

"You killed—!"

"A waste! A stupid, unnecessary waste of a strong soldier who could have fought well for King Charles!" He grabbed the goblet from the trembling steward and drank it in one swallow, dashing the cup to the floor. "Bring me another!"

I stood still. I know the look of a man who wants to beat someone. I held my head high and looked him in the eyes.

"He challenged me. In front of the men I must lead, he drew his sword and swore he would not follow a—" Raymond broke off.

I watched him in silence as he glared about the room.

The steward came running with a second goblet. Raymond drank it in one long swallow and handed the empty goblet back.

"The others will follow me now." He turned and walked to the stairs, his hard footsteps echoing in the empty hall. I drew a deep breath as he started up the stairs. He would never be able to silence every man who called him such names.

Well, he had silenced one.

I stood beside Raymond in the pre-dawn darkness waiting for his war-horse to be brought to the mounting block. He was massive in his thick leather armor and boots. He had not told me the details of his commission, but I had heard the rumors of civil unrest in the northern region of the kingdom. Several counts were involved in a vendetta that was laying whole villages to waste and making our trade roads unsafe.

"Are you..." I hesitated. A woman did not ask a man if he was afraid before he rode to battle. "Are you anticipating a long absence, my Lord Husband?" It was the first time I had called him that. He turned to me with a smile.

"Will you miss me, Madame Wife?"

"I do not want to order too many provisions. I will not be entertaining while you are away. The food would go bad."

He laughed that hearty laugh of his. I frowned to hide the pleasure I had begun to take in hearing it. He laughed again. "I expect you will see me in a month, two at most," he said. Seeing his horse being led out of the stable he started toward it.

"Are you not even going to bid me goodbye?" *Had I got up in the dark to watch him mount his horse?* He had not come to my bed since our wedding night, which admittedly was a relief, nor once spoken to me in private, which was not. I was left to stew over what my role in his household was, and whether he no longer cared for me, and that led to wondering what Cicillia had told him. I had not thought of a way to ask her without revealing as much as I learned.

Raymond stopped and turned back to me. He smiled broadly. "I believe you want to be kissed!" he announced, and before I could answer, he lifted me off the ground and kissed me long and soundly. I was so startled I kissed him back. His arms tightened around me, pressing me against the hard leather of his armor. Hard enough to prevent the piercing of an arrow or a sword? Of their own accord my arms encircled his head and held him to my lips.

I was breathless and a little dizzy when he set me down. Guilio had never kissed me like that! Raymond drew his finger along the curve of my cheek, looking at me as though he would memorize my face. I felt an odd impulse to kiss his finger before he withdrew it. Fortunately, I did not. I managed to scowl severely at him, trying to hide the upward tremble I felt at the corners of my mouth. In response I received another of his laughs, this one a low chuckle. "I shall look forward to our reunion, Madame Wife," he said.

I blushed furiously. My foolishness had given him a false message. But as I watched him mount I was struck once again by the thought that he might die, and I had not the heart to discourage his hopes.

The horse pranced sideways, feeling him in the saddle. He reined it in and brought it near me again. "My steward has my will," he called down to me. "I have left you all your gowns and jewelry, and your bed. See that you get them, if it comes to that."

"Come home and see to it yourself!" I snapped. But secretly I was astounded. Such a fortune! I could return to Sicily and live there a wealthy woman. Or stay here quite comfortably, perhaps even set myself up as an herbalist. Who would have thought he would do such a thing? I had not even been a true wife to him. I vowed to be more pleasant to him when he returned. Beneath my dutiful, guilt-inspired resolution I felt a shiver of anticipation. "Come home," I said again, quietly, as he rode off.

Raymond rode home victorious five months later. He had soundly beaten the armies of the quarreling counts and confiscated the sacked villages in King Charles' name, along with a great bounty of holdings, quarries, castles and money in recompense for the trouble they had given their king.

I heard him arrive, first through the rumors in the market place, then in a thunder of hooves. I ran to the main road in time to see him sweep by, leading his weary but triumphant army. His armor was dirty and stained—with rust, I hoped—but he sat his horse proudly and did not appear wounded. When they had passed I ordered my servants to "buy more of everything: meat, fish, the root vegetables your master likes, flour for pastry—we will feast tonight," and hurried home ahead of them.

I called to Cicillia to wash my hair in rose water and sent another servant to invite the merchants who were his friends to dine with us. He would have to report to King Charles first, who knew how long that would take? I had time to decide what I would wear, to wonder why I was going to all this trouble and consider calling the servant back, to change my mind and send an order to the kitchen to make sure they made Raymond's favorite sauce, to change it again and order my own favorite so Raymond would not think I had thought too much about him. I reminded myself I had promised to be a better wife to him, and that was all I was doing. The giddy feeling in my stomach was only hunger.

I chose my red kirtle, for a celebration, and clasped above the lacing on my breast the engagement brooch Raymond had given me. Its black pearl shone at the center, with the two topaz gems gleaming fiercely against the red silk. I slipped onto my finger the ruby ring he had given me before he left, remembering the importance he set on impressing his wealthy friends. I snapped at Cicillia twice while she was braiding up my hair—I should have an older maid who knew how to do hair properly! I caught myself, a fisherman's daughter, saying such things, and sat in chagrined silence while she finished, then told her she might choose a ribbon for her hair from among mine.

It was all I could do not to run downstairs when I heard Raymond's boots on the hall floor, but I remembered how tired and hot he had appeared riding past the market, and sent Cicillia to let him know I would meet with him when he had washed.

As soon as she left I realized what he might think. Of course he had washed his hands and face before he spoke with King Charles. I had told him to come home and had kissed him back—how often I had relived that kiss during these months—and now I wanted him to wash for me more thoroughly than he had washed for the King of Naples? I flushed with shame, but Cicillia was already gone.

I sent a servant to the kitchen to tell the cooks we would eat as soon as Raymond was ready. I ordered another to ride to the merchants' homes and invite them to come now with their wives, for our supper was prepared. When Raymond emerged from his bath I was already greeting the first of our guests and need not be alone with him for several hours. I smiled at him as he entered, as though to say I had known he would want to be free of the dust and dirt of travel before greeting his friends.

That night Raymond came to my bedchamber. He stopped at the door. I was sitting in my chair by the fire with my hair combed out, a black tumble against the white of my night-gown. I knew he would come. He stood in the doorway, a large night shadow half-lit by the flickering wall sconce.

"Come in," I said when he made no move to enter.

He approached me, carrying two cups of mulled wine, and set them on the table before lowering himself into the other chair.

I took my cup and sipped the warm sweet wine. "King Charles was pleased with your success?"

Raymond cocked his head with a smile. I felt an answering one lift the corners of my lips and fought it.

"He has given me one of the manors I confiscated for him. At Aversa."

"A manor?" I sputtered, coughing on the mouthful of wine I had swallowed too suddenly. "A manor at Aversa? Given to you?"

"We have a summer home." He chuckled, low and pleased.

I took another gulp of wine to stop my coughing. *We. We have a summer home.* I shook my head.

"Are you pleased?" He was grinning broadly now.

"We have a summer home." I was overtaken by a fit of giggles. Raymond laughed with me.

"Would you like to see it?" he asked.

"Of course! I will see it when we go there for…" Another giddy giggle escaped me. "For the summer!"

When our laughter subsided, we sat watching the fire and finishing our wine. I imagined us traveling to Aversa, trying to convince myself it was real. The King had a castle there, Matriona had gone with the royal family as nurse to the little princes, but I had been left in Naples.

The silence lengthened. I became aware of Raymond watching me. He had finished his wine; was he thinking of staying? If so, he could not know about Guilio. Or did not care. He had been a heathen for years before converting. Who knew how many wives his father had had?

"What are you thinking so seriously, Madame Wife?"

I set my empty cup on the table. "I think of many things. I thought of running away when I first came to your house."

"Every night when I returned I wondered if you would be here."

"You hired Cicillia to make sure of it." I stared into the fire, but I could see his slight grimace at the corner of my eye. "Tell me what she told you of my past." I said it calmly although my heart was racing.

"She did not tell you?"

"I did not ask her."

He nodded as though he had expected as much. "It is better if there are no secrets between us."

Secrets are often necessary, sometimes useful, and never completely absent between people. Nonetheless, I nodded. Men do not like to think their wives have secrets.

"Cicillia told me you are married and have a son back in Sicily."

I sat very still in my chair, fighting to keep my face impassive. He knew. He had known all along. Or had he doubted her? "She is not from Trapani," I answered carelessly.

"Her mother knew a woman in Trapani, a cousin who married a fisherman there. When you left your husband to go with the Neapolitan army, there was talk."

I had been going to ask him whether he believed this girl, but there was no point denying it now. What did he mean by 'talk'? Better the truth than what he might be thinking. "I came as nursemaid to Prince Charles. I have never been with any man but my husband."

"That I know." He smiled slightly. "I lived at the castle also. There is always talk among the men about those women who are willing to warm a man's bed."

I flushed, remembering that he also knew the reason I had fallen out of Princess Violante's favor. A minor transgression now, compared to the sin of bigamy. A sin he had knowingly forced on me!

"Yet you married me. Knowing I was married to another man!" I glared at him, my voice rising. "You knew all along! You forced me to marry you, knowing I should not. Knowing I would be committing a mortal sin!"

"Have I asked you to consummate our marriage?"

"It is no marriage, nor ever can be." I huffed in my chair. Why did he have to tell me? Why tonight? How could I go to Aversa with him now? I fumed in silence.

"I will see that no one learns of it."

I looked at him. If he had known... "Cicillia...!"

"Cicillia is our servant. I pay my servants a good wage and treat them well. In return I demand their complete loyalty. Cicillia knows this."

"I will be executed if it is discovered."

"There is nothing to fear," he put his hand over mine. "You have nothing to fear, Philippa. I will protect you."

I snatched my hand away. "I cannot!" I cried. "I am married to another!" I shrank against my chair, away from him.

He looked at me a moment. "Very well," he said.

"You knew!" I cried as he got up from his chair. "You knew all along!"

"I knew. But this was the only way I could think of to protect you."

Raymond's second mission was to the south. He told me no more than that, and I did not ask. I stood beside him wrapped in the cool silence I had maintained for weeks, waiting for him to leave. Before he mounted his horse, he turned to me. "This may be a long campaign." He leaned in to embrace me. I turned my face away, offering only my cheek.

He did not kiss it. Instead he murmured, so only I couod hear, "Go and have Cicillia pack your things, then. Be sure to take your jewels. I will wait."

I stepped back and stared at him. Was he putting me out on the streets? Had I provoked him too far?

"Come," he said, still quietly. "It is time to choose. I will take you south with me, and see you safely back to Trapani, and to your loving husband."

My mouth dropped open. I shut it with a snap. How dare he! I wanted to slap him, but he would not have allowed it in front of the servant holding his horse at the mounting block. I leaned forward, causing him to bend again to hear me. "I have a better idea," I said.

"Why don't you keep going when you get down south? Why don't you find a boat that will take you back to your little village in the jungles of Africa?" I turned with a swish of my kirtle and marched back into our house.

There was silence for a moment that made my back tingle, and then a huge gust of laughter that could be heard even when the door closed behind me.

I grabbed my green headdress and yanked it from my head, the pins tearing strands of my hair off with it, and hurled it across the hall. He knew full well I would not go back to my village; he only wanted to make me admit it! I could still hear his laughter outside. Servants scurried aside as I stormed up to my chambers. I slammed the door behind me and threw myself into a chair. I was so angry I wished... I wished he would...

Go back to his little village in the jungles of Africa? I pictured him in Africa riding one of the grotesque animals painted on his walls, and chuckled.

Did I really say that to him? I covered my mouth with my hands and laughed. *His little village...* I bent over, laughing *...in the jungles of Africa...* I pressed my hands to my mouth and laughed silently, helplessly, my eyes streaming. If I was proud and ambitious, so be it; I could throw the same accusation at him! Let him paint his walls how he liked, he would never return to his humble origins.

He had laughed, too, after a moment. I started laughing again at the thought of that moment. I would like to have seen his face then! Pity I turned my back so quickly. But after that moment, how he had laughed!

Oh, this was an interesting man.

If only I was not already married.

Chapter 19

August-October, 1346
Castle Capuano, Naples

lizabeth, the queen mother of Hungary, seethes with fury over the delay in bringing her son Andrew's murderers to justice. We learn she has written Pope Clement that if the murderers are not punished Hungary will intervene and see to it themselves. The threat is real, and grave. Her son, King Louis of Hungary, would relish an excuse to invade Naples and claim it as his own, and with the Neapolitan dukes fighting amongst themselves it would be near to impossible to present a unified resistance. The Pope responds at once by authorizing Bertrand del Balzo, chief justice of the Kingdom of Naples and cousin to Hugo del Balzo, to act on his behalf to judge and sentence everyone responsible for the heinous murder of the prince, and to conduct their swift punishment.

This ushers in another round of gruesome tortures. Day and night we hear screams rising from the dungeon and moans from the prison cells. I do not want to think about what is being done to them, or wonder what lies they are confessing to make it stop.

When two guards enter our cell and come toward me I stand up straight. I am shaking so badly I am sure they will notice despite my attempt to hide it. Have I been accused by the others? Are these men taking me down to the torture room or outside to be put to death? I turn a last, bracing look on Sancia, wishing there was time to tell her how proud I am of her, to exhort her to have courage… and then they drag me out.

It is a long hall, lit sparingly. On either side I hear the agony of my fellow inmates as I walk down it. My heart stops when I recognize my sons' voices moaning from behind the iron doors of their cells. At least they are alive, but it is poor consolation for their suffering. When we reach the stairs and I am led downward I know my fate. I feel faint, thinking I would rather have been taken up and outside to my death. Then I raise my head and steel myself for what will come. Despite my resolve, it is not long before my screams and moans contribute to the hideous cacophony of the dungeons. Sancia, too, is tortured, though only once. Her condition is obvious now and possibly shames them.

The torture continues until Bertrand del Balzo and his committee of jurists announce they have uncovered multiple plots against Andrew's life, and confessions enough to condemn us all. We are uniformly divested of our titles, robbed of our lands and wealth, and sentenced to death. Our guard gleefully tells us the news as soon as it is made public.

My son Robert and the Count of Terlizzi are the first to be executed. From a small window in my cell I watch my son, bound in iron chains, being dragged across the courtyard and prodded up onto a prison cart. The guard attaches his wrists to the pole in the center of the prisoner's cage on the wagon bed, forcing him to stand where all can see him. Terlizzi, similarly bound and nearly fainting with fear, is hoisted into a second cart. An executioner climbs up into each prison cart, hauling the tools of his trade: whips and knives, branding irons and a pail of red-hot coals. Already I can hear the howling of the crowds lined along the streets of Naples, waiting with their hands full of stones and rotting fruit to throw at the prisoners while the executioners flay and burn them. This gruesome parade will wind all through Naples before they reach the place where they will be executed.

"They are being taken to the beach outside Castle dell'Ovo, where a great pyre has been built on which to burn them," our guard gloats. He rubs his hands imagining it, which is all he can do since he must stay to guard our prison and will miss all the fun.

I watch the carts leave, Terlizzi already screaming while my Robert endures his approaching death with grim stoicism. He looks up at the castle wall just before they pass out of sight. I hope he sees the face of one who loves him behind the iron bars of my tiny window before he plunges into the sick mass of hatred that Naples has become.

When he is gone Sancia falls against my shoulder, sobbing. I hold her, staring dry-eyed out the window, hanging on to the last sight of my son. I do not allow myself to weep, for if I once begin, I fear I will never stop.

I am denied even the comfort of knowing he had a Christian burial. We learn that the bodies were pulled half-burned from the pyre, the hearts and lungs torn out and eaten, and the rest cut into pieces and dragged by hooks through the mud and sewers of Naples. When their flesh was gone, the bones were taken by craftsmen to form dice and knife handles. "And that will teach the black-skinned son of a slave to aspire above his station," our guard finishes his account with a satisfied smirk. "And to conspire against a royal prince," he adds as though it were an afterthought.

A week later my younger son Raymond and Nicholas of Melizzano suffer the same ignoble death and mutilation of their remains.

My husband Raymond, dead five years now of a fever, was buried in the church near our home, after a magnificent ceremony with almost regal rites. His position as royal seneschal of the kingdom was given to his son. And now that son, and his brother, the seneschal of the court, are fallen so low they are not even given the meanest Christian burial. It is the poison of envy and prejudice that has done this.

Nightmares plague me day and night until I no longer know what is real and what is only in my mind.

Raymond comes to me, as young and confident as the day I first saw him, when he looked across his kitchen at me and smiled the way a man smiles when he sees something he wants.

"What are you doing here?" I ask him. "Have they accused you, also?"

"Grandmother, I have been here all along," Sancia says. I feel her unwind the bandage and examine the burns on the tender sole of my foot. I wince as she pours a little wine upon it, a trick I taught her to avoid infection, but otherwise I ignore her, gazing at my Raymond.

"They cannot accuse me," he says, laughing. "I have escaped them!"

"I lost it all," I tell him. "Everything we built together. Every manor and castle, and all our lands. All our titles, all our money, all my jewels and dresses. Even our home is gone, taken from me..." Tears leak from my eyes. I have never allowed myself to weep in front of him, but I am old and weak now and full of pain. I cannot stop my tears.

"Do not fret, Grandmother." Sancia murmurs, tying the bandage again. She begins examining the wounds on my arms and legs, pouring a few drops of the precious wine onto the worst ones. We used up our herbs and medicines long ago.

"What did I tell you? For people like us there are only two places in society: at the very top, or at the very bottom," Raymond warns me, as he did in life. His face is stern.

"I could not protect them," I continue, accepting his blame. "It has all gone, all our strength and our wealth, and I have nothing with which to keep them safe..."

"Shhh, shhh. I am here with you, Grandmother."

Raymond is fading. I stretch out my arm toward him. "Our sons are safe with me," he calls, his voice reaching me from a great distance. And there—I can see them—standing in his shadow, tall and whole. Charles, our third son, is with them, dead at seventeen from a wound sustained on military campaign with his father, so long ago. Raymond could not prevent the blow that sliced his thigh to the bone and for all my skill in healing I could not draw out the poison that had spread while the wound festered all the long ride home.

"Look to the living," Raymond calls to me as his image disappears. "Not everything is lost."

I feel the cool touch of a damp cloth as Sancia gently wipes my brow. I look up to see her bending over me, a worried frown creasing her brow. "You must eat something, Grandmother," she says. "Please, let me feed you."

For her sake I nod. She fetches a bowl and a spoon. I try to eat the lukewarm fish stew she spoons into my mouth, but after a few swallows my throat seizes. I turn my head aside, closing my mouth.

"Some small ale?" she asks, putting the bowl down and lifting a mug to my lips. I take a sip and swallow with difficulty.

"We have not seen Beatrice lately," I mumble.

"She left, Grandmother." Sancia says, holding the cup up again for me to drink. "Remember? She came to tell us she was leaving Naples to find sanctuary with her family."

I nod although I do not remember. I let Sancia coax me into one more swallow of ale. Only half of it goes down, the rest dribbling out the side of my mouth. I close my eyes.

She leaves me to rest. I do nothing but rest, and yet I am always tired.

Two little girls with golden hair run smiling toward me along the garden path, as pretty as any flowers in the kingdom. A third child follows behind them laughing, their constant playmate. She is dark-haired and dark-eyed with nut-brown skin. She is trying too hard to keep up, her little face pinched, her eyes darting left to right, anxious even at play. I wonder if I have made a mistake, but I do not go to her, or comfort her, or acknowledge the uneasiness she hides. She must learn to ignore the cruelty of the other children, jealous of her closeness to the little princesses. She must learn to live in this aristocratic court with her brown skin. When she trips and falls I wait for her to get up, resisting the urge to go to her as I would if one of the princesses fell. She gets up slowly, her face scrunched up with the effort not to cry.

Are you hurt, Sancia? I ask, kindly but not so sympathetic that it will loosen the tears she is holding back.

"Are you hurt Sancia?" I repeat.

"Not very badly this time, Grandmother."

I open my eyes. Sancia, all grown up, is standing beside my bed, patting my hand. For a moment I am disoriented, until I remember where I am and everything comes back. I groan, remembering my sons. Sancia grips my hand making me focus on her. She looks bruised and tender but she does not stand as though she is in great pain. Her swollen belly pushes against her kirtle. Perhaps they felt pity, the jurists overseeing our torture, eliciting our 'confessions'. More likely they had already received the false confessions and names they needed from the others. I close my eyes as despair rolls over me again.

"Grandmother," Sancia says. "You must live, Grandmother. I cannot go on without you."

I look at her dully.

"And I must live." She takes my hand and places it on her belly. I feel a solid little kick. "He is alive, Grandmother. My son's life has begun." She holds my hand there a while longer. With every quiver of movement under my palm I feel my own life quickening, my heart reviving. The room comes into focus. Sancia's breathing and my own fill the silence. I grit my teeth against the pain in my body and the grief of my loss. But I do not move my hand.

"Robert," Sancia says. The infant kicks as though he knows his name already, startling smiles from us both. My face feels stiff, as though my very skin resists the act of smiling, but little Robert kicks again, insisting on his right to make us smile.

I sit up with Sancia's help and force myself to eat. My granddaughter has been strong for both of us long enough. Perhaps

Queen Joanna will rescue us yet, as she hopes. Most of Joanna's former courtiers have been executed by now. I cannot understand how she has managed to keep us alive. But alive we are, so perhaps she has some power still. I straighten my back and raise my chin.

"You must send for a priest."

"Grandmother, you are not dying!"

"Not for me, Granddaughter." I nod at her belly. "Your child has quickened. He is alive. He cannot be baptized yet, but we will have a priest bless him and commend him to Our Lord's mercy."

Sancia pales. "You believe he will die." She puts her hands protectively over her womb.

"I think it is less likely if Bertrand del Balzo knows he has been committed to the care of Our Savior, who said: It were better for him that a millstone were hanged about his neck, and he cast into the sea, than that he should offend one of these little ones. I want a priest and a witness, and I shall quote Saint Luke when the blessing is finished. That will make those jurists think twice before inflicting harm on an infant God has quickened to life."

She grasps my hands, her lips curving into a smile which I have not seen there for many weeks now. I bless my poor dead King Robert for the many lengthy religious lectures he forced his nobles and advisors to sit through, earning him the name Robert the Wise. If I had not learned Latin and memorized my Scriptures at his court it would have been a miracle. And now, those weary hours may save my granddaughter's life.

Our guard relays Sancia's request to the jurists, who cannot deny us a priest. Two of the jurists serve as witnesses, at my request. Sancia and I kneel in turn and murmur our confessions, and are blessed. Then Sancia, in a clear, carrying voice, asks the priest to bless the quickened child. I smile to myself at the jurists' surprised expressions. Hah! They had thought the request would be for me. The priest lays his hand reluctantly on Sancia's womb. I pray fervently for the infant to kick, and am gratified to see the priest's face when he does. To his credit, and my relief, he performs the blessing and commends the infant to Our Savior. Then it is his turn to look surprised, and a little offended, when I quote Scripture. But when I ask, "Those are Our Lord's words, are they not, Father?" he nods confirmation. I turn to the jurists, one frowning while the other stands with his stupid mouth hanging open, and thank them most humbly for bringing the priest to us. The frown turns into a glare; the other blinks, snaps his mouth shut, and inclines his head to the priest. They know full well the message we have sent them and their committee, for none can deny that the child is innocent of any treason.

We have no money now, but our guard, despite his jeering, is honest. He has been paid in advance by Beatrice and he sees that we have food. I suspect he has been told he must keep us alive for whatever hideous death they are planning, but I do not give voice to that thought. Instead I tell myself that we will live to see little Robert born and Louis of Taranto, God willing, will have beaten his brother's army by then. I only wanted to safeguard Sancia, but now I realize I must see my grandson born. I cannot be sure any other midwife will be sent when Sancia's time comes.

The days pass slowly. I try to remain cheerful for Sancia's sake. I pretend we are shut in an ordinary woman's confinement, for it is near the time for her child to be born.

The bread is stale and the ale is thin and the cheese is hard, but none of them is as difficult to force down my gullet as hope, and yet I force it down, and smile, for the sake of Sancia and her baby. And there is also Maroccia, I remind myself, safe outside of Naples with her father, the Count of Marcone.

I have lost all track of time. Our little window tells us night from day but I had not the foresight to scratch it on the wall and now it would be meaningless without a reference point. I am desperate for news of what is happening in Naples, but our guard, knowing he is torturing us, ignores my questions.

One day we are surprised to have a visitor. Blanche, Beatrice's former maid, enters our cell, her face strained with fear. With good reason, for it is dangerous to visit convicted traitors. She is carrying a loaf of fresh bread; the smell of it makes my mouth water. But it is the basket of fruit over her other arm that I can barely tear my eyes away from.

"Giovanni bade me come," Blanche whispers, her eyes darting round the cell, looking everywhere but at us. We must be a sight, with no water to bathe ourselves or wash our hair, barely enough to keep our hands and faces clean, with no change of clothes for weeks now and the wounds from our torture still raw.

"How good of you to come. Thank you for the fruit." I strive desperately for something normal to say for the sake of the guard no doubt listening at the door. "Is the queen safe? And the little prince?" I whisper.

She shakes her head. "The Duke of Taranto entrenched in Castle Nuovo, the queen his prisoner." She places the basket on our table and says more loudly, "It is my Christian duty to exhort you to repent your hideous crimes." She lowers her voice again: "My brother gave me this for you." She slips a letter out of her bodice and onto the table. I recognize the writing as Joanna's and snatch it up with a shaking hand. Sancia maintains the conversation with Blanche while I scan it quickly.

I have word that Louis of Hungary intends to attack the Kingdom of Naples. To prevent this and appease his anger over his brother's murder, Pope Clement is sending his legate, Cardinal Bertrand de Deux, with instructions to prosecute even members of the royal family, should he judge them guilty. He proposes to have Charles Martel taken to Avignon to be placed in the Pope's care.

There is neither signature nor royal seal, nor anything to show the letter has come from Queen Joanna. This and the desperate tone of the abrupt message tells me all I need to know of her state of mind. The very possibility of losing her son will have Joanna wild. My heart sinks at the clear warning that she cannot protect us much longer.

I retrieve my ink and quill from their hiding place and set them on the table. My hand shakes as I turn Joanna's note over to write my answer on the back of her vellum. My own supply is finished. That will send a message also.

Blanche and Sancia stand between the table and the door, shielding me from sight in case the guard comes in. I would only have an moment to hide everything, not nearly enough time, and the ink would be wet, but Blanche's brother told her to wait for an answer and I cannot fail Joanna. I write as quickly as I can, praying for enough time.

The best defense against foreign attack is a stable kingdom unified around a clear line of succession. Naples would be well-advised to follow the example of King Robert the Wise sixteen years ago.

I dare not take longer. The guard will wonder why Blanche is taking so long to deliver her fruit, and open the door. I cap the jar of ink, scoop it and my quill into the sachet and slide it under the mattress. I blow on the vellum and wave it to dry the ink before rolling it and handing it to Blanche. She tucks it into her bodice and we all sigh with relief.

"What of Louis of Taranto?" I whisper.

"He is still waiting with his troops on the hill overlooking Naples." She shrugs. "No one knows what he is waiting for."

The latch to the door alerts us that our guard is coming.

"What month is it?" I ask quickly as she ties on her cape.

"In two weeks it will be September."

We have been locked in Castle Capuano since March 16th—five long months. That evening I begin scratching the days off on the wall of our cell.

Three weeks later I wake to hear all the bells in Naples ringing. It is already mid-morning, I judge by the light coming in through our little window. When our guard enters with our midday meal I ask what is happening. He hesitates, the expression on his face conflicted between the pleasure of keeping us in ignorance and the eagerness of being the one to share important news. I take a bite of the stale bread, feigning indifference.

"Today," he says gravely, preening with importance, "the little Prince Charles Martel has been given his title, Duke of Calabria, and named heir to the throne of Naples in a ceremony presided over by Cardinal Bertrand de Deux on behalf of His Eminence, Pope Clement VI. All the nobles in the kingdom have come to bow before him and swear homage to him as their future king. And you," he sneers, "did not even know of it!"

I, who was once the queen's chief advisor, he means. I make myself appear dismayed, for I want him to enjoy telling us news. But inside I am smiling. Joanna has taken the advice I gave her. Sixteen years ago, when Joanna was four years old, her grandfather King Robert unified the kingdom by holding a formal ceremony of succession for her. Charles Martel, now two years old, son of the Hungarian Prince Andrew, is now the legal and proclaimed heir to one of the greatest kingdoms in Europe.

I hope the Neapolitans are re-united around their queen by this proof of a stable succession, not to mention the delight of a lavish ceremony. No doubt Joanna threw coins generously during the parade to the Cathedral of Santa Chiara, and had little Charles Martel throw some, also. I hope the Hungarians are mollified by having their prince's son receive his due. I hope Pope Clement takes note of Joanna's wise statesmanship. I hope Duke Robert of Taranto chokes on his frustration and rage.

I do not have long to enjoy my small victory, for the next day Sancia goes into labor.

Chapter 20

Summer, 1302
City of Naples

That summer, while Raymond was fighting in the south of the kingdom, Violante became ill. All of Naples knew the princess was ill, but she had been ill so many times, and always recovered. I went to the basilica and prayed for her like everyone else, but it did not comfort me. I did not trust the court physicians with their leeches. I should be taking care of her, making her herbal teas to bring down the fever, reminding her of her two young sons to bolster her strength.

Prince Robert had taken a mistress who had presented him with a son just before Violante's fever began. Robert had claimed him, although he was still a bastard. They called him Charles of Artois. Another little Charles named for his Grandfather, King Charles II. The little prince I had brought into this world and nursed for two years was four now, a strapping lad, clever and healthy. Did he remember me? I had gone to play with him and his brother Louis a few times after I left the nursery and entered into Violante's service, but he had not seen me for over a year now.

I caught my wandering thoughts and brought them sternly back to my prayers for Violante's recovery. My knees ached from the hard floor in front of the statue of Holy Mary. I thought I had said enough about Violante for Mother Mary to get the gist of what I wanted so I moved on to Raymond, away in battle six months now.

I prayed he might have some common sense to balance his ambition and his daring, and if that was too much to ask, that his soldiers defend him loyally while he led them to victory. I thought about our summer manor and wondered if I should pray for... and decided against it. *Bring him home,* I ended my prayer for Raymond, which made me remember my suggestion when he left and caused me to laugh. I received the frown of a nearby priest and bent my head again contritely.

Holy Mary, you are a mother yourself, save and guard my child, Antonio. Keep him healthy and strong and remind those who care for him to be patient and kind. I tried to picture Antonio. He would be five years old now, with the round cheeks, wide eyes, and tender mouth of babyhood still. I imagined him running about on sturdy legs and calling to his half-sisters in a high-pitched child's voice. Make them love him, I prayed, and not resent him for being the child of their father's second marriage. I sat back on my heels, then added one more thought: remind his grandmother to tell him his mother loved him. I made my obeisance and rose. The statue's face was kind, but on the other hand, she was made of marble. I slipped some coins into the priest's hand to soften her stone heart.

Violante died a few days later, despite the prayers of all Naples. I mourned her sincerely, for she had treated me better than I deserved, and I prayed for her soul to ascend to heaven soon. It would have been presumptuous of me to wear the white of mourning. Instead I put on for the first time the yellow dress Raymond had given me, with its white undershift, and I had a simple white headdress made. I stood on the street with my maid and one of Raymond's house guards beside me to watch the procession for her funeral and interment in the cathedral of Santa Maria. When I saw Prince Robert ride by wearing white, I suddenly remembered my great-grandmother's prophecy: *she will be mother to a queen.*

The thought startled me. I was married. Twice over! My great-grandmother's prophecy was wrong. Surely I could not be expected to have three husbands!

Prince Robert turned his head and looked straight at me. I felt the same jolt of excitement he always invoked, a queasiness in my stomach and a rush of blood to my neck and cheeks. His face was a mask of princely sorrow but I was certain he recognized me. I had come here today for that one glance, I realized, gazing after him. I put my hand to my cheek in horror. Impossible!

How could my great-grandmother see my future the day I was born?

This girl will travel far from home…

Even so, she must have been wrong about the rest!

… and rise high above her station…

"Is there anything amiss, my Lady?" my maid asked anxiously, peering at me.

I looked around wildly. Who could tell me news of the fighting in the South?

"My Lady?" Cicillia asked again, her face wrinkled with anxiety.

I took a breath. "Nothing is wrong. We must go home at once when the procession is finished."

I sent Cicillia to fetch Raymond's steward as soon as we walked through the door. "Have you heard anything?" I demanded as soon as the man entered my receiving room. "Your master!" I snapped when he stood looking confused. "Have you heard anything of your master?"

"His army wins every battle they undertake, Madame. He will return victorious when he has subdued the rebels who refused to pay King Charles' taxes or obey his laws."

"Yes, yes, his army is winning battles. But is he well? Has he been wounded? Is there a fever in the encampment?"

He studied me. "Have you heard something, Madame?"

"No, nothing. Why would I ask you if I knew? I only…" I shivered.

When I did not continue, he said, "There are always rumors about a great man, Madame. And your lord husband is a great man. He is also a very good warrior."

"You have seen him fight?"

"Only at practices, Madame. But none can match him."

"It will make him too confident. He will be bold when he should take care."

"That is possible, Madame." His expression disagreed with his words. I did not know Raymond had inspired such loyalty in his servants.

"The men he leads, do they follow him willingly?"

He hesitated, seeming to decide something. "Not at first, Madame. But when they rode back with him in triumph after his last campaign, they were his to a man."

"They admire him?"

"They love him, because he is careful of them. He will not squander their lives, not even the lowliest. I have heard of a time he saw a dozen of his men trapped by the enemy. He fought his way to them, rather than leave them stranded. He will not send men into a hopeless battle while he watches from a hill, as other generals do."

"And are they careful of him as well? Will they keep him safe?"

"If it is in their power, or die trying."

I frowned. I had wanted more certainty that that. "Get your writing materials. I will send him a letter."

The steward smiled. I would not have thought it possible had I not seen it. The man had always made me uncomfortable with his solemn demeanor. "It will cheer him greatly, Madame," he said.

I almost changed my mind at that, but he had already gone for them.

"My lord husband," I began when the steward had settled into a chair with his writing tablet on his lap. "I admonish you to take care."

The steward marked it down and looked up at me.

"That is all."

"That is all?"

"Yes. So I said." I frowned at him. Was he waiting for me to add some endearment? I was not sure I wanted Raymond to come home.

The memory of Prince Robert's glance still made me shiver. Had he remembered me in my yellow dress at court when he saw me in the crowd? What if my great-grandmother's prediction did come true? There was only one way I could be mother to a queen…

If only I was not married!

I did not know what I wanted. But what I did not want was that I—or my great-grandmother's prophecy—should be the cause of any harm to Raymond. If I was the catalyst, it was my duty to warn him. My mother's belief that a prophecy comes true in the telling, especially a prophecy of death, kept me from saying anything more direct. And I did not want to sound like a superstitious fisherman's daughter to Raymond's dour steward.

"Do you wish to tell him of what he should take care?"

"Of everything! Very well, add: Do not trust to your good fortune. It may fail you now."

He stared at me until I scowled, and then he wrote it down. I watched him move his plume across the page. As soon as he was finished I dismissed him, with the order that he send my letter at once.

Each day I waited feverishly for news about my second unwanted husband. When Raymond's steward approached me in the hall where I was discussing the coming week's provisions with the head cook, I broke off mid-sentence.

"A letter has arrived for you from your lord husband," he said, bowing.

"Bring it to my presence chamber at once." I left the cook with only half his instructions and hurried up the stairs, wanting to be alone when I heard whatever news it brought.

I was too anxious to sit, but paced the floor while I waited, oblivious to the girl kneeling before my fireplace lighting a fire against the cool day. Raymond had not written to me in all the weeks he had been gone. Why now? He could not have received my letter yet, so it was not a reply. Would it be to tell me he had been badly wounded? That he had contracted a fever? He might even now be dead!

Why I should care so much was beyond me. He had married me knowing he should not. If his death was now required for the prophecy to come true it was his own fault. But I did not want him to die. Had Violante died because of the prophecy? I wrung my hands. If only I could escape this terrible prophecy!

"Read it!" I cried, the moment the steward arrived. He glanced toward the chairs.

"I cannot sit and neither will you. Read the letter at once!"

The steward opened the letter with infuriating slowness. My fingers curled with the urge to snatch it from his hands. But I could not read it myself. And why not? Why had it not occurred to me to learn to read? I must see to that soon.

"My most gracious lady wife," he began. "I think of you with fondness—"

"Disregard the endearments. Get to the news. Why is he writing? Has he been wounded?"

The steward looked up open-mouthed.

I took a breath to calm myself. "Read the letter to me."

"My most gracious lady wife, I think of you with fondness and I hope…"

I watched the logs in the fire smolder, curbing my impatience, as he read to me.

At length he reached the point. "I am writing to inform you of a loss I know you will feel most keenly. I have learned that your uncle Guilio met with a fatal accident while on his fishing boat. I cannot say how long ago this happened, for I have only just learned of it from one of my men. Guilio's son, Antonio, is living with his maternal grandmother and will inherit all his father's holdings when he comes of age. Your uncle's daughters are living with their paternal grandmother. At my instruction, my man left money for the boy's care and small dowries for the girls, as I know how tender-hearted you are. I send my deepest sympathy for your loss and hope you will find consolation in knowing your uncle's children are well-cared for. I will not take up your time with news of my many victories, but know that I am well and will have happier news to share when I return home to you."

I was no longer listening as the steward read Raymond's final sentences. Guilio was dead, and Violante. The prophecy was coming true! Raymond would be next!

I sank onto a chair. Thank God and all the saints Antonio had not been on the vessel with his father! Tears came to my eyes.

"Madame!" The steward took a step toward me. "Shall I send for your maid?"

"Leave me." My voice was little more than a whisper. I reached out my hand. "Give me the letter and leave."

I stared unseeing into the fire. It was a terrible thing to be ruled by a prophecy.

I started when a knock came at my door. A servant entered carrying a jug of wine. I had not realized my throat was so dry and drank the cup he handed me in one long swallow. He poured a second cup and left.

The wine revived me somewhat. Guilio was old and the seas were often rough. One did not need a prophecy to explain a fisherman lost in a storm. And had I not told my mother when I left that no prophecy was binding?

I straightened in my chair. And if it was not the prophecy at work here?

What was one of Raymond's men doing in Sicily? Specifically, in Trapani? Raymond was fighting in Calabria, within the Kingdom of Naples. A chill went through me. Why could he not say how long ago Guilio had died, when he had learned so many other details?

I crushed the letter in my hand and threw it into the fire.

224

Two weeks later Prince Robert was publicly betrothed to Princess Sancia of Majorca, the eldest daughter of the King of Majorca. A strategic marriage; her father was uncle of the King of Aragon who was the elder brother of King Frederick III of Sicily. King Charles was still determined to regain Sicily. Prince Robert, I was certain, had had no more choice in his marriage than I.

I wept when I heard the news.

My great-grandmother's prediction had been thwarted after all. I would never be mother to a queen.

Raymond arrived home unharmed, leading his triumphant army through the streets of Naples. Crowds of citizens cheered them as they passed. Calabria was once again obedient to King Charles' laws, and the southern trade routes secured. Naples appreciated those who protected its trade.

Each time Raymond returned victorious from battle more of Naples' prominent citizens sought invitations to our dinners, eager to attach themselves to his rising star. Our large dining hall was filled with friends come to dine with us on his first night home, nearly fifty in all, fawning on the unbeatable new general. Raymond thrived on the attention. Did he not know how false their friendship was?

After enduring hours of detailed descriptions of Raymond's various battles and the tactics he had used to win each one, I finally retired while Raymond saw our last guests out. I was seated in a chair by the fireplace in my chamber when Raymond entered, followed by a servant carrying mulled wine. Raymond lounged against the cushions in the chair beside mine while the servant poured the wine and left. He must have noticed how quiet I had been during the banquet in his honor, but he gave no sign of it.

He took a sip of wine and set his cup back on the table, watching me the whole while. I kept my face averted.

"I have a village," he said casually. "And a small castle beside it," he added, when I turned to stare at him blankly. "A very small castle, it is true, but the next one will be larger."

"You are serious."

He laughed. "I won a great victory. A number of victories, amounting to a great one. King Charles is a monarch who shows his gratitude. Next week I am to be knighted."

"You will be knighted?" I felt foolish repeating his sentence, but it was beyond belief. "Knighted?" I asked again, as if I might have heard him wrong.

He nodded solemnly. "Knighted."

I should have congratulated him. Instead, I laughed.

He frowned. "You find me amusing?"

"Why did you not tell our guests? I would have liked to see their faces."

His frown turned into a conspiratorial smile. "I am waiting until it happens."

I laughed again, and raised my cup in salute. "Sir Raymond." I drank.

'Lady Philippa."

I coughed on my drink and took a second swallow, not quite looking at him. I did not know whether I believed it yet; it was not a thing one could take in all at once. I glanced down at my fine silk kirtle. The topaz and ruby gems sparkled on my brooch.

"What are you thinking, Philippa?"

"I feel like I am at a masque. Wearing my new silk kirtles and fancy headdresses, with precious jewels on my breast and neck and fingers. I am always afraid I will do something, say something. That I will open my mouth and my... my rough Sicilian accent will emerge and I will be exposed for the peasant I am."

"You are fortunate that you can don the mask. At least you can make them forget, see something beautiful that might fit into their narrow aristocratic world. No matter how well I speak in how many languages, how elegantly I dress, how capable I am at court and on the battlefield, no matter what title I hold, now or in the future, they will always see my face, my hands, and know me for an imposter." He stared down at his hands, turning them over and back. "I can never escape my origins."

"Then we shall not, either of us. Let us throw it in their faces that despite our origins we are smarter, richer, more successful, more favored at court than any of them!"

He smiled his beautiful smile, the darkness of his skin only making his smile shine brighter. Was I once afraid of his smile? I leaned forward now and kissed it, feeling the hardness of his teeth, the softness of his generous lips, the curve of his smile under my lips.

"Have you finished your wine?" he asked when I drew back.

"No."

He smiled. "Finish it," he said softly. "It is late. I have waited a long time for this night."

Abruptly, and even with some regret, I remembered his letter and the questions I had waited for this evening to put to him. I took a quick sip of my wine. Did I want to know?

I tapped my fingers on the chair's arm, glanced at him and looked away. Want or not, I had to know the truth. I set my cup upon the table between us and drew in a breath. "Did you murder Guilio?"

He barely hesitated, slipping into the masque again as easily as a leaping fish slides back into the water. "I have never set foot in Sicily."

So calm, as though he had been waiting for my question. "Did your man... did you have him..."

He raised an eyebrow. "I was told it was a fishing accident. I assume he fell from his boat during a strong wind."

"Guilio has been a fisherman all his life. He would no more fall out of his boat than you would fall off your horse."

"Men have done so in battle. Often."

"Tell me the truth!"

"Why are you upset? He was stupid and greedy, a dangerous combination."

"You knew him so well?" I asked sarcastically. "And yet you never met him."

"He gave you up!" Raymond's fingers brushed my cheek. "He had you and he gave you up. Did he imagine another man would do the same?" His face hardened. He cradled my face in both his hands. "Or was he waiting for the day another man would not?"

I pulled away and stared at him without speaking.

"Sooner or later he would have heard of our rise in fortune. But you are safe now." He stretched out a finger and idly stroked the back of my hand lying on the chair arm beside his.

Did I even know this man? He thought his skin gave him away, but he was wrong. Nothing gave him away. He was as calculating and ruthless as any aristocrat. I drew my hand out of his reach. "Are you willing to do anything?"

Raymond straightened and leaned toward me. How tall he was, and strong. The muscles in his arms and chest moved under his white shirt.

"*Anything* is a very broad term."

"It is."

"One day, Philippa, you will give me strong sons and daughters as beautiful as you. Do I truly need to explain this to you?"

I looked unwavering into his eyes, my face expressionless.

"Our children will never see the mud huts of Trapani or Africa. They will be raised in wealth and luxury." He waved his arm to indicate the manor around us. "But do not fool yourself. Everyone who looks at us, all these new friends who fawn on me, they will always see a fisherman's daughter and an African slave. They will be waiting for something—anything—a rumor, a slip-up, a loose thread from our past, to pull us down again. I will not be caught like my father, trusting and unprepared, unable to protect my wife and children! So yes, I will do what is necessary to keep you and our family safe."

Raymond reached for my hands, twisted in my lap. His eyes held me, daring me to be as honest as he. I had not felt grief at the news of Guilio's death—why should I? He had bedded me as a wife, but treated me as a servant and a pawn. He would have been willing to ruin me for a good price. Raymond was right about him. Guilio was as greedy and dangerous as the lords King Charles had sent Raymond and his men to subdue.

The first time I saw Prince Robert on his war horse in Sicily, I thought that he looked every bit the warrior, a natural leader of men.

Raymond did not look the part when he rode off to his first battle, but I saw a similar look on his face to the prince's: proud and confidant.

When they rode back, they were his to a man. Now I understood his steward's words. All my life, with my father, with Guilio, at Castle Nuovo and here, I had kept one eye on the back door. I woke in the night planning my escape route. And now this man, this leader of men, the greatest warrior in the kingdom whether he looked the part or not, had sworn to keep me safe. And I believed him.

He smiled as though he knew the moment I yielded. I let my hands uncurl inside his. Had he not provided for my son and my mother, and even for Guilio's daughters? I offered him a tentative smile.

Raymond leaned across the little table between us and cradled my face in his huge hands once again. I raised my chin as he leaned toward me, warm where his palms cupped my face, my mouth parting even before his lips touched mine. *His to a man,* I thought, surrendering. I, who had never surrendered to anyone.

He lifted me and carried me to our bed.

Chapter 21

October–December 29, 1346
Castle Capuano, Naples

Philippa, Philippa," the little princesses cry, running to me with arms outstretched, anticipating my embrace. "Philippa…"

Their cries recede. No, not Philippa… they do not call me that, they call me…

"Grandmother!"

I open my eyes to find Sancia shaking me. "You must wake up, Grandmother, we have a visitor."

I close my eyes again. She pulls the blanket aside, urging me to sit up. I shiver. Why is it so cold in here, and damp? I open my eyes to demand a fire, and everything, the dirty, dark cell, my conviction, my poverty, my pain, my grief, comes back to me.

"Grandmother," Sancia says again. Her voice is flat. Ever since her son was stillborn, she has been like a ghost. And I have been no better, the two of us slipping deeper and deeper into despondency.

I should not have encouraged her to hope. What chance did the infant have, born into this filthy, stinking, jail cell, of a mother tortured and half-starved throughout her pregnancy? Perhaps it is best he died, for his father has shown no interest in claiming his son or his wife again and has left Naples. At least he took little Maroccia with him. I sigh and let Sancia help me off the cot and onto a chair.

I hear coins clinking at the door as the guard is bribed to keep silent, and then a woman enters our cell. Her cape and hood hide her face. When she pushes back the hood I am shocked to see Princess Maria, Joanna's younger sister.

"Philippa!" she runs to me as though nothing has happened between us since she was a child princess under my care. I return her embrace. Even if she knew about our torture in her husband's dungeon, there was nothing she could have done. Charles of Durazzo is not one to listen to the pleas of his young wife. And she was in confinement, I remember now. I hold her at arm's length. "Maria...?"

"Oh, no," she shakes her head. "The baby is well. Another little girl." She smiles sadly, then raises her chin, a gesture I recognize. "A healthy, beautiful little girl."

"That is good, Maria," I say. There is nothing to be gained by telling her of her husband's role in our suffering.

She bites her lip. So she would do as a child when she was troubled. How young she is, only seventeen. I wait. She could never keep anything in, little Princess Maria, unlike her sister Joanna who listened to advice but always kept her thoughts to herself.

"What am I to do?" she cries. "My husband has learned that Joanna wrote to Pope Clement to arrange a marriage between her son and a princess of France. Charles wanted... that is, he hoped..." she stumbles to a stop.

Is it possible she can feel no regard for my circumstances, no impulse to ask what she might do for me? She bites her lip, watching me, her face pale and anxious. Ah yes, only too possible.

"You and Charles have three suitable daughters," I say wearily.

She nods eagerly. "Just so! And Charles is furious! I think..." she lowers her voice to a choked whisper. "I am afraid he may have... have written to King Louis of Hungary... to offer his support. If they attack us!"

Sancia gasps. I find myself leaning back, away from Maria. I, a convicted traitor, putting distance between myself and a real one.

"What shall I do, Philippa?" she whispers, wringing her hands. "I wept and begged him not to, but he would not listen. I told him I would leave him—" She breaks off, her hand stealing over her mouth with remembered horror. "He... he said he would kill me if I tried."

"You should not have come here, Princess. It is not safe." *For her or for us.*

"He is out dining and drinking. He will come home late and fall into his bed stinking of wine." She wrinkles her nose. "I cannot tell Joanna. She is practically a prisoner at Castle Nuovo. But what shall I do if Charles betrays Naples?"

I shake my head. "Go home to your husband. You must not be discovered missing. If you hear of anything... anything imminent... from Hungary, you must get word to Joanna. Or... send a message to Louis of Taranto and his soldiers on the hill. They will have to be warned. If you hear of anything definite."

Sancia and I do not speak of her visit after she has gone. We are shaken by what we have heard. Princess Maria has never been strong or steadfast, but a traitor to her country? I must get word to Joanna of Charles of Durazzo's betrayal, but I have no way of reaching her.

I wait impatiently, praying for Blanche to visit us again soon. When she does, it is all I can do to sit quietly sipping a cup of the wine she has brought us while she and Sancia exchange pleasantries until the guard leaves. As soon as the door closes I retrieve my writing supplies, whispering that I have a message for Queen Joanna.

"I have news for you, also," Blanche says, her voice hushed. "Catherine, Empress of Constantinople, died this morning."

I straighten in surprise. "Catherine of Taranto? Dead?"

Blanche nods. "This very morning, after a brief illness. The news has not been made public yet. My brother got word secretly to me and ordered me to come at once and tell you."

The last of Joanna's former council, Countess of Taranto, Empress of Constantinople, Robert and Louis of Taranto's mother, dead. I shake my head, speechless. I need time to sit and absorb the news. Joanna will be in shock, her last and greatest ally—most of the time—now gone. But how long will the guard leave us alone?

I unwrap my writing materials and use my dinner knife to cut off a piece of my last sheet of vellum. Quickly I write: *Organize a state funeral for your noble aunt. Be sure to lock the Castle gates.* I think a moment and add: *Beware! C.D. has promised his full support to Hungary.* I underline the word full. She already knows Charles of Durazzo is no friend of hers, but now she will understand that all the Neapolitan nobles allied with him—his full support—are not to be trusted if Louis of Hungary invades Naples.

A week later, our guard enters the cell chuckling. We act nonchalant as we take the pot of thin stew he has brought for our supper, not asking what has amused him, or what might be the cause of the church bells ringing throughout the city. He hands me half a loaf of stale bread to go with the stew, and I set it aside for tomorrow. His offerings are erratic. Sancia thanks him. He stands waiting for me to question him, but I do not give him the opportunity to thwart our curiosity.

"You hear the bells?" he finally cannot help asking, annoyed.

"Yes," I reply without even a glance his way. "What is it to us?"

"Nothing!" he roars. "Except that your last ally has died. The Empress of Constantinople. Her funeral ceremony was today at San Domenico."

I look shocked. Sancia drops her spoon onto the table and puts her hand to her cheeks. It is a good performance and the guard looks smugly satisfied.

"And you find her death amusing?" I say, hoping to rouse him into spilling more news. I must know whether Joanna followed my counsel.

"I do not!" He draws in a phlegmy breath. "What I find amusing is how little our clever queen needs your advice. For when Duke Robert of Taranto rode out with his men to join the procession behind his mother's casket, Queen Joanna had her palace guards evict the rest of the Duke's retainers, unprepared and leaderless, and lock the gates of Castle Nuovo behind them!" He begins to chuckle again until the phlegm catches in his throat and makes him cough.

"A clever move," I agree, trying to look surprised rather than delighted. My suggestion worked! Joanna is freed of her unwanted suitor at last.

"How did Duke Robert take it?" Sancia asks innocently.

"Purple!" the guard guffaws. "His face turned bright purple! He screamed and beat at the gate! But there was nothing he could do." He rids himself of the phlegm on the floor of our cell.

I drop all pretence and laugh at the thought of Robert of Taranto's helpless rage. I have not laughed this hard in many months and sound, no doubt, a little hysterical. The guard's smile turns nervous. He leaves, shaking his head at the crazy old woman.

I do not care. I laugh, wiping tears from my eyes at the same time. With one stroke Joanna has unified her country, secured the succession to the throne, taken steps to gain a valuable ally in France, and regained her sovereignty and freedom.

Even sick and rotting in this cursed cell, I have proven myself an accomplished councilor. I feel my confidence returning and straighten my back, holding my head high. Queen Joanna is not beaten, and neither are we.

At the end of the month our guard informs us that four sisters from the nearby convent of Poor Clares have moved into Castle Nuovo with the queen. "Much better companions for a righteous queen than you and your ungodly family," he sniffs. I ignore the insinuation, the old accusation that we led Joanna astray, sowing discord between her and her husband. Instead I am pleased to hear the approval in his voice. Joanna is regaining her people's support. No one can question her virtue now, surrounding herself with such holy women, not even her spiteful Hungarian relatives.

It is a wise move, connecting her with Queen Sancia, her saintly grandmother, in her people's minds. Queen Sancia was named the protector of the Spiritual Franciscans and their sister order, the Poor Clares, with their shorn hair and coarse grey robes. Queen Sancia, whose devout faith none questioned because she had three sisters of the Holy Order as her personal attendants. And now Joanna has four. I smile at Joanna's cleverness. She is a pious young woman—how could she not be, raised by such a grandmother—but she has also learned that the appearance of virtue is as important as virtue itself.

That night I dream of my son Robert. Not as I last saw him, going to his death bruised and burned with his head held high, unafraid. I dream of happier times, of Robert's birth.

"You have a son." The midwife wipes him clean, swaddles him, and puts him into my arms. He has not cried. His eyes are open, gazing around as though in wonder, completely relaxed in my arms. He is so beautiful, this dusky little boy with his cap of black hair already beginning to curl and long, dark lashes framing his wide brown eyes. When did I stop seeing dark skin as ugly? He is not so black as Raymond and I almost regret it, for Raymond's dark body is as mysterious and fascinating to me as the night sky. But our son's lighter shade is proof that he is mine as well as his father's.

The door opens and Raymond enters. He ignores the protests of the midwife and my female attendants, smiling broadly at me as he crosses the room with his giant strides. I smile back, not at all surprised. Lesser men may fear losing their manhood in the presence of a woman at her full powers, but my husband, this giant of a man, all taut muscle and formidable strength, moving with an assurance that commands any room he enters, laughs at such feeble superstitions. I hold out his son to him like a battle prize and his smile erupts into a laugh of delight.

He has not brought me jewels or other baubles, as men bring their wives to thank them for their labor. Everything he owns is mine; so he told me the night we consummated our marriage. This infant is a gift to both of us.

Raymond stands beside my bed gazing down at our son. His laughter is gone, his face serious, tight with emotion.

"What is it?" I ask.

"I will never let him be afraid," Raymond vows.

Robert blinks up at Raymond and purses his tiny mouth as though considering his father's promise. I think of Raymond's terrifying childhood, the abuse he must have suffered as a child slave, of the many times I was beaten at home, or feared I might be cast out penniless when I first came to Naples. I reach out my hand. Raymond clasps it as we stare down at our perfect son. I cannot trust my voice. I squeeze Raymond's hand and he tightens his grip in a wordless oath between us.

This child will never learn to be afraid.

I wake smiling from my dream. For a moment I can still feel Raymond's hand gripping mine. We were more than husband and wife, more than lovers. We were a little island unto ourselves, surrounded by those who would tear us down. I bore Raymond two more sons and a daughter, and each one strengthened our bond. We were each other's only family; kin and blood and dynasty, lineage and line. Surrounded by those who had had all that for generations, who were born a link in a long, unbreakable chain, we only had each other, the six of us. But we were enough.

I lie still on the cot, my eyes shut, reliving the past. The day I returned to Castle Nuovo and presented myself to Queen Sancia, determined to help my husband raise up our family. I had a new green kirtle made, with seed pearls sewn around the neck and down the length of the sleeves, and wore my most expensive jewelry. I was older than most ladies-in-waiting, but Queen Sancia was a serious young woman and appreciated my maturity, and I had not forgotten all I had learned as Violante's primary attendant at Castle Nuovo.

Raymond and I advanced together, he to ever-higher military commands as he proved himself a fierce warrior and a capable strategist, and I to greater positions of trust as mistress of the queen's jewels and lotions, and later her trusted advisor. When young Charles, his father's only heir, married Marie of Valois, I performed the same services for her. Ah, our glory days, in the sophisticated and learned court of King Robert and Queen Sancia, as our family grew and our wealth and lands increased, and our titles and position rose in the Neapolitan court. My Raymond achieved the highest post in the kingdom, the seneschal of the Kingdom of Naples, and when he was given that title, I was equally honored and promoted…

I sigh. That was the year Prince Charles died, in November, 1328, of a sudden fever. The little prince my mother brought into the world and handed to me to keep alive while she saved his mother, Princess Violante. The infant I wet-nursed so long ago, little more than a girl myself, and so earned my passage to Naples. Perhaps it was the stories of how I saved his life by breathing my own life into his mouth, or healed his fever on the ship, that earned me my appointment, on his death, as guardian of his two-year-old daughter, Joanna, the heir to the throne of Naples.

When her mother, Marie of Valois, died three years later in 1331, I was honored once again. I was named surrogate mother to the two little princesses.

Every time Joanna and her little sister ran to me, calling "Mother, Mother" in their lisping, childish voices, I knew that my great-grandmother's prophecy was real. Every time I reprimanded them for unbecoming behavior in a royal princess, and heard Joanna's contrite, "I am sorry, Mother," or little Maria's unrepentant "yes, Mother," with her bottom lip pushed out, I knew that my great-grandmother's prophecy would all come true. However often I denied it and told myself no prophecy is binding, I knew in my heart it was all bound to happen, including the terrible ending my mother whispered in my ear.

I open my hand, releasing the memories.

"You are awake," Sancia says. "I have saved some bread to break your fast."

"What is it?" I ask, noting the strain on her face.

"The guard has told me Cardinal Bertrand de Deux has arrived."

No more notes come from Joanna. The Cardinal is advising her now, and she must listen if she wants to keep her crown.

Day after weary day passes, with no visitors, no news of what is happening except the meager bits of information our guard lets slip. The Cardinal is staying at Castle Nuovo. He intends to reenact the homage ceremony of succession for little Charles Martel, giving it the legitimacy of Papal approval.

Each time the door to our cell opens my heart stutters, certain they have come to execute us. Our guard knows this, he sees it in our faces. He has begun to stamp his feet outside our door, as though there were many men standing there, before opening it to bring us our meal.

I count the lines scratched on my wall one evening and realize it is December. They will be preparing for Yuletide in the castle. Here in our dreary, damp little cell the thought is preposterous.

The bells of every church and cathedral in Naples ring out on Christmas morning. Sancia and I awkwardly wish each other a happy Christmas, neither meeting the other's eyes. We have been entirely forgotten.

Not entirely. The disembodied voice of my great-grandmother comes to taunt me in the moments just before sleep and at the edge of waking:

"This girl will travel far from home and rise high above her station. She will be mother to a queen. Prepare yourself, for the end will be swift. She will die cruelly and all she has accomplished will come to nothing, crushed under Fortune's wheel."

I push away the dire prophecy and say nothing to Sancia, but I cannot dispel the gloom that has once more fallen over us.

Four days after Christmas we hear it: the tramp of several pairs of boots approaching our cell. Sancia stands up, her eyes wide in her pinched face. I stay seated, waiting.

The key rattles in the lock of the door to our cell.

I straighten my shoulders and hold my head high. From the moment I left my Sicilian robe in the dirt at Trapani I was committed to the golden crown prince and his unpredictable wife, to glorious Naples, the jewel of the Mediterranean, the sun-lit city of intellect and art and trade... and to the destiny my great-grandmother saw at my birth.

The door swings open. Four armed men march in. Two of them seize Sancia. She gives a little gasp but does not resist. The other two grab my arms and haul me up from my chair. We are hurried down the hallway and up the stairs and out into the front courtyard.

After so many months in our dark cell, I am blinded by the sudden sunlight and stumble. Even before my eyes adjust enough to see, I hear the roar of the people waiting on the streets to vilify us.

I shake off the arm of the guard who caught my stumble and walk toward the waiting wagons proudly. I do not fear death. If I had stayed in Trapani I would have died years ago, worn out with hard work and old before my time. Instead, what a life I have lived! Bowed to by counts and countesses, the confidante of kings and queens, my advice has ruled a kingdom! The things I have seen and done, the policies I and my family have implemented—a life worth living no matter what the cost.

"Courage!" I call to Sancia as they hoist me into the prisoner's cage on the wagon bed. I stand tall with my head high as they bind me to the pole in the center of the cage. Staring straight ahead I begin to recite the Lord's Prayer in Latin in a loud, clear voice. After a moment Sancia joins in from the second wagon.

The wagon shifts as the executioner climbs in behind me. The cage door clangs shut and we jerk forward.

"Maroccia," I hear Sancia say as my wagon passes hers. She does not sound afraid. She sounds like she is murmuring a blessing.

I never got to see Maroccia walk. I close my eyes and imagine her toddling forward on her fat little legs, crowing with pride at her clever accomplishment. A little countess already, with her father's noble blood in her veins. She turns to peek back at me over her shoulder, and gives me an impish, dimpled grin.

Walk, Maroccia. Walk into the future.

Maroccia takes another step and claps her chubby hands, laughing.

I feel my lips curving upward. I want to laugh with Maroccia. I want to clap.

My great-grandmother was wrong.

She did not see all that I have accomplished. She did not see the influence we had, the things that Fortune's wheel can never crush. And she did not see little Maroccia walk.

Little Countess Maroccia.

The Neapolitan nobility—perhaps one day the Angevins themselves—are marked forever with the blood of a fisherman's daughter and an African slave.

Author's Note

Most of the people and main events in this story are historically accurate. I have invented their conversations and a few scenes, such as the opening scene at the river and the scenes between Philippa and Raymond. The facts of this story were recorded by Boccaccio, a contemporary of King Robert, who visited Naples often and knew not only the royals but also Philippa and Raymond. Boccaccio wrote a full chapter on Phillipa's life in his book, The Fates Of Illustrious Men. (Frederick Ungar Publishing Co., New York, 1965) In this account he speaks disparagingly of Raymond, echoing the sentiment of the times: "What a ridiculous thing to see an African from a slave prison, from the vapor of the kitchen, standing before Robert, the King, performing royal service for the young nobleman, governing the court and making laws for those in power!" He records Philippa's rise in the court of King Robert and Queen Sancia, stating, "...for nothing serious, arduous, or great was accomplished unless it was approved by Robert, Philippa, and Sancia." I also read Joanna's biography, (The Lady Queen, by Nancy Goldstone) which quotes letters and court records of the time.

I have tried to portray Naples in the 14th century as accurately as I can, by travelling to Naples twice, speaking to historians there, and visiting the streets, castles, and cathedrals mentioned in the book which still exist. However, it is likely I have made some errors, for which I beg my readers' indulgence.

The 15th Century picture of Naples on the back shows Naples as it would have looked when Philippa was there, although the long pier would not have been there then. The cover picture is a painting of Philippa made to go with Boccaccio's account of her. It was painted shortly after her death, and depicts the major events of her life: breastfeeding infant Charles, her marriage to Raymond, and in the top right, which has been omitted on the cover, her death.

About the Author

Jane Ann McLachlan was born in Toronto, Canada, and currently lives with her husband, author Ian Darling, in Waterloo, Ontario. They spend most days sitting in their separate dens typing on their laptops, each working on their next book. When they get out it's usually to do research.

Between books, Jane Ann enjoys gardening, quilting, travel, spending time with family, and getting away from the cold Canadian winters. She is addicted to story, and reads just about any kind of book, but she writes mostly historical fiction set in the Middle Ages and young adult science fiction and fantasy.

You can learn more about her novels and joining her launch team on her author website: www.janeannmclachlan.com

Find resources for creative writing on her website for writers: www.downriverwriting.com

If you have enjoyed reading The Girl Who Tempted Fortune, please consider leaving a review on Amazon.

The Girl Who Tempted Fortune is the second novel in the Kingdom of Naples series. If you enjoyed it you will also enjoy *The Girl Who Would Be Queen*.

The Girl Who Would Be Queen:

Ruling a kingdom in the 14th Century was no task for a woman.

When King Robert of Naples died in 1342, beautiful, sixteen-year-old Joanna and her younger sister Maria became the heirs to one of the largest, wealthiest and most sophisticated kingdoms in Europe.

Born in a male-dominated world in the passionate south of Italy and surrounded by ambitious male cousins with an equal claim to the crown, will these sisters be able to maintain control over their kingdom? With only their wits, beauty, and the love of their people to aid them, Joanna and Maria, bound together by their strong love and fierce rivalry, are prepared to do anything to hold onto their beloved Kingdom.

But can they survive a kidnapping, court intrigues, civil war, and a royal murder from tearing their Kingdom apart? Find the answer in this gripping true story of 14th Century Europe.

Praise for The Girl Who Would Be Queen:

"Absolutely fascinating!"   ~D. D., Amazon reader

"Be prepared for the ride – once you start, you won't want to stop reading until the princesses meet their fates."
~ Barbara B., Amazon reader.

"I couldn't breeze through this detail-rich book, nor could I put it down. It's a historical drama, first and foremost, but one leavened with romance, betrayal, greed and discovery."
~R, Campbell, Amazon reader.